HIGH

HOLIDAY

PORN

HIGH HOLIDAY PORN

a memoir

EYTAN BAYME

ST. MARTIN'S PRESS ≈ NEW YORK

www.stmartins.com

Designed by Steven Seighman

The Library of Congress Cataloging-in-Publication Data is available upon request.

ISBN 978-1-250-06722-7 (hardcover)
ISBN 978-1-4668-7523-4 (e-book)

St. Martin's Press books may be purchased for educational, business, or promotional use. For information on bulk purchases, please contact the Macmillan Corporate and Premium Sales Department at 1-800-221-7945, extension 5442, or write to specialmarkets@ macmillan.com.

First Edition: August 2015

10 9 8 7 6 5 4 3 2 1

To my parents. With love . . . and apologies.

CONTENTS

HIGH

HOLIDAY

PORN

CHAPTER 1

STAAARVING

THE FORBIDDEN DUNKIN' DONUTS was only a few blocks from our home. As my mother walked us past the storefront, I caught a brief glimpse of the cream-filled, jelly-engorged, and rainbow-sprinkled beauts on the wall behind the register. How fun it would be, I thought, to bite into one of each before offering the clerk my thorough ranking from least delicious to most. As my mother held my hand against my little brother's stroller, making sure I kept at her brisk pace through the crowds, I resisted and craned my neck to savor the view a few moments longer.

"Maybe I could have a doughnut?" I asked, feigning innocence.

"Eytan," my mother spoke sternly, "you know very well they aren't kosher for Passover."

It was true, aside from matzoh, the holiday dietary restrictions forbid anything with flour in the ingredients. But I thought that maybe since she had walked us past the shop and since I wanted a doughnut at that very moment, perhaps she would overlook the rules and let me have the treat. Every moment had led up to one another too precisely for this to be one big coincidence.

"The answer is obviously no," my mother continued.

I rolled my eyes and shook my head in a great show of frustration. "Uch," I grunted.

The sidewalk teemed with people going about their days. Some carried four or five shopping bags of groceries; others wore suits and clutched leather briefcases. These strangers could eat doughnuts whenever they wanted, and they probably thought we had lost our minds to follow a religion that prohibited such a delicious food. I tried to catch their eyes and silently communicate that I was the same as them. That people like us knew that God wouldn't put things like Pizza Hut and Burger King on this earth if He didn't mean for us to try them. Wordlessly, I implored a half dozen sympathetic-looking commuters spilling from the side of a city bus to, please, talk some sense into my mother.

All I wanted were the simplest pleasures the world had to offer, but life is so unfair when you are a six-year-old Jewish boy.

That evening I sat down with my extended family for the Passover Seder. In the center of the dressed-up dining room table, a clear glass bowl of water held a thin layer of delicious salt at the bottom. I kneeled in my chair and leaned over to swish my forefinger in the mixture a few vigorous times.

"Eytan!" the women in my family all called out at once.

"We have to eat from that!"

"Gross!"

"Behave!" cried three different generations on my mother's side.

"Sorry," I said with an embarrassed frown while, ever so slowly, bringing my finger to my mouth and sucking off the savory juices. They all shook their heads.

"Please sit back," my mother said.

"But I'm staaarving," I whispered to her from my seat.

"Shh."

Arranged around the salt water were more forbidden food items: a boiled egg, a saggy radish, a charred chicken neck, something maroon. I sat up on my knees again and knelt in for a good whiff.

"Sit back now, Eytan," said my mother sharply. She knew that I knew these wrinkled foods were off-limits. They were set aside, special for the Passover Seder, as symbols of how difficult life was for the Jews during the time of Moses. The salt water and bitter radish represented tears shed and hardships endured as slaves in Egypt. The maroon glob was supposed to be the mortar we used to build whatever the Pharaoh forced us to—pyramids or something. And that delicious egg and neck were the covenant between God and the Jews, or maybe they were the fragility of life. Whatever. They reminded me only of how hungry I was and how long it would be until the food was served.

"Eytan, would you like to do the *Ma Nishtana*?" asked my grandfather, in a thick Magyar accent, before I got the chance to pounce on the holy offerings. My *nagypapa*, as we called him, was a perpetually smiling Hungarian man. He sat at the head of the table behind a large stack of matzohs. His wife, my *nagy-mama*, sat at the opposite end looking bored.

I stood up on my chair, in dress pants and white oxford shirt, and frowned at my parents. Every Modern Orthodox kid over the age of three knows the *Ma Nishtana*, or "Four Questions," and was probably being told to recite it at this very moment. The questions kick-start the Seder, which can last anywhere from three to six hours, with dinner served halfway into the program. At six, eating before the rest of my family was not an option, yet I was already famished.

"On all other nights we eat bread," I sung in the original Hebrew, a little louder than a whisper, "but on this night we eat matzoh. Why? On all other nights we eat vegetables, but on this night we eat bitter stuff. Why? On all other nights we dip our food once, but tonight we dip it twice. Why? And on all other nights we sit straight up, but on this night we slouch on pillows. Why?" I didn't know or really understand most of it, I thought as I finished the tune. All I could think about was leaning back down into my half-deflated pillow and maybe trying to nap until the meal was served.

"Very good, Eytan!" My mother beamed as I finished.

"Eytan, that was beautiful," said my aunt.

My *nag ymama* and *nag ypapa* smiled at each other and at their daughters.

"Thank you," I said shyly, looking at everyone and no one all at once.

The Seder continued and I sat back down next to my three-year-old brother, Yehuda. He was like a Russian doll with smooth, grapefruit cheeks that my sister and I called Chubs.

"Lady, you got a fat baby," a nurse told my mother at the hospital when she had given birth to Yehuda. Even at that age, my baby brother seemed to understand the insult and had despised cracks about his weight ever since. Chubs, Husky, the Round One, and another dozen names my sister and I came up with all pissed him off equally.

As he shoveled a few specially prepared chicken pieces into his face, I stuck my forefinger into his Chubs. If he could eat and I couldn't, I should at least be able to take a few satisfying stabs at him.

"Uhhh," he said with his mouth full, swatting my hand so he could chew in peace. His cheek was soft but firm. I loved the way it popped back into its original shape when I removed my finger. For a moment afterward, Yehuda continued eating as though nothing had interrupted him, but like a selfish cat, I wanted to feel more of him against my body.

I wrapped my hand under his chin and pressed both of the Chubs together, prodding him with different finger variations as if he were a chunk of meat. I slid my fingers back toward his neck and then softly toward his mouth, wishing that I could roll around and bury myself in his face.

"Stop it, Eytan!" he wailed, waving his log-like arms in each direction and upsetting *Nagymama*'s silverware.

Under normal circumstances, this was the ideal reaction. *Is that really the loudest you can scream?* I might have taunted him, while sneaking a tickle on his stomach or brushing my arm against the soft skin of his back. But here, in front of extended family, where the fuse on my parents' patience was short, I needed to calm him down.

"Shh, it's okay. I was kidding," I whispered.

"Just a moment," my father said to his brother-in-law. "There is no real historical evidence of a Jewish presence in what we today call Egypt."

Historical accuracies of the Bible were common conversation topics around my dad, a professor of Jewish history and director at a Jewish nonprofit organization. "Some say it's a metaphor," "There's a larger concept at work here," "It's an interesting set of circumstances," were all familiar sound bites at our dinner table. I had a difficult time paying attention to anything more complex than a game of patty-cake, so of the ideas that followed, I usually caught only a word or phrase, such as "continuity" or "another set of circumstances" or "pass the salt," and decided that it was the main point of their discussion. It was like grabbing a single leaf as an entire pile flew down the street.

"I understand, Steve," my uncle shot back. "The 1967 Israel borders would obviously not hold up in a biblical courtroom."

"S'not funny, Eytan!" Yehuda shouted.

"That's enough." My father scolded me. "Eytan, stop picking on your brother!" Without skipping a beat, he then put his hands in the air and returned to his brother-in-law. "All right, all right!" he said. "Agree to disagree, agree to disagree."

I slumped back in my chair and grimaced by the edge of the table.

"Very interesting," said *Nagypapa* to his sons-in-law, indicating that the Seder should proceed.

My brother continued devouring his poultry bits in a trance, the entire episode behind him in a matter of moments, yet as the dust settled behind the trail of adult conversation, I seethed inside. Yes, I had pushed a button too hard, but was it fair to discipline me after I had sung the Four Questions?

I huffed and breathed loudly, trying to better express my unhappiness. "Hmmph," I said, looking around to see who was noticing.

Oh, I shouldn't have spoken so curtly to you, I hoped my father would say. *Won't you please accept my apology and these macaroons to eat?* Yet no one paid me any attention whatsoever.

I slid deeper into the pillow behind me, my Gumby-like body swimming in the vast dining room chair. The pillow was supposed to make us feel like kings relaxing on thrones and celebrating our deliverance from Egyptian bondage, but true royalty would never be starved while forced to listen to Passover commentary. Where were the pewter platters of figs and dates to grab freely from? A king would not be screamed at for mushing his brother's face; he would be given other faces for each hand to fondle as the Seder progressed.

I drifted farther down into my chair until my head hit the pillow and my knees settled on the creaky surface below. Goodbye, cruel table, I thought and flopped onto the hardwood floor.

Before me lay two rows of feet, split into a narrow valley along the center. At the head of the table, just beyond my *nagy-mama*'s legs, I spied the kitchen lights glaring off aluminum foil–wrapped warming trays and a pot of what had to be chicken soup. It was the promised land of steaming, meaty treats, and so, just as Moses parted the sea and led the Jews out of bondage, I crawled on my belly, between shifting and crossed legs— my suit collecting matzoh crumbs, boogers, and whatever else lay under the dining room table of our Bronx apartment.

"Eytan, get off your tummy this moment!" my mother whispered when she peeked below the tablecloth and saw food and dirt smeared into my holiday dress clothes. I shook my head and continued crawling toward my *nagymama*.

To my left, my nine-year-old sister, Ilana, sat like an adult, with one leg over the other. Such a faker, I thought.

On the right, my aunt Anna held my uncle Jack's hand tightly on her thigh in a display of affection that I had never seen between them. Above the table, everyone acted so proper and seemingly interested in the Passover Seder. Down here, though, their body language said otherwise.

My father, who was always telling us when he was quoted in a newspaper or had been praised by someone at synagogue, had removed one of his shoes and was scratching his heel with the other loafer. Earlier that year, he said it was rude to tuck only the front part of my shirt into my pants, and had called it "uncouth" to fasten only the top button on my suit. As I paused to enjoy the floorboards pushing against my body, I wondered if he would have taken off his footwear if he knew someone was watching.

As I inched closer, it became clear that *Nagymama* was engaged in her own covert affair. She lifted an object above the table, out of sight for a moment, before returning it to her lap. I crept nearer until the round, spongy, khaki-colored object in her hand came into view. She lifted it up and brought it back down again, smaller this time. It glistened from the kitchen lights behind her and my mouth dropped open in shock. She was eating a matzoh ball!

I peeked my head out while she stared intently across the table, as though deeply interested in whatever her husband was saying, but I knew different. I recognized the signs: the half smile, slightly too wide open eyes, and extreme stillness. *Nagy-mama* was a pro, but I was a budding student of the art of pretending to pay attention to holiday ceremonies and biblical lessons. I had an uncanny ability to make people think there was nothing more interesting to me than whatever Jewish-related stuff they were spewing, while in reality I was busy counting carpet threads.

As *Nagymama* lifted her arm to steal another bite of her treat, I put my hand on hers. For a moment, she pulled up harder, as if my hand were a stumbling block between the snack and her mouth that she had to bully her way out of. But I held fast and rode her arm up a few inches until she realized that something was physically keeping her back. Slowly, methodically, attracting the least attention to herself, she craned her neck and looked down at me.

"Ahh," I whispered at her, with my mouth wide open like a hungry chick waiting to be fed. I had no intention of making a scene. As long as I got a little taste, no one had to know that she was eating this early in the Seder.

She cocked her head thoughtfully, the way a giant would after catching a tiny man rummaging through his cupboards, and for a short moment the world seemed to stand still. But then she jerked her arm away and popped the remainder of the matzoh ball into her mouth.

"No!" she said with her cheeks full, not caring that the rest of the table could clearly see her eating. "Eytan, you wait!"

I stared up at her dumbfounded, realizing that the food was gone but not quite understanding what had happened, like the picture on the television turning off before the sound cut out of the speakers. Yes, my *nagymama* was older and cooked all the food and gave birth to my mother, who then gave birth to me, but still, everyone should be equal. Everyone should eat at the same time. I slid back on my belly underneath the table, mashed my face into the floor, and tried to force out some tears.

"It's not fair!" I whined. "I'm sooo hungry!"

No response.

"Please!" I pleaded in a full-blown temper tantrum. "Please, just give me something to eat!" Yet no one seemed to notice me at all and the Seder continued with a song about a goat.

Why doesn't anyone care? I wondered. There were two hours before the meal would begin, yet here was *Nagymama*, someone supposed to be setting an example, chowing down on delicious soup parts.

"Ittt's. Nooot. Faaaaaaair!!!!!" I screamed while kicking my legs out in a partial breaststroke. And still, no one even bothered to pause and tell me to shut up. They seemed to have other, more important things on their mind, such as holding their wives' hands or ripping runs into their stockings or the meaning of Passover.

What was the use of it all, I wondered, as I stared at a stray bit of matzoh by the tip of my nose. I must be a different breed from these people. They would probably sit back idly and sip their second cups of wine while I got lynched for wanting a bite of food. "Don't mind Eytan," they'd say, as the air cut off and I released my bowels into my pants. "It's just one of his phases."

Jerks, I thought as I closed my eyes and rested my cheek flat against the hard wooden floor. They wouldn't know fair if it bit them in their faces. I slid my hands underneath my crotch. One day, I'm going to leave here and start my own Seder, I thought as I pressed toward the floor. A Seder where we eat at the beginning and where we leave the TV on before the holiday starts so we don't break the rule about turning on the TV on Passover. I pushed my butt and chest hard toward the floor. And we'll leave the turned-on TV in the hallway, right outside the dining room so it's visible from the table. That's a Seder! My legs came up, slightly off the ground. I could not press hard enough. As I pushed down with my body, I pushed up against myself with my hands. I forgot about my brother's cheeks and *Nagymama*'s betrayal. I forgot about not being paid attention to. I forgot that I was hungry. I forgot everything. I pressed my hands into my groin one more time harder, longer, and then relaxed.

I closed my eyes. I was calm. I drifted off as I heard my *nagypapa* ask my mother to pass a bowl of boiled eggs around the table.

CHAPTER 2

ROCK BOTTOM

THE DISCOVERY WAS LIFE CHANGING. It was liberating. It got my mind off everything unfair in the world and it felt really good. Shortly after Passover, I began pressing against myself anywhere I felt the urge: family gatherings, department store aisles, anyplace with a gym mat on the floor. I didn't care who saw me or what they thought of it. It was my favorite activity.

My mother, a social worker for the elderly, invented the term "rocking" as a polite way of referring to it.

"How was Eytan in the traffic on the way back from Brooklyn?" my father asked one day after we arrived home from an afternoon of dress-suit shopping in Boro Park.

"Oh, he was fine," she said. "He rocked in the backseat for most of the ride." It had a nicer ring than "He jerked off the whole way home."

Aside from calling it something other than what it was, my mom and dad were okay with it. They may not have encouraged me to do it wherever I pleased, but they never told me to stop once I had started.

Um, are you not seeing your son getting off on the floor in front of you,

Steve? I imagined my father's friend asking him during Friday night services in a synagogue pew.

What's your point, Sid? my dad would respond, looking up from the Hebrew-English Talmud he was reading. *He's six years old. He does what he wants.*

Perhaps, of course, they could not wait for me to grow out of this embarrassing phase but were too worried I would become some repressed sexual predator later in life if I could not experiment with my body as I saw fit. Better to get the public jerking off out of my system now than when I had found a job and was trying to raise a family.

"Yehuda," my father said to my brother one night as he was tucking him in across the bedroom we shared, "can Eytan borrow your penguin?"

"Fine," he replied, pulling the bird out from under his covers and tossing it across the room.

My father knew about the hands-free method I developed, which involved lodging my brother's shoe-sized, stuffed animal beneath me, and he was happy to accommodate my needs.

Sometimes my behavior tested his patience, like when he came to pick me up from a birthday party and had to search through the house until he found me lying facedown on the basement floor. But it wasn't the act that upset him, rather that it made him late.

"There's Eytan!" the mother of the birthday boy said after leading my father on a hunt around the house for me. "I think he might have been down here the whole party."

"Wouldn't be the first time," my dad replied. "Time to go, Eytan. It's a great day for up," he continued, quoting the Dr. Seuss book. "And the party ended twenty minutes ago."

One evening I was in the middle of a spirited session

beneath a glass dining room table at our parents' friends' home. We were eating the Friday night Shabbat dinner, and I had again snuck underneath mid-meal to grind against my fists. With the glass tabletop above me, diners had a front-row seat for the show.

"You're rocking," said my sister. I looked up from the floor to see her sitting beside me with outstretched legs and arms propping her up. Above us, the diners were midway through a salad course.

"What are you doing down here?" I asked.

"It's boring up there."

"Obviously," I said.

"Rocking is like . . . weird," Ilana said.

"No, it's not. It's natural." This was my reasoning. There were no artificial ingredients or apparent negative effects. It felt good and could be done without the aid of anyone or anything. It was all natural, like a bowl of Kix cereal without any extra sugar or cocoa powder sprinkled on top.

"Rocking is not natural," Ilana said.

"So why are you sitting next to someone who's rocking?" I pointed out.

"It's gross," she said with finality.

"Shut up, Ilana!" I screamed.

Clank clank, went the table above us. We both looked up and saw our mother pointing the handle of a salad fork at us through the glass. "That's enough," she said, her voice muffled through the tempered tabletop. "Leave your brother alone."

I cocked my head and gave my sister a toothy smile, my license to rock renewed.

Life was black and white. Schoolwork, washing my hands, and listening to adults talk were painful chores that I stayed far away from. Rocking was one of the most pleasant things I knew and helped me forget what I could not avoid. So I rocked until it hurt, which it never did.

"Isn't that painful?" one of my first-grade teachers, Morah Gurion, once asked in the middle of class as I bent over my desk, grinding the edge closest to me while clutching the far side for leverage.

"Painful?" I looked up incredulously. "No, it feels good."

How could this crazy woman think rocking hurt?

She spread her lips and forced a smile. "Well, maybe you should take a break then?"

"Nah, I'm okay."

My school taught a double curriculum, with Hebrew and Judaic courses in the morning followed by English, math, science, and liberal arts courses in the afternoon. The day lasted more than ten hours and I had trouble paying attention to most of it, so I would often rock right through lessons and zone out for long stretches at a time.

By the third grade, the inappropriateness of my behavior began to weigh on my conscience. One afternoon, as I pressed forth against a firm corner of my chair, the only student standing during a quiet math exercise, a classmate began pumping his fists in the air and screaming at me from across the room.

"Go, Bayme! Go, Bayme! Go, Bayme!" he said, laughing short and maniacally.

"That's enough," our teacher cut him off, before turning to me. "Eytan, please sit down."

I rubbed myself against the chair a few more times, like sucking down a couple of sips of a soda before tossing it away unfinished, and took a seat. Mortified by the public jeering and my teacher's backhanded agreement with it, I kept my eyes straight ahead, focusing on a spot on the blackboard at the front of class. I shouldn't rock in public anymore, I thought, but within moments the urge crept back up on me. So I crossed my legs and lodged my elbow into my groin for some slight relief— the quiet snickers of my heckling classmates just a few feet away.

I was never bothered by the awkward stares and disapproval of my parents, siblings, and teachers, but nothing was worse than the shame a peer could inflict.

"Please don't make me go," I begged the next morning while clawing at the front door.

"Not an option," my dad replied firmly before scooping me off the ground and carrying me to the school bus.

And yet, I still rocked on. Everywhere. I could not easily give up on something that provided so much relief.

One afternoon a month or two later, I sat in a Hebrew class with a dire urge to go to the bathroom. I kept shifting around in my hard plastic chair, sitting up straighter and contorting my torso in an awkward attempt to hold it in until the end of the day. Next to me sat Shlomo Sasson, a gangly redhead whom I shared a desk with. I jealously watched him fly through the fill-in-the-blank assignment we were all working on. In fact, my entire class seemed to be writing answers down without any other care in the world. No one fidgeted or had their hands under their butt like I did. They looked like students modeling for a private school brochure.

Sweat formed above my lip and I held my breath for several seconds at a time. Using the school toilets wasn't an option. Someone could throw a stink bomb into the boys' room and proclaim me responsible for the wretched smell seeping out, or they could clog up the sink outside the stall and flood the entire bathroom with me in it.

All of sudden, something shifted at the other side of my pants. Like a breeze tossing a dandelion, the switching from one butt cheek to the other had attracted the attention of the front of my trousers.

C'mon, Eytan, I imagined my crotch talking to me in a high-pitched Brooklyn accent, *just a couple of rocks to help your old buddy out.*

I had to respond. I wasn't strong enough to ignore it and knew that rocking would bring some kind of relief from the pressure I was feeling. I stood up, still shifting from one leg to another, grabbed the far side of the desk and jammed my crotch into the edge closer to me. I lifted my legs up into the air and rocked, back and forth on my groin, toward a calm and soothing place.

Thanks, guy, mmmmm, my crotch said, as I tilted my neck up toward the ceiling and closed my eyes. A classmate or two might have started to giggle, but I didn't care.

Slowly and then very quickly, my underwear filled up with everything I was trying to hold back. It was hot and, for a few moments, terribly satisfying, like setting a bag full of juice cartons on the kitchen counter after carrying them all the way from my mother's car outside. I opened my eyes and froze while still balanced against the white laminate desk. Within moments I was covered in sweat.

"It smells like a crap!" Tzachi Abramovich shouted from the row behind me. The entire class cracked up.

"Excuse me, Tzachi," our teacher, Morah Perez, retorted. "We don't talk like that."

"What? I'm just being honest," he replied. "It smells like a crap. What else am I supposed to say?"

Everyone was laughing.

"Enough!" she shouted.

The class died down slightly and those who could returned to their assignment. I was still rocking against the desk, unable to move. If I could keep this awkward position for the rest of the day, I thought, then once the bell rang, my classmates would file out and leave me by myself to run home under the cloak of night. It was an ingenious plan. I would essentially become invisible.

"It's this guy!" shouted my desk partner, Shlomo. He stood behind me with his hand raised high in the air, a single pointy finger extended down toward my elevated bottom.

The class erupted in a silent, slow-motion montage. All around me, my classmates' eight-year-old mouths gaped in horror, their eyes squinting in uncontainable hilarity. Tzachi and his desk mate, Ariel Samson, were in the midst of some jerk-off dance where they rubbed their hands in front of their crotches and shimmied their hips. The girls avoided staring at me altogether and shook their heads in disgust. With my body leaning over the top of my desk and my feet just off the ground, I was a platter on display for anyone to step right up and take an investigative whiff, as Shlomo had done. Morah Perez, our tight-lipped teacher, offered me a barely sympathetic look before uncrossing her arms and ever so slightly raising a palm in the air in a gesture that said, *Get up.*

Slowly, I pushed myself off the desk and stood up before lowering back down into my seat.

"Stop!" Morah Perez said sharply, freezing me in place before I could sit down in my own filth. "Did you go to the bathroom in your pants?"

I nodded, tears beginning to stream down my face. It seemed the class was laughing louder now, even clapping.

"You need to go clean yourself up."

———

That night I came home crying.

"Everyone knew it was me because I was rocking," I said to my mother through thick tears.

She held me tight as I sobbed. "I'm so sorry, honey."

It felt so good to admit.

"Maybe it's time to stop?" she gently suggested.

"I know," I blurted.

I hit my rocking rock bottom that day—the lowest point in my young life. I'd love to say that stopping was easy and I never did it again, but for another few months, if my mother dragged me to Marshalls to buy school clothes for my sister and me, I spent the hour rocking in an aisle. Here and there during school, I snuck some quick rocks against a desk or chair back. And during Shabbat afternoon meals, I continued to pleasure myself, but usually behind a locked bathroom door and not under a dining room table.

CHAPTER 3

HIGH HOLIDAY PORN

As I FIDGETED in the seat next to my father, the rabbi delivered an angry, brimstone sermon about sinning. I bent down to have a look at the congregants' feet in the next pew and then wrapped the tassels of my dad's prayer shawl around my finger until it turned purple. I had to get out of synagogue and breathe the fresh Riverdale air or watch the mailman push his neat blue cart down the block. Services had been running for almost five straight hours; this was how people went insane.

Yom Kippur is the holiest and most frustrating day of the Jewish calendar. For twenty-four hours, observant Jews don't eat or use electricity. They spend the day in synagogue, where prayers proceed, without a break, from seven in the morning until eight in the evening. Prayers are followed by sermons, which are followed by more prayers, fund-raisers, Torah readings, sermons, and still more prayers.

That Yom Kippur morning, I joined my dad in synagogue a reasonable two hours late.

"Hi, Daddy," I said, taking a seat next to him in the wooden pew.

"Nice of you to join us," he said, looking at his watch. "How about some praying?"

On my seat was a thousand-page leather-bound volume of the entire Yom Kippur service. I picked up the tome and scowled, immediately regretting my decision to show up.

"Urrrrg," I said softly enough so that only my dad could hear. "Can I take a break?"

"No, you just got here."

"Fine," I moaned.

Over the next few hours, I shifted in my seat and scrunched my face into exciting new shapes. I said a few prayers here and there, but whenever I opened the book, it was usually to calculate how many pages were left until the service was over. Page 427 was 611 pages from the final 1038th page. Page 428 . . . 610 pages to go. 429 . . . 609. The end seemed impossibly far away and once the rabbi began his sermon, we set the book aside. Time couldn't be measured by the pages anymore. He was adding filler to the already tremendously long service.

Outraged and confused, I leaned my head on my father's shoulder and closed my eyes. I might have slept for a day or a moment, but when my dad gently woke me, people were getting out of their seats.

"What's going on?" I asked, bleary-eyed.

"*Yizkor* prayer," he told me. "Only people who have ever mourned an immediate relative are allowed to be here for this one."

I jumped off the bench and smiled at him. "Sweet! See you later," and I marched out of the sanctuary just as chipper as someone who has never lost a loved one would.

We lived across the street from the synagogue, on the first floor of a six-story, redbrick, co-op apartment building. From the corner outside shul that sunny September afternoon, I could see the window of the room that Yehuda and I shared. Diagonally across the street was a giant public junior high school with a gray and yellow facade. I was relieved to have fled prayer services after being cooped up in them for so long, yet as I paced the sidewalk, looking up and down the double yellow lines along the empty street, I grew antsy. There was nothing to do, no games to play, and no TV to watch or food to eat.

Leaning against a parked car, I wondered what exactly was going on in synagogue behind me at the moment. Was some special weird mourners' ritual taking place? Would they try to summon the dead? I imagined the ghosts of all those late relatives flying above the heads of the congregants through the vast sanctuary hall.

Wooooooo! they howled. *Don't tell anyone who isn't in here!*

I turned around to sneak back inside and investigate further as my best friend Gilad came striding out toward me. Gilad was a gangly nine-year-old with a blond Jewish Afro he wore proudly. He earned the highest marks in our class of sixty students, while I usually scored the lowest. On Saturday afternoons during Shabbat lunch, his family discussed topics foreign to me such as current events, culture, and sports. During these interminable debates, I shifted couscous from one side of my plate to the other until the meal was over, or I excused myself to play Legos with his four-year-old brother.

"Eytan!" Gilad shouted.

"Good to see you." I nodded and shook his hand. In the

hallways at school, we high-fived each other or bumped shoulders, mimicking the way cool people acted, but here we gripped each other's hands and shook vigorously. It was how adult men greeted each other at synagogue.

"How's your family?" I asked smoothly, taking the role a little further.

"Fine, thanks for asking," he said earnestly. "I got fifteen minutes before the dead people prayer is done. Where should we go?"

"There," I said, pointing to Junior High School 191. The four-story building stretched from corner to corner and reached back halfway to the next avenue. Behind it lay a baseball diamond, four basketball courts, handball courts, and a small wooded area.

"Good call," he said, and we grabbed each other's hands to safely cross the empty street.

Under his shirt, Gilad wore *tzitzit*, a four-cornered religious garment with spaghetti-like fringes hanging from each end. Jews wore the tassels to signify their observance, but I avoided them whenever possible because they were itchy and sometimes fell in the toilet bowl if I was not careful. Usually, when my parents checked to see that I was wearing them, I would make a painstaking show of taking off my shirt, pulling the *tzitzit* over my head, and then shimmying back into my rumpled clothing. Then, on the bus to school, I would pull the holy undergarment off and stuff the tassels into the bottom of my knapsack. If my teachers ever asked to see if I had them on, I would secretly reach into my bag, yank off a couple of strands, and tie them to my belt loop beneath my untucked shirt. Gilad's *tzitzit* blew in the cool September air.

When we reached the curb of the opposite sidewalk, we shook loose each other's hands and began walking through a covered passageway, into the belly of the empty public school.

At our school, our classmates were all white, observant Jews. Boys wore yarmulkes, long pants, and collared shirts, while girls wore dresses that fell below their knees and elbows. The only non-Jewish person I knew was Rhondie, the woman who dressed like a nurse and came once a week to clean our apartment. J.H.S. 191, with its sturdy construction and multiethnic student body, was mysterious and sexy to us. All these different-looking people who could ride in cars on Saturdays and eat the food at Burger King must have kept some deep secrets waiting to be discovered along their school grounds. It felt as though we were walking through an old mine, hoping to come across a scrap of gold someone had overlooked. A vacant lunchroom was visible through a large window we passed on our left.

Most of 191's students came from Kingsbridge, a less afflu-ent Bronx neighborhood to the south of Riverdale. If classes were out at my school or I pretended to be sick and stayed home, I watched from my window the large, unaccompanied waves of dismissed students pile onto city buses that drooped under their weight. Sometimes they opened the emergency exits and tossed their classmates' knapsacks and baseball mitts out onto the side-walk. Once in a while a fight broke out on the street and sucked the cheering mass of bodies toward it, leading it, like a magnet attracting iron shavings, wherever the brawl meandered.

Dismissal at my school of five hundred students was a well-orchestrated event. Each class was summoned via loud-speaker and marched single file to their chartered yellow school buses waiting for them at the front entrance. Once the buses were full, we could exit the long driveway and head home only after the assistant principal inspected and con-firmed that each of us sat safely in our seats.

In the empty 191 campus, Gilad and I took a footpath along the fenced-off wooded area behind the main building and looked for openings until the chain link met the baseball diamond. Past an empty dugout, we slipped inside a narrow gash in the links and discovered an old concrete path rambling through a woodsy courtyard. Weeds grew out of the cracks in the ground and a creepy silence hung in the air.

"Awesome!" I cried at the sight before us.

Strewn around the forest were large gatherings of empty bags of Doritos, Swedish Fish, Charleston Chews, and every other non-kosher-candy wrapper imaginable. It was as though a corner store had been shaken over the woods and all its contents had tumbled out for the students to plunder. I imagined that this was where J.H.S. 191 must have held their non-kosher junk food eating functions. Just like my school had special Israeli Independence and Holocaust Remembrance Day programs, perhaps public schools celebrated their freedom to sample all the different types of treats that the Old Testament forbade.

"Smell this," I said to Gilad as I picked up an empty bag of Cool Ranch Doritos. It was a flavor that I had heard about on television but had never tried because there was pork or shrimp or caviar or something in the seasoning that prevented it from being kosher. I stuck my face in the bag and breathed in something similar to old cheese with a hint of mildew.

As we squatted over the gathering of debris, huffing the various empty bags like addicts, something farther down the path, amid a gathering of Crazy Calypso potato chip bags, caught my eye. Slowly, without standing, I squat-walked over to the pile and used a branch to flick the trash away from the object.

My eyes widened and I felt a cool breeze on my lips. The hardened concrete path stung through the thin cotton knees of my suit pants, yet I hardly cared. "Oh my God," I said, "it's a porn!"

"Wha??" screamed Gilad, dropping the bag he was inhaling and scampering over to me.

"Shh. Shh," I said, worried that people would hear us deep in the empty woods.

We knew about porn but had never seen more than the tops of shrink-wrapped copies of *Penthouse* and *Club International* that sat behind *Esquire* and *GQ* in the local newsstand's racks.

"No. No. Please. Excuse me. Too young," the newsstand owner once snapped at me when I folded down the top of a *Men's Health* to get a better view of the *Hustler* behind it. Like a bungled heist, I bolted out of the shop and down the block to safety.

The fifteen faded black-and-white pages of the public school porn had been weathered from dirt and rain. Many were crumpled, some stuck together. The cover was missing. I picked it up with both hands, my mouth hanging open moronically. Each page of the porn featured several very small, neatly arranged pictures of women displaying their private parts. They all had big hair and dark cheeks, and some had their hands near their pubic regions. Next to each photo was a title and price. It was a catalog for other pornographic magazines and videotapes. Most of them cost $39.95.

"Yes!" I screamed toward the sky. "Thank you!"

We were like oil men and black crude was spewing from the ground beneath us. Gilad let out a gradually rising "ahhhh—" sound that got louder and faster until it peaked and burst into a laughing fit interspersed with out-of-breath "Holy crap"s.

"Who's gonna get to take it home first?" he asked finally, after we calmed down and flipped through each page.

The thought of sharing the porn pained me. This was the most valuable object I had ever held. I didn't want to split custody of it with Gilad, wondering if he would take proper care of it when I was not around.

"I don't know . . . ," I said. "How am I gonna get it from you when it's my turn to have it?"

As we silently pondered the valid logistical concern, the Bible story of two women who fought over an infant in King Solomon's court came to mind. One woman claimed the baby belonged to her, while the other said she was the mother. The king said there was no way to know who the true parent was so the baby should be sliced in half, with each woman caring for one part.

"I got it," I said to Gilad, and tore the porn in two, giving him seven pages and keeping eight for myself.

"Genius," he said and I beamed proudly. Gilad knew I was a poor student, but he trusted my street sense in times like these.

"Okay, I gotta get back to shul," he said while stuffing his pages beneath his *tzitzit,* against his bare chest.

"I'm gonna go home first," I said, before sliding my half down the sleeve of my suit jacket and heading back out to the street.

Moments later, I ran up the stoop to our first-floor apartment, my arm bent at the elbow and my fist above my heart to keep the porn from sliding out. *Please don't let anyone be home. Please don't let anyone be home. Please don't let anyone be home,* I prayed silently. Yom Kippur wasn't the day to be asking God for favors, especially ones relating to hiding things from my parents, but I didn't know who else to turn to.

"Hi, Eytan!" yelled my mother from the living room when she heard me enter.

"Hi, Mommy, I gotta make!" I screamed back and ran to the bathroom, slamming the door and locking it behind me.

Carefully, I pulled the porn from my sleeve and sat on the toilet. The pages felt frail, like a text that belonged in the rare books section of a library. I worried that the oils from my palms would corrode the paper fibers.

The girls all had similar body types: full thighs and enormous breasts. I scratched some dirt off a page and revealed a tiny photo for a video called *Orient Express*. My porn felt weighty, heavy with substance.

I placed the porn by the corner of the bathtub on the black and white tiled floor and slid down onto my stomach. Any concerns about keeping my holiday suit clean were far in the back of my mind as I slid my hands beneath me.

In the year since I had stopped rocking in public, I had orchestrated elaborate sexual fantasies in my mind each night. In one, a younger girl that I was secretly in love with would come over to help me with my homework and end up giving me a bath instead. In another, I was a member of the 1986 Mets team and my mattress would transform into one of my teammates' wives. Rocking was not just about feeling good any longer; it had become sexual, something that I wanted to do with, or at least near, a girl.

Now, on the bathroom floor, it felt different. My mind wasn't working while I was pushing against myself. I didn't have to think in order to feel good, the fantasies were all laid out there on the floor before me. *Sex Boat Party 14*, *Tales of She-Man 3*. It was as though someone was there with me, guiding my mind.

"Everything all right?" my mother said from behind the bathroom door.

My body quaked at the jolt of the surprise, like a flash of

lightning with no thunder to follow. For a few moments, I lay there motionless, trying to register what was going on outside the door.

"Yah?" I said finally, as much a question as a statement. Could she somehow know what I was up to?

It had been a long time since she had seen me rocking, and embarrassed by my past, I had worked hard at making it seem as though I had outgrown that phase of my life.

"Yehuda, shut the door," I'd say to my brother before we went to sleep at night. Our bedroom door unsticking from its frame and swinging open would give me a few extra seconds to pull my hands out from under my crotch should my mother or father burst in.

"Everything all right?" my dad asked one evening when he popped in to see if we were asleep.

"Yeah, I was just practicing a snow angel," I had responded weakly after quickly sliding my arms away from me and brushing them back and forth on the mattress.

"I'm in the bathroom," I said to my mother as though it weren't obvious. I wondered if my voice sounded different while lying horizontally with my hands underneath me.

"Okay," she said finally. "I'm going back to shul. Should I wait for you?"

"No, that's all right. I'm gonna be a little bit," I said, breathing a sigh of relief as her footsteps faded away.

CHAPTER 4

SO ABOUT THAT SIN ...

THE WORLD WAS UNFAIR and I was angry about it. Sometimes I would storm into my sister's room and kick her in the leg simply because she was older and allowed to watch an extra half hour of TV. Unprovoked violence like this troubled my parents, and they sent me to numerous specialists to try to corral it. One of these pros must have suggested the journal.

"The next time you feel like you need to hit someone," my mother said to me when I was seven, "I want you to write about it in this."

She handed me a book the size of a cigar box. It had a dark green, padded cover. I turned it over in my hands and flipped through the shiny, empty pages, trying to understand what this was all about.

"You need to channel your frustrations onto this," she continued, placing her smooth white hand on the front, "instead of your brother and sister."

I pursed my lips and looked up at her knowingly before fleeing to my room and promptly tossing the journal behind my bed.

Two years later, that Yom Kippur afternoon after my mother had left the apartment, I reached down between the wall and my bed and pulled out the diary for the second time since she had presented it to me.

WHAT A BITCH!! began the only entry I had made a few months earlier. It continued for a page and a half about the unfair way my *nagymama* hadn't let me watch TV one evening at her home. I carefully inserted the porn between the pages that followed and closed the book.

Next to my bed, a double window looked out at the synagogue and the junior high school. I opened the left side and lodged the diary outside, underneath an air conditioner unit in the right window frame. It was the perfect hiding place, I thought, because it was not technically in the apartment.

Several times during the Yom Kippur service, we recite a prayer called *Al Chet*. Roughly translated to, "So about that sin . . . ," it is a list of fifty evil acts such as speaking in false tongues, having impure thoughts, or insincerely confessing. With our heads down, we beat our fists over our hearts and recite verses such as, "So about that sin where I disrespected my parents [chest smack] . . . so about that sin where I lied under oath [chest smack] . . . so about that sin where I murdered a small bird [chest smack] . . ."

Back in synagogue, services seemed to fly by. I wasn't missing TV or food. I wasn't even that bored. I was simply content thinking about the next time I could look at my porn.

Close to the end of the service, I walked to the front of the sanctuary and peered down the aisle where Gilad and his father and brothers sat. He was urgently reading from a prayer book, striking his porn-protected chest at each line of the *Al Chet*.

———

Over the next two weeks, my porn and I had an intense love affair. Most nights, after school, I would retrieve the journal from its hiding spot and dash into the bathroom to study its features. It made me feel whole. If I was upset about not being chosen to play softball during recess, or jealous of a video game system a friend had, I wasn't as angry as I usually was. My porn was at home, patiently waiting for me.

"You don't know how to tag!" screamed my classmate Asher, as he continued to play after I had sacked him during a game of touch football.

Normally, I would hurl every manner of curse word I knew at such a blatant school yard offense and demand he stop the play. Instead I came at him harder and brought him down a second time. "Cheater," I said softly after the play went dead.

I was calm and content. Channeling my frustrations into the diary wasn't nearly as effective at soothing my nerves as hiding X-rated material in it had been.

One night, as I was returning the porn to its spot underneath the air conditioner, my fingers slipped and the journal fell to the sidewalk below. I watched in disbelief as a light wind teased the hard green cover slightly open and then quickly closed. One strong gust could easily send it flying down the street, so I pulled myself inside and ran toward our front door.

"Eytan, where are you running to at this hour?" my father asked as he was underlining an entire page of a hardcover book in the living room.

"Um, my things fell out the window by accident. I just need to go grab them," I blurted and jetted out the door before he could respond.

The sidewalk was cold under my bare feet as I turned a corner and saw my porn laying on the ground only steps away. The walkway was empty, but as I ran across it, I felt as though

I were trying to beat out a herd of hungry opponents all wanting to get their hands on my adult mag. Finally, when I scooped it into my arms, I breathed a sigh of relief. My porn was mine again.

I slipped it beneath the elastic waistband of my shorts and went back inside.

"What exactly fell out the window, Eytan?" My father confronted me as I came back into the apartment.

"Oh, nothing," I said nervously. "I made a mistake."

He towered over me as I inched away. I just needed to get back to the safety of my bedroom and this whole fiasco would be behind me.

"What were you running out the door for?" he continued. "I don't appreciate things falling out of my windows. Are you playing with He-Man figures?"

My dad forbade us from playing with He-Man action figures because he thought the cartoon was too violent. "No He-Man and no *Married . . . with Children*," he often said. "Too much violence and too much filth!"

"Uh, no," I said, thankful for an opportunity to answer honestly. The journal was rapidly slipping from my waistband, though, and I needed to get back to my room fast.

Just then a brilliant idea came to me. "No, Daddy. Not He-Man," I said. "I thought one of my books fell out the window, but I must have been wrong."

Books were my father's weakness. The walls of our apartment were lined floor to ceiling with his bookcases. They were the first thing any visitor saw when they entered, and my dad was always eager to give "tours" on the various subjects they covered. He usually read five to six at a time. One for the subway ride, he'd explain, another for before dinner, another for after, another to read while watching sports, another for synagogue, and others for who knows what. Since kindergarten, he had never been without a book.

"You never know when you might need one," he would often say.

When he wasn't reading, his favorite thing to do was to talk about books.

"Reading anything interesting?" he would ask my friends when they came to visit.

"I dunno," they usually shrugged.

And so, any talk about books easily sidetracked him.

"Oh," he said to me that night with the porn in my pajama bottoms, "which book?"

"One of my Matt Christopher ones," I told him. "I actually need to check that it's still in my room." And I bolted to my bedroom to return the smut to its hiding place, safe and sound.

My porn and I continued our affair uninterrupted for another week or two. Often I tried to will the girls inside to come to life. I'd squint my eyes and pucker my lips, hoping that one of those frizzy-haired ladies would pop off the crusty pages and let me sit on her naked lap.

One afternoon, I stepped off the school bus to a commotion underneath my window. Tallahassee, the superintendent of our building, was surrounded by four or five kids from Junior High School 191. He pointed a broomstick up toward my porn as the students all strained their necks to gape at the action above them.

Tallahassee then tried to flick the book out from under the air conditioner.

"Oof," he grunted while jumping inches off the ground. His stick had hit the binding of the book and moved it slightly to the left, but it hadn't fallen down.

As the nightmarish porno rescue operation unfolded before my eyes, one of the kids threw a stone up at the book. It clanked against the back of my air conditioner before, thankfully, falling to the ground porno-less.

"Don't you throw any rocks at my building!" shouted Tallahassee.

"But it's ours," the kid shouted back. "We saw it first!"

"Get out of here now before I call the cops!" he retorted, shutting the kids up but not scaring them away.

It was a beautiful day in late September. There wasn't a cloud in the sky and only a light breeze rustled the branches of the trees lining our block. Tallahassee wore a plain white T-shirt and Dickies brand work jeans.

"Eytan! Is this yours?" he called to me while pointing the stick at the journal. "Why you putting things outside the windows?"

I was stunned silent, unable to bring myself to respond with more than a shrug of my shoulders and a nod of my head. Tallahassee shook his head and turned around to have another go at the porn. But before he could, my mother emerged from the back entrance of our building around the opposite corner.

"What's going on?" she asked.

"Mrs. Bayme," said Tallahassee, resting the broomstick against the side of the building, "the kids were throwing rocks at the window, trying to get your son's book."

"What book?" she asked, as he pointed the broom up to the ledge under the air conditioner. She looked around, confused and irritated, before catching my eye.

"Eytan, why is that up there?" she demanded.

"It's ours!" shouted a feisty 191er.

Tallahassee took another two-handed go at the book, this time sliding it out and sending it flapping down to the ground like a dead pigeon. The pages of porn came flying out and scattered all over the sidewalk by my mother's legs.

"It's porn!" cried one of the students. The rest of the crew looked at me and started cracking up.

Tallahassee smiled sheepishly and peeked at my mother, who seemed to be at a loss for words.

"Are these yours, Eytan?" she asked.

Suddenly, the 191 kids swooped in, snatched up the pages, and ran down the block.

"Thanks, Eytan!" one of them coolly shouted, sending howls of laughter from his friends. I couldn't feel that shamed by them. After all, I had found the porn in their school. They were just coming to reclaim what was rightfully theirs.

"I'll leave you guys to it," Tallahassee said. "No more of that stuff outside the window, Eytan, okay?"

I nodded silently, loathing the words "that stuff," but missing him once he left me alone with my mom.

"You know that's not what women are really like?" she said with her arms at her waist.

I frowned, nodded.

"I can't have that in the house," she continued.

She didn't have to explain further. There was no shelf in our observant home for the porn. My dad's bookcases were filled with works on modern Jewish literature, history, and political theory. Porn was for people who watched wrestling, which I was forbidden to tune to during my allotted half hour of TV each night. People who wore tank-top undershirts kept pornography. Not us. Our coffee table was covered with issues of *The New Yorker*, the *Forward*, *New Republic*, and *Psychology Today*.

"I won't allow it in the house," my dad had said when we asked to subscribe to *TV Guide*. How could they let a porn in?

"Sorry," I mumbled to my mother before gathering the porno-less diary in my arms. "Can you please not tell Daddy?" I begged.

She paused for a moment.

A what, my father might have reacted, *like with naked people? How could this happen to us?*

My mother probably foresaw his dramatics. "Okay," she said. "But no more girlie magazines. Next time it's going straight in the incinerator."

CHAPTER 5

SLUTFES

MY RELATIONSHIP WITH porn continued even though my mother had warned me against bringing it into the house. I hid porno mags behind my bed and underneath the bathroom sink. I ordered movies from Spice Channel on our cable box and slowly downloaded erotic literature in the early days of the Internet. Each time, I got caught.

One afternoon while I was at school, Rhondie, our Seventh Day Adventist cleaning lady, pulled an issue of something called *60 Plus* out from under the sink and gave it to my mother before I got home. It was one in a vacuum-sealed three-pack of magazines that I had purchased for an allowance-crushing $26.99. Sandwiched between copies of *Lips* and *Eager Beavers*, and featuring mostly naked older women holding sex toys or cocktails, *60 Plus* wasn't even a publication I particularly enjoyed.

When I arrived home that afternoon there was a yellow Post-it note stuck to my pillow that read, *See me. -Ma*.

I dragged myself out to the living room, knowing that whatever this was about wouldn't be good, and presented myself before her.

"You got my note?" she asked without looking up from a copy of *The New York Times* laid out on the coffee table before her.

"Yeah, what's the problem?"

"Rhondie found your elderly ladies magazine while she was looking for the Windex."

"What even is an elderly ladies magazine?" I instinctively protested.

"You know very well what I'm talking about, Eytan." She looked up. "Why would you hide it where we keep the cleaning supplies?"

I had not considered that anyone would root around underneath the sink. I never used any cleaning products and couldn't imagine anyone else needing them either. But I had made a sad oversight. Rhondie had been our cleaning lady since I was four years old. For a long time she was the only black person I knew. At that young age I didn't understand anything about race and it was important that I made sense of our differences.

"Rhondie is dirty because she is black," I sang to her when I was five years old. I hoped that my rhyme would put Rhondie and myself in context, that it would clarify the difference between me and her, as I was sure that she was just as confused about my skin tone as I was about hers. But instead, Rhondie dropped the vacuum cleaner on the carpet in Ilana's room and stormed off to confront my parents. They had to convince her that I was just a child and didn't understand my words, and that they were not raising racists. Eventually, they persuaded her not to quit.

"Rhondie was very upset," my mother continued at the kitchen counter. "She thought you left that magazine for her."

"What!" I exclaimed. "No! It was just a stupid place to hide it."

"So you admit that it's yours?" My mother caught my lie.

I groaned and gave in. "Yes."

"It *was* a stupid place to hide it. A very stupid place," she said. "You know that's not what *older* women are like?"

My mother was a geriatric social worker, who tended to the needs of the elderly and their families every day. I couldn't tell if she was making fun of me or offering me instructive advice about her area of expertise. Either way, I nodded and said, "I know."

"No TV for two weeks," she sentenced.

"Ma, come on."

"And I think you should apologize to Rhondie."

"What?" I cried. "She should apologize to me. She got *me* in trouble."

"You want no TV for a month?"

The next time Rhondie was at the apartment, I approached her as she was putting a stack of folded towels away.

"I'm sorry about the thing you found," I mumbled at my mother's urging.

Rhondie continued in the linen closet without answering, her back toward me.

"I wasn't trying to tell you anything. It was just a magazine I had."

Nothing.

"Anyway," I offered one last time. "I'm really sorry."

Finally, without looking at me, she responded, "I thought this was a nice home when I started working here," she said. "A nice home and a nice family, until I met you."

A few months later, Yehuda was angry at me for trading away his prized Ozzie Smith rookie card for an unopened box of

1991 Fleer wax packs. In retaliation, he fished out an erotic audiocassette I kept hidden in the space behind my bed and presented it to my mother.

"Look what Eytan has!" Yehuda exclaimed, proudly holding the recording up to her at eye level. A half-naked, long-legged woman bent over and peered back at my mom from the hard plastic cover. This was the lady on the tape who, in a Latin American accent, moaned things like "Oy, Papi," and "I love it, Papi." I winced at the implication of being related to her but couldn't deny that it sounded pretty sexy. Not that my mother needed to play the tape to understand what was on it, though; she just looked back at the girl on the front, frowned, and revoked my Nintendo privileges for the next two months.

"Enough of this!" she said to me, her patience for my affliction wearing very thin.

"You jackass," I muttered to my brother. We marched into the main living/dining area, where I swiftly pushed him back onto my leg behind him. He reached his hands out to grab me for support, but I jumped out of the way and let him crash to the floor unobstructed. His head made a dull thud against the hardwood, like a Skee-Ball hitting sidewalk pavement. Then he let out a piercing shriek followed by some quick sobs, and I knew I had taken this too far.

"Crap," I cried and dashed around the other side of the dining room table in cowardly retreat.

Yehuda slowly stood up, clutching the back of his head and glaring at me.

"You're dead," he said calmly, sniffing back tears.

"I'm sorry!" I cried.

"Too late for sorry," he replied and ran at me with his arms out. I continued around the table, dodging the tall wooden chairs, trying to keep the dining set between us.

"Stop running!" he screamed.

"No way!" I screamed back.

"Enough!" My mother raised her voice from the next room.

I ran off, away from the dining room, and drew Yehuda into the narrow kitchen. Our mother's recently installed granite countertops lined either side, and at the end of the room, a window looked down onto the street below. With my back toward the window, Yehuda entered the kitchen and trapped me.

"Relax," I tried to reason with him. "Mommy said enough."

"Shut up, Eytan. You could have broken my skull." He swung at me, but the kitchen was too cramped to wind his punches far back enough, so I fell into him and took a couple of his weak jabs as a show of goodwill. Now we were tangled up together, like exhausted boxers. I tried hugging him and lightening the mood, but he still meant business.

"Get off me," he seethed. "This isn't a joke." He then snatched my nipple below my shirt and tried to squeeze it off.

"Whoa!" I said, swatting his hand away. I pushed him up against the fridge, lodging my feet into the bottom of the cabinets opposite him. With my arms firmly against his shoulders, I wedged him hard against the refrigerator, like a steel toe boot in a door. He wasn't going anywhere.

"Relax," I whispered, my face only inches away from him.

He looked at me and frowned before checking to make sure our mother wasn't anywhere within earshot.

"Fuck you, Eytan," he whispered. "Fuck you so much." The F curse was new to Yehuda, and even though it was an exciting and strong word, he kept it sacred and rarely uttered it. I sprinkled it liberally and often incorrectly wherever I felt the urge, like when I told Gilad, "It's so fucking that the school bus picks me up first in the morning and drops me off last at night." But when Yehuda spoke it, he expressed a deep and crucial

anger. In fact, Yehuda was so beside himself that it was difficult to maintain a straight face and I couldn't help but crack a
quick grin.

"Like I said," he assured me, "you're dead."

I held him against the fridge for a few more minutes, but
the situation was growing dire. At some point I would want to
watch TV or go to the bathroom or get something out of the
fridge.

"If I let go of you," I asked, "will you promise not to come
after me?"

"I can't promise that."

"Will you at least give me a chance to run?"

"I can't promise that either," he said wryly.

Yehuda was three years younger than me, but he was physically larger. While my father often referred to me as the "Splen-
did Splinter," I liked to tease Yehuda for having to wear
clothes that had the word "Husky" printed on the inside label.
Once, I had even introduced him to a classmate as "my slightly
overweight, younger brother."

If I didn't escape Yehuda's wrath that afternoon in the
kitchen, I was sure he would leave me with some permanent
physical damage. Only one option came to mind.

I stared him in the eye and said, "I'm really sorry about
this," and slammed my knee into his crotch. For a moment,
after I loosened my grip on his shoulders and he slumped down
to the floor, he seemed to be asking me, *Why? Why would you do
such a thing?* Then he let out a shriek unlike any I had heard
before. It was as though an air horn were crying over the death
of his too young, air horn child. High and loud and long and
utterly devastating.

Oh fuck, I thought, and ran out of the kitchen past my
mother, who emerged urgently to attend to her wailing youngest.

"What's going on?" she shouted, panning her head back and forth.

"I'm sorry!" I screamed and continued into the bathroom, the only room in the apartment that locked from the inside. After fifteen minutes, Yehuda's cries settled and my TV punishment was extended three more months.

While my parents grew tired of grounding me for all my filth and filth-related acts of terror, Gilad managed to amass a three-foot stack of dirty magazines that he kept in a run-down shed in the woods behind his house. Once a week, he opened the hovel up to our classmates, who, for a small fee, could borrow a porno mag for a few nights. He had become an entrepreneur as I developed a dependency.

Pleasuring myself to porn felt good, but there was more to it than that. Pornographic magazines were preparing me for sex. They showed me where to put my hand on a girl and the type of face I should make while it was there. They showed me things to do with my mouth, tongue, arms, and knees. When I did finally get a girl, I would surely be able to impress her with all the information I had gathered. Surely.

There was something spiritual about porn as well. One morning my classmate Yonatan Zimmerman told me that during prayer services he would ask God for certain baseball cards necessary for his collection. After praying hard enough, he said he would find the cards inside packs that he purchased later in the day. Miracles were occurring and all I had to do was pray. So, eyes closed, standing straight up with my feet together while swaying back and forth, I would mouth the words, "Please give me a girl. Please give me a girl. Please give me a girl," during the three prayer services I attended each day at school. I promised God everything: I'd be nicer to my family. I wouldn't curse so much. I would wear the goddamn four-cornered tasseled garments He insisted upon. All I asked for in return was some open-mouthed kissing, to feel some boobs on my thigh, maybe a hand job. But none of it ever worked, and it only led me to squeeze my pillow harder each night. So I took it to the next level: I began to study.

Jews are known as people of the book. Four times a week, we publicly read chapters from the Bible. When we aren't doing that, we study endless volumes of Talmudic thought, breaking down and critiquing the Bible like law school students. My father's collection of texts on Jewish history and literature was a tool to get closer to God and connect with his fellow Jew. I took his approach and applied it to my own interests. Since pornography was the book of sex, the more I looked at it, I reasoned, the closer it would bring me to getting laid. This was it, sex, right here on the page. It was elementary: If I wanted to learn how the Jews lived under Roman rule, I read Josephus. If I wanted to know how the gearbox on a car worked, I read *The Way Things Work*. If I wanted to have sex, I read porn. And so I read a lot of it. I read *Hustler*, *Penthouse*, something called *Bobby Sock Girl*, and anything else I could get my hands on and keep away from my parents before they threw it down the garbage chute.

Logically, I wasn't sure how all this would help me have sex. After all, dirty magazines weren't introducing me to any girls. But I hoped that maybe all the smut would show God how much I wanted one, and then perhaps a woman might come knocking on my window and slide into my bed somehow. Yet after years of poring over girlie magazines, I hadn't even kissed a member of the opposite sex. It was time to try something else.

One Shabbat afternoon, I stretched out on my bed with one of Gilad's *Hustler* magazines as the rest of my family prayed in synagogue across the street. The issue had an article about hunting small game with an automatic rifle and a piece called "Acting Gay to Get Girls." There were crude, full-page cartoons featuring impossibly big-breasted women and short, balding men with giant penises poking out of their pants. In one cartoon, a dazed couple took a break from what appeared to be a wild night. Dildos and puddles were strewn all over the picture, and the woman was marking a board that kept track of his and her orgasms. She was in the lead. I didn't understand. Were orgasms something that people recorded? Since I had never had sex, I assumed I was simply not in on the joke, and I didn't laugh, thinking that the more I respected the act of sex—whether in my mind or on the page—the closer I would get to actually experiencing it.

Toward the back of the magazine there was a directory of phone sex lines. The pages contained hundreds of phone numbers beginning with 1-900 or 976 and ending with easy-to-remember dialing codes such as *S-E-X-X* or *H-O-T-F-U-C-K* or *D-R-I-P-P-I-N-G*. Here, a discerning phone sex customer could find someone to discuss practically any topic. If he was interested in talking to girls with large breasts, he could dial HUGE-CANS. If he was interested in girls with sex on the mind, try WETSLUTS, or if he wanted to get straight to the point, the FUCK line would be a good option. Each number was listed under a photograph of a naked girl, who was presumably the person on the other line. The girl at HUGECANS had very large breasts and the girl at SHEMALE had a penis. Most of the calls cost four to five dollars per minute and could be charged to your phone bill or drawn directly from a bank account.

The hotlines were enticing. An actual person was on the other line with the same filthy thoughts as me, or was at least paid to pretend that she had them. It was a free-for-all. I could tell the girl what was happening to my body, and even if I was nervous or shy, she had to listen. I wondered what kinds of things she would talk to me about. Would she breathe heavily and whisper a lot? Would she call me baby and say things like "Ooh"?

It was ideal. Pornographic magazines left me alone with my thoughts, without any actual human contact. The phone offered someone to cavort with, a partner to alleviate my sexual frustration. She might find me charming and want to meet in person. Even if she lived across the country, I would find a way to get to her. This was a phone sex operator, after all, and if she wanted to meet, it would mean that we would have sex, something a bus ride of any length was worth.

In fact, since I wasn't the average phone sex caller, she probably would really like me. I was young and inexperienced, but eager to learn and came from a good family. I would be a welcome change from her usual callers, who were probably all old, overweight slobs living with their mothers. It was true that I too lived with my mother, but I was only twelve, so she would understand.

I pulled the phone next to me and scanned the options on the page. The SLUTFEST line had a picture of a beautiful woman in nothing but a blue bikini bottom and red lipstick. She looked over her shoulder and twisted her body toward the camera with an arm covering her breasts. The photo wasn't overt; there were no explicit private parts on display. Instead, it was suggestive, as though I were a welcome intruder in her bathroom and not someone who put a quarter in a machine to see her play with herself. Simple, elegant, sold.

On Shabbat, using the phone is strictly forbidden, but right at that moment, when I was supposed to be in synagogue, was the only time I would be alone in the apartment. There was no way I could do it while my family was home and risk having them pick up the receiver and listen in. It would be suicide.

Oh. My. God. Eytan, I imagined Ilana saying to me, *that's disgust-ing!* Her eyes would be closed and her chin up, she would hold her wrist to her chest as if swallowing back vomit. *What if those people found out where we lived and tried to kill us? I'm telling Mommy.*

I had no choice but to violate Shabbat. One little phone call, I told myself, wouldn't hurt anybody.

I lifted the phone off the receiver and slid a finger onto the button beneath the earpiece, so it was still technically hung up. I took a deep breath and rolled around on the bed until the handset fell out of my hand. By performing the sin in such an inconvenient manner, I thought it might make me look slightly less guilty in God's eyes.

With the phone off the hook, I put my ear to the receiver and listened to the hum of the dial tone. Shabbat had officially been broken and God wouldn't charge by the minute, so I may as well go ahead with the call.

I dialed 1-9-0-0 and stopped. The ad said that for every minute, $3.99 would be charged to my account. Each month, my father sat over our bills, pen in hand, and scanned them for unfamiliar charges. Technically speaking, though, by making this call I wasn't *bringing* any porn into the house, as my mother had warned against. Aside from the listing, there were no pictures of naked people involved, just a voice on the other line. Could this really be considered porn?

The Shabbat issue was more difficult. My parents were at synagogue and thought I was sitting in the back of the sanctuary, praying or analyzing the Torah portion, or maybe even talking to a nice Jewish girl who I would someday marry, have children with, and carry on the traditions of the Jewish people. Staying at home to violate the Sabbath was certainly grounds for a stiff two-month TV ban.

I needed this, though. I was never going to get a girl to touch me, and since I wanted this so bad, maybe God would intervene and disguise the bill creatively so it looked like a regular phone conversation that didn't occur during his obligatory day of rest. Screw it, I thought, I'll deal with the repercussions later.

S-L-U-T, I dialed, *F-E-S* and it started ringing before I could hit the second *T*. It was an unnecessary letter, sloppily included only to make "SLUTFES" sound better. It rang a second time and I swallowed dry and hard. This was it. Buyer's remorse aside, I was going to talk to someone who wanted sex.

"Hey there, sexy," a female voice purred. "You've called the hottest line in the phone book." It was a recording. "Sexy and interesting singles are waiting to hear from you. Press 'one' to talk to beautiful girls in your area. Press 'two' if you're looking for hot guy action." While I was hoping to talk to a live person, I had to admit that this was probably the sexiest voice I had ever heard. I pictured the woman licking her lips and twirling the phone cord with a painted fingernail. I pressed 1.

The sound of glasses clinking and a thrum of voices in a dining hall filled the other end of the line. "Mmm, thanks for pushing the right button," the recorded girl continued over the noise, "so many beautiful women are waiting to talk to you. C'mon, the party is just getting started."

It wasn't exactly what I had expected. I had hoped to talk to a professional phone sex operator skilled in the art of turning on twelve-year-old boys. When was I going to be told to grab myself or rip off all my clothes? When would she demand that I try giving myself a blow job?

I had been on the line for a while. Time seemed to go fast when each minute cost $3.99. Across the street, synagogue congregants were milling about on the sidewalk in front of shul. The men wore tasseled prayer shawls over their shoulders. They stood around discussing the rabbi's sermon while their sharply dressed, yarmulked children ran up and down the stairs leading to the sanctuary entrance. That's where I should be, I thought, reading from a prayer book and staying awake for the rabbi's sermon, not ramping up obscenely priced phone sex bills.

Here I was, frivolously spending my parents' money on something they had not budgeted for. Something not part of the weekly grocery store purchase or the dry cleaning bill. Something that didn't even fall under the category of "stupid waste of money," like cable TV or a palm reader. This was a "holy shit, Eytan has some seriously antisocial behavioral problems" expense. Something shifted in my pants.

The recorded voice was playing a loop. "Mmm, thanks for pushing the right button," she said, despite my not pushing anything. "So many beautiful wom—" The words cut out and there was a dead silence, as though I were listening to a piece of sponge cake. Then it clicked and there was a different type of silence, a silence behind the silence, like a high-end refrigerator. I heard something breathe and my stomach fluttered. Someone real was on the other line, but I was frozen. I couldn't speak. What if she knew I was twelve? I thought. What if I said the wrong thing and she thought I was some sort of freak? My nerves rapidly turned to frustration. Dammit, this wasn't supposed to be like talking to girls in real life! I should be able to say whatever I wanted. I was paying for this!

I opened my mouth and forced a sound out, "Hul—"

"Hallo? Anybody out there?" someone said, cutting me off. The voice was different from the recording. It was Southern and sounded older . . . and belonged to a man.

I didn't respond.

"Hallo?" he said again. "Is anybody out there?"

This was not a sexy woman. This was an actual phone sex caller, a real one, not a sexually frustrated kid spending his parents' money. He could be a criminal, I thought, a sex criminal or a drug addict. He was probably in a one-room apartment or basement somewhere spending his last dollar on the SLUTFES line.

"I can hear you breathe," he said, "and I'm payin' fer this call, so speak up."

A fracture of confidence breeched my anxiety. I wasn't on my own any longer. It was a framework I could work within. It was filling in the blanks. I was being told what to do.

"H . . . Hello-o," I said, elongating the last vowel. I sounded different, more feminine.

Sylvia Sapperstein was an elderly Jewish woman from Long Island whom I had created to prank-call dentists' offices and wig stores.

"Well, hello there. How are you?" the Confederate asked.

"This is Sylvia. Sylvia Sa-apperstein, hu-low." Sylvia always started this way; she was a bit of a yenta and couldn't help but lead the conversation her own route.

"Oh," he said, caught off guard, "what's a . . . going on?"

"How-a you?" Sylvia asked. "So whatta ya ware-ing?"

"Um, not much," my john said.

"Oh, all right." Sylvia was in control, but I was controlling Sylvia, like a sex operator marionette. The tingle in my pants was gone, but something wanted me to keep Sylvia on the phone. It made no sense. The per-minute cost of this call was astronomical, and when my father saw the bill, there would be hell to pay.

How could you, Eytan? I imagined him saying. *A one-nine-hundred number? And on Shabbat! What would the rabbi think? What does the phone company think? Whoever sees this bill will think we're phone sex addicts.*

And maybe that was it. I couldn't tell my father straight out how often I thought about sex, and I was too scared to tell him that I secretly wanted to see what happened when things such as the phone, TV, and Nintendo were used on Shabbat. It was simpler and less immediately painful for Sylvia to have her way and let the phone company break the news to my dad in a month's time.

"Well, I'm ware-ing a teddy," Sylvia said.

"A what?" the man asked.

"Ya know, a teddy . . . thing." I had once read about teddies in a sex toy catalog. They looked like small dresses that barely covered a woman's breasts and vagina. "I bought it at the lawn-juh-ray sto-we."

"I'm so hard."

Whoa, I thought. I was in deep.

"O . . . kay," Sylvia said, unsure of herself.

"I want you to touch it."

"Umm . . ." Eytan said.

"I want you to suck it."

"I . . . I . . ." It was too much. I couldn't maintain the charade without cringing. I took a breath. I wasn't ready to help a strange man pleasure himself.

"You sound like a nice man. What's ya name?" she asked.

"John," he said.

"Well, I just lo-ove that name."

"I want you to taste it, Sylvia."

"O-kay," I said, "Um . . . taste, taste, taste. Yum?"

At that moment, I heard the front door of our apartment open and shut.

"He-llo!" my father shouted.

"Who's that?" John said.

I sat there with my mouth open. My father was two rooms over. There was ample time to hang up the phone and make it look like I was busy not violating the Sabbath. But something kept me lingering there, like a wild animal idiotically waiting for a station wagon to come along and plow right into him. I could give up right now and let my dad find me. He'd walk in and I would throw up my hands. *This is it, Daddy,* I'd say. *What can I tell ya? I'm breaking Shabbat and I call sex hotlines.* I felt a calm wash over me.

"Hu-llooo," said John impatiently.

Jesus Christ! What the hell am I thinking? Hang up the goddamn phone!

I quickly put the receiver down and ended the call. Technically speaking, I had broken Shabbat a second time by cutting the electrical connection, but there was no time to mull it over. I lay down and pulled the covers up to my chin with the phone somewhere underneath. An unfamiliar swell of sleaze formed over my skin.

"Eytan," my dad said, surprised to see me in my room, "I thought you were in shul?"

I felt transparent, as though the call I had made was an active juice, a phone sex juice, secreting from my body and disintegrating my suit and the blanket covering me. It was so obvious what was going on here, I thought. "Yeah, I, uh, just needed, uh, to have a rest," I said.

"Um, okay." He squinted his eyes before continuing, "Well, let's go. You're already late." He turned and walked out.

I pushed the covers off me, sat up on the edge of the bed in my now wrinkled suit, and shuttered. What had I done?

Three weeks later I was alphabetizing my CD collection when my father called me out to the dining room table.

"Eytan!" he shouted. I was wondering when this would happen, dreading it like an exam I didn't study for. I walked out to the dining room in slippers and shorts as my dad sorted through tri-folded papers.

"Did you call a . . . a sex . . . chat phone number?" he asked, confused and angry. He had difficulty even saying it. It was probably the first time he ever had to acknowledge the existence of a sex chat phone number in his life. These were things beneath him, disgusting, crass, uncouth things that existed in a rarely opened filing cabinet in the back of his mind somewhere. When he purchased *The New York Times* at a newsstand and happened to catch a glimpse of the cover of a *Tit Parade* magazine, it barely registered. For him, there were no thoughts like, *Hmmm, interesting, but I really shouldn't.* It was simply, *Oh, there's that thing that doesn't impact my life. Let's get back to thinking about why synagogue affiliation rates in the 1950s were so high, yet attendance so low, as I walk to the subway.*

"It wasn't me," I cried.

"Oh, really, then who was it? Your mother? Your sister? Your brother?" He paused. "Me?"

The logical person to pin the blame on was my brother, but we both knew that he didn't have the nerve to make such a phone call. In bed at night, while I came up with long-winded sex fantasies, Yehuda often meowed and pawed at the air in front of him while deep in slumber. My brother wasn't the type to bring porn home. He wanted to be a cat and change his name to Cookie when he grew up. I, on the other hand, had an evil side. I had awful grades. I liked seeing things get hurt. I was known to tie my feline-esque brother to a chair, tip him over, and then lodge him under the bed. I was capable of bad things.

"This is truly disgusting, Eytan," he said, "even for you."

"I know," I broke down, "it's bad." But it didn't seem that he had investigated the matter fully, because there was no talk about breaking Shabbat. I gave in and took the blame, hoping that he wouldn't think too hard about the date listed on the phone bill. The smaller offense in lieu of the larger.

"Sixty-eight dollars," he said. "How could you?"

That seemed pretty high. I tried doing the math in my head, but at $3.99 per minute, all I could come up with was that it was more than ten minutes.

"No," I said, feigning shock and disappointment at myself as if I really should have known better. "Let me see that. That must be a billing error." Yet right there next to the 900-number with a description of the charge as "Media-Erotic, LLC," it said $67.86.

"Sixty-seven dollars," I corrected him. "But even that can't be right."

"I don't care, Eytan. I'm not calling the phone company and fighting over a sex chat phone call. You're paying for this."

"Okay," I said, "I'm sorry."

"And I'm not telling your mother. This is too embarrassing."
Sweet!

"Never again. Am I making myself clear?"

"Yes, I'm sorry."

"Now go to sleep," he said.

"But it's only six o'clock!" I cried.

He seemed flustered. This was clearly not something he had ever dreamed his son would get involved in. Higher education degrees, agreeable girlfriends, annual charitable donations were all things that I could imagine him imagining for me. This probably never factored into his plan. He had to get his thoughts straight.

"Well, just get out of here," he said. "I . . . don't want to see you right now."

I shuffled back to my room, grateful it hadn't gone worse, and resolved to keep my "baser interests," as my father called them, out of my parents' view.

And in a sense, I did, because the following year, my friend Jared got his own phone line that he was responsible for paying for himself.

"So you're the *only* one who sees the bill?" I asked, sitting on the floor of the bathroom that adjoined his tiny bedroom in his parents' Upper East Side apartment.

"Yup," he said, and I promptly racked up four hundred dollars in debt that my parents never caught wind of.

CHAPTER 6

MY CREEPY HORSES

THROUGHOUT ELEMENTARY SCHOOL, I fell in love with one girl after another. In first grade, there was Aviva. In the second grade: Sarah and Nechama. Third and fourth grades: Jocylyn. Fifth grade: the twins Danielle and Sasha. I never dared talk to any of them. Instead, I fawned over them from across the lunchroom or hoped that they would mistake me for a rock star and chase me down the school hallways. At night, I would usually play my stereo at full volume with the speakers facing out the window and dance on my bed to songs like C+C Music Factory's "Gonna Make You Sweat." I wanted anyone on the sidewalk underneath my room to think that I was a bandleader and we were rehearsing our hit in my bedroom. Hopefully Miriam or Dana or whomever it was that I couldn't stop thinking about at the time would happen to pass by and be impressed.

I know that song, she would think when she saw me lip-synching Color Me Badd's "I Wanna Sex You Up." I never realized that was Eytan's band. I'm going to talk to him tomorrow.

No one ever mentioned my evening performances, though

I imagine that congregants leaving the synagogue across the street after nighttime prayers enjoyed some part of it.

That Bayme kid is lead singer of Boyz II Men? they may have thought. He sure has range.

In the sixth grade, there was Jodi. She was a skinny, long-haired fifth grader that I was hopeless over. It was easy to fall for Jodi because she was the same height as me. I thought that if she lay down on top of me, every upward-facing surface of my body would be covered by every downward-facing surface of hers. With our arms and legs spread, like human asterisks, our noses would smoosh up against each other's and bend out of shape. Naked or clothed, I thought it seemed like the ultimate form of intimacy.

I was terrified to ask if she felt the same way, though, so I stalked her from a safe distance. As she passed me in the school hallways, her wavy brown locks bouncing over her shoulders, I imagined her sitting on a chair in front of my parents' bathroom mirror.

Don't worry, I'll be very careful, I'd say with a pair of scissors in my hand as I trimmed the hair that sometimes got tangled in her plastic-frame glasses.

Jodi preferred heavy denim skirts that fell to her ankles and floral print, long-sleeve shirts that buttoned to her neckline. She dressed in the typical Modern Orthodox female manner and could have been a spokesperson for a matzoh or gefilte fish producer.

On days that the sixth grade's recess overlapped with the fifth grade's, I bolted out of the school doors and onto the playing field to catch glimpses of her. I loved the way she walked across the playground while talking to her friends at the same time. She was like a stuffed animal that could move on her own and converse and hang out. I wanted to be her friend, maybe laugh at an inside joke we shared, casually put my arm around her or let her fall asleep on my shoulder on the bus ride home. I even wanted to be friends with her friends, to be a sensitive yet practical ear that they could talk to about *Little House on the Prairie* or *Rainbow Brite* or whatever it was that girls talked about.

These were all impossible fantasies, though, formed late at night, while tightly wound in a blanket. How would I ever make her mine? In what setting, physically, would we be able to lie down on each other? Not my apartment. Perhaps the forest? Would she get freaked out there? Did she even know that I knew that she existed? When our eyes met and she caught me staring at her across the kickball field, did she actually see me or was she looking at something behind me that my head happened to be in front of?

I was becoming infatuated, driving myself crazy with desire. Somehow, I had to let Jodi know about this very particular relationship I wanted us to have. So I decided to write her an encrypted letter that only mentioned our initials. This way, if I was ever accused of liking her, I could deny the whole thing.

E.B.? Why that could be any number of people who are in love with J.B., I would explain to a jury.

E.B. in the sixth grade, I wrote in two different-colored pencils, *is in love with J.B. She is beautiful. I want to go horseback riding with her. Regards.*

The letter confessed my feelings and I hoped that something might happen with them once they existed in the world. Perhaps Jodi knew of a stable where we could rent a bareback horse.

No, I'd say sitting behind her, *no need to kick the creature. Just stroke its soft hairline. It's called a mane.* It didn't matter that I had never once been on a horse and was easily frightened by small dogs. This was how it would be when Jodi and I were together.

My friend Gilad was also troubled by girls, yet he chose to be upfront and ask them to marry him or be his very serious girlfriend.

"I'm going to ask Shira to go steady with me today," he once said.

"But have you ever spoken to her?" I asked.

"Not really." He shrugged.

He was too straightforward and aggressive, and I counseled against the approach. My note, on the other hand, had a coolness to it. *This is what I feel*, I was saying. *Take it however you see fit*. In fact, it was not even specifically addressed to Jodi. It was simply a statement to the person who received the note.

Oh, you happened to read that letter, I was trying to say. *Yes, I suppose it does have to do with you. You are certainly welcome to respond if that is what you wish.*

Adults didn't ask people to marry them the first time they met. They said things such as "Regards," and since I was older than Jodi, this showed her how mature I was.

Even if you don't feel the same way that I do, I was saying, *say hello to your parents for me.*

The next day at school, I staked out Jodi's classroom until she and her classmates left for recess. At her desk, she had a turquoise plastic pencil case and a purple folder. All day, these lucky school supplies got to sit inside her knapsack on the back of her chair and wait to get handled by Jodi herself. She used the same Ticonderoga brand #2 pencils that I did, but there was something more dignified about hers. The lengths seemed statelier than mine. The eraser heads were more rounded than mine, as though she eliminated her mistakes in a more correct manner than I did—in the way that the Dixon Ticonderoga

Company designed errors to be erased. There was something sacred about her workplace. Everything on it seemed to be in a specific, designated location. Even the torn-up bits of paper under her desk, which were ripped with a level of precision that I could not match, were in the exact place they should be. That was the way to tear up paper.

If Jodi's belongings were a course, I would never fail an exam on them. I could have studied them for hours, memorizing the edges of her folders and notebooks until I was ready to teach the class myself. But I had to leave; anyone could have seen me there. "Sixth Grader Snooping Around Fifth Grader's Stuff," the headline splashed across the weekly school newsletter would read. Name-calling and rhyming teases would make their way through the hallways. "Pedophile" was a new word some boys in my grade had learned from *The Howard Stern Show* and they were eager to throw it around.

"She's a total peda," Gilad had said about a cranky secretary in the administrative office. I could not let myself become the target of such a dynamic new insult, so I pulled the letter out of my pocket and threw it down on Jodi's chair before running off.

Our 1970s-era, open-plan-style school had no walls. It was designed as one giant room built into the side of a hill, with mezzanine levels for each grade. After dropping the note, I was worried that Jodi would mistake it for a piece of garbage and brush it off her chair without opening it. So I retreated to an area overlooking the fifth grade and waited, half hidden, as her class began filing back inside.

Jodi soon pranced in, her long hair keeping up like an aerobic streamer. I held my breath and watched her scoop the note off the chair, carefully open it, and examine its contents. Satisfied with what I had seen, I began to leave, but then I heard her scream.

"Look at this!" she shouted and four of her girlfriends huddled around to have a peek. I couldn't make out exactly what was being said, but their erratic giggles seemed to have a meaning of their own.

Is this guy for real? I imagined one said.

I bet it's that Eytan Bayme guy who's always staring at you, another might have said.

Oh my God, what a freak!

My face flushed red and whatever relief I felt from leaving the letter was replaced by a knot slowly tightening in the center of my belly. This was it, I thought, the worst possible reaction: public humiliation. As they continued their gigglefest, I ran off to the dark synagogue to ponder my next move.

Thank God I left it semi-anonymous, I thought, as I listed the other E.B.'s in my grade. I would feel bad pinning it on my good friend Elie Blumenthal, but wouldn't hesitate to in the end. In matters of social homicide, it was every man for himself. The problem was that Elie and his family had moved to Israel for the year, and it would be hard to believe that he sent the letter to Jodi's seat from overseas.

Elana Brand was also similarly initialed, but she was a girl and I didn't think anyone would believe that there was so bold a sixth-grade lesbian at our private Jewish day school.

There were no other E.B.'s in my grade. Once Jodi took a look at the school phone list, she could easily deduce that it was me, Eytan Bayme, who was so terribly in love with her. Why did I have to leave such a dumb note? Couldn't I have just gone up to her and asked a question about schoolwork or the bus ride home or the lunch menu and seen where things went? She would have no idea that I wanted to steal locks of her hair and keep one of her shoes in my baseball card drawer if we talked about a few things not having to do with how crazy I was for her.

I had screwed myself. And so, with no other choice, I went into hiding. I began by spending recesses in the library, a place I absolutely despised for having nothing but books everywhere. There I would hang out with two nerds who always kept a pencil and piece of graph paper handy to draw diagrams that helped explain their discussions about chess and the interminable computer game "Dungeons & Dragons." These recesses were hell on earth, but I felt that I had to endure them because had I spent them on the field with the rest of the fifth and sixth grades, Jodi and her friends were likely to approach me and point or laugh or lay some other unthinkably awful act of terror upon me.

At lunch when I had to be in the same room as the fifth graders, I tried to sit in a far corner, away from their seats. This way if she approached me, I would have enough time to slide under the foldout lunchroom table and hide. I still kept her in my line of sight, but I never let my stares linger. If her head moved the slightest inch as she chewed on a tuna sandwich or twirled spaghetti and sauce onto a fork, I immediately looked elsewhere for fear that she would catch me ogling and offer further proof that I was E.B.

An entire year of shame and self-torment passed without saying a word to Jodi. I managed to ignore her so thoroughly that there was no way she could think I was her secret admirer. If I passed her in the hallways, I would come to a complete stop and fiddle with my watch intensely or rifle through my bag as though I had misplaced something deeply important, and only dare look up from my charade after she was long gone.

Dodging efforts were going smoothly until I was forced to

participate in a choir recital before the entire school. Getting onstage in front of people was not the concern, as I had sung and danced in school plays in the past, but this performance was during school hours with Jodi in the audience. I would be on display in front of all my peers, giving Jodi the perfect opportunity to embarrass me publicly and tell everyone that I thought she was beautiful.

As the recital date approached, the knot in my stomach grew tighter. I thought about not showing up and maybe hiding in the library during the performance, but the musical director had given me solo verses, and I would let the whole choir down by skipping it.

On the big day, the thirty other choir members and I lined up in rows on a bleacher on the school stage. I scanned the sea of faces filling up the gymnasium in front of us. Everyone was there: all my friends, all my teachers, people whom I had known since I was three. And there in the center, in her glasses and scrunchie, was Jodi. She looked as beautiful as ever, and oh my God, she was staring directly at me. I quickly looked down at my palms and began to sweat. What was I going to do?

The music started and the choir began singing, but I was too nervous to participate. What if I looked up and our eyes met again? It would give her all the evidence she needed to prove that I wrote the letter. I pulled a piece of scrap paper from my pocket and stared at it intently. Then it came to me. I looked at the blank page harder. There was nothing written on it, but that made no difference. The idea was to appear too busy to sing. As my choir mates ran through a Hebrew song about harvests, I put a hand to my temple and tried to appear as though I were grappling with a very difficult and convoluted equation. The deeper I was in thought, the less likely Jodi would get up and out me as her stalker. Who would interrupt a person so busy and vexed by something he was reading? I thought. It would be too rude, even for a note-sharer like Jodi. And if I was wrong and Jodi was so disruptive a person, someone who had no problem interrupting me in the middle of such a seemingly important letter, the audience would surely take my side. I would be victim to a delusional girl.

What? I would respond angrily when the music stopped and Jodi waved my letter high in the air. *I'm just trying to get through this very serious correspondence. What does any of that have to do with me?*

At one point in the performance, I sat down in the bleachers, hidden from the five hundred students in the audience and surrounded by the legs of my fellow singers, so I could better pretend to focus on my blank note. When it was time for me to sing my solo verses I popped up and delivered clipped, bored versions of them as if I had better places to be, before ducking back down again. The performance ended without a scene. My plan had worked.

A few months later, our grades began praying together each morning. This meant that every day Jodi was sitting somewhere behind the *mechitza*, a sculpted metal grate that separated the girls' side of the synagogue from the boys' side. The sanctuary was a circular room much smaller than the cafeteria, and it would be difficult to remain invisible throughout the forty-five-minute service.

The first few weeks were miserable. I was constantly worried that she would giggle at or about me. Each time I saw a girl talk to her, I thought they were discussing what a shameful little person I was. Unable to control myself, I would sometimes steal glimpses of Jodi's perfectly hazel eyes, and the few times she caught my gaze, she returned it with a knowing look that said, *Oh, you again. I know about you and your creepy horses.*

Soon I realized that if she were going to accuse me of something, she would have done it already, and I relaxed a little. I stopped worrying so much about what she was thinking and came to enjoy being in the same room with her each morning. The close proximity excited me, and I began daydreaming of the life we could have together. I imagined her wearing a white button-down shirt and khaki pants as she hung our freshly laundered sheets on a rope behind the immaculate Westchester home we lived in. At the local park, we would play lighthearted, sexually charged one-on-one basketball that led to sex acts behind a short wall separating a woodsy area from the swing sets.

I started coming to prayer services full of energy, hoping to appear like a fun guy who everyone wanted to be friends with. I memorized crude jokes that morning disc jockeys told and repeated them to my classmates at prayer. They smacked their knees and tried to hold in laughter. I am so funny, I thought. You could have had this, Jodi.

My long-term hiding plan had only a few more weeks to go. The end of the year was approaching, which meant that I was about to begin a full Jodi-less summer.

One Saturday night, a few months after my twelfth birthday, I was watching TV with my mom in her bedroom. At that age, most Saturday nights were spent in front of the television with her. Usually, we tuned into reruns of a sitcom called *Small Wonder* about a robot girl with an electrical outlet under her arm, followed by *Saturday Night Live*. Most weeks, my dad would come in around 1:00 a.m. and say that it was time to "hit the hay," and usher me into my room, bleary-eyed and already half asleep.

That night, shortly before *SNL* began, the phone rang.

"It's for you, Eytan!" my father shouted from the other side of the apartment.

"Really?"

"A girl!" he said.

Something wasn't right. Girls never called me. I had learned my lesson the hard way and avoided any unnecessary conversation with them, fearing that something incredibly stupid might come out of my mouth, such as "I love you," or "I think about you sometimes during long car rides and in the bathtub." It was simpler to avoid talking altogether.

My mother looked over at me and smiled. "Aren't you going to answer it?" she asked.

"Yes. Obviously," I told her. I slowly picked up the phone next to the bed and listened in. On the line, I could hear the basketball game my father was watching in the other room as he waited for me to answer.

"Hello?" I asked nervously.

"Hi, is this Eytan?" asked a nasal feminine voice.

"Yes," I said, beginning to shake. "Who is this?"

"This is Jodi," the voice said, and I was almost certain I could hear faint giggles—not the giggle of one girl but the giggles of many. Who knows how many? Perhaps her entire class was on the other line.

"Oh," I said, "hold on a second."

I pulled the phone off my ear and covered the mouthpiece with my hand. What the hell was going on? Why would she be calling me? Maybe she had come to her senses and decided that she loved me. Maybe she wanted to lay all our feelings out and sort through them once and for all. Maybe it had just taken her a long time to realize how great I really was.

"Who is it?" my mother asked, smiling.

"Nobody! Jesus!" I stammered.

"Okay," she responded, still smiling.

"Daddy! Hang up when I tell you to!" I shouted back across

the apartment. I didn't know what I was in for. Would she make fun of me? Would she ask me on a date? Would she want phone sex? Whatever it was, I needed to take this call in my own room.

"Okay!" my father screamed back. I placed the phone back on the receiver and ran out of my parents' room. It was only fifteen feet to my bedroom, but I couldn't get there fast enough. I didn't want to leave the love of my life waiting on the phone for too long. I slid across the hardwood floor in my socks and burst through my "No Parking"-sign-covered door as my little brother smashed two Teenage Mutant Ninja Turtle action figures together.

"Get out!" I told him.

"No, I'm playing," he said.

"I said get out! Now!"

"I said no! I'm playing!"

Precious seconds were wasting away. There was no time to chase Yehuda out of the room we shared, so I called him an idiot and picked up the receiver, stretching it out as far from him as it would go.

"Hello?" I asked.

Nothing.

"Hello?" I said again.

Nothing.

I pushed down on the call button and the hum of a dial tone rang in my ear. The line had been disconnected. I was on the cusp of putting an end to the torment that filled me. I could have told her or whoever it was that I wrote that letter because my feelings were simply too overwhelming to bear.

My heart sank. Over time, my longing for Jodi had begun to fade, but now I immediately missed her again. Even if she and her friends were calling to make fun of me, I wanted to hear what she had to say. I wanted to feel close to her. If it wasn't her, I wanted to hear the impression. I wouldn't know the difference.

I sat there staring at the phone dumbfounded, looking perhaps like I was going to cry, because my brother asked, "What's wrong with you?"

"Nothing! Goddamnit!" I said.

"Nothing goddamnit *you*," he said. "I was trying to be nice."

I ignored him and ran out to the den, where my father was watching a Celtics game.

"What did you do?" I screamed.

"I hung up the phone, like you asked," he said.

"You hung up the phone before you were supposed to!"

"Excuse me, Eytan," he said. "You said hang up, so I hung up."

"I said hang up when I tell you to! You hung up before I got to the phone!"

"Who was that?" my mother asked as she came out of her room.

"Nobody!" I shouted louder.

"If it was nobody, then why do you care?" my father asked.

I couldn't handle his logic games. "Baaaah!" I screamed in frustration and jumped on the couch face-first.

"If it was so important, I'm sure whoever it was will call back," said my mother.

But no one called back, and I was left with only my imagination as to what Jodi and her friends would have said to me:

We know you, Eytan. We know you dream about being our friend and getting to know our mothers, imagining us naked in a secluded outdoor area, raising children with us in some suburb. We understand exactly how you think. In fact, we know what you are thinking before you think it, and we think it's despicable. Laughable. Keep dreaming.

I was better off for hanging up on whoever it was. My father had actually done a service for me, for all the further heartache that talking to whoever was on the other line would have caused. The raspiness of the caller's voice was nothing like I had imagined Jodi's to be like, so why open up a scab that was mostly healed and ruin the fantasy? What Jodi and I shared was heartbreaking, but no less special. The memory of it needed to be preserved like a prehistoric mosquito in amber. Besides, other girls were bound to start calling me at some point soon.

CHAPTER 7

BAR MITZVAH BULGE

ONCE AGAIN, MY EYES settled upon Cantor Ratner's bulging pants. His wasn't an inappropriate bulge, rather it was the bulge of a second stomach. One stomach swelled, stretching his white button-down shirt above a black leather belt, while the second protruded wide and blunt like the tip of a giant's thumb beneath his gray slacks. Aside from the plastic-covered dining room chairs and the menorah-filled breakfront, the Cantor's apartment had a shortage of interesting things to examine, and so I always came back to that inflated lower midsection.

There he was, sitting next to me at his dining room table, the third book of the Old Testament open on the plastic-covered tablecloth in front of him. His chair was tucked in, yet I was still trying to catch a glimpse of that crotch. *Stop it, Eytan!* I told myself, but it was like trying not to stare at a burn victim or a female classmate's chest. I could not help myself. The man had a massive fat deposit on his most precious property and I was a skinny twelve-year-old unable to pull my polluted little mind away from it.

Just a few minutes earlier, the Cantor's wife, Mrs. Ratner,

had greeted me at the door to their apartment. Like my wid-
owed *nagymama*, the Ratners always kept the thermostat in their
home hovering just above eighty degrees, and whenever I
visited, their shared appreciation of an overly heated home
made me think that the three of them would make great friends.

"Would you like a snack, Eytan?" Mrs. Ratner asked me
from the kitchen as I laid my knapsack and winter jacket on
the floor beside the dining room table.

"Um . . . thank you," I said before she placed a delicate plate
of stuffed cabbage in front of me. I was always unsure of what
to talk about with older people who were not blood relatives,
but manners made things easier. I said "thank you" when someone blessed my sneeze, I said "you're welcome" when someone
thanked me. Manners were an easy-to-follow script that crossed
generational boundaries.

"Would you like some more?" she asked after I finished.

"Please," I told her, confident that the right words were
coming out of my mouth.

The Cantor himself soon shuffled into the dining room
clutching a Bible and wooden lectern that he unfolded and
placed on the table.

For a few decades before I was born, Cantor Ratner had
led the prayer service each Shabbat at our synagogue. By the
time I started meeting with him, he was officially retired, yet
all the congregants still referred to him as "the Cantor." It was
a fitting title. From his booming voice to the larger-than-life
surfaces that compromised his body, everything about him was
cantorial. Here he was, engulfing my shrimpy paw with his
beefsteak hand or turning a sturdy-looking dining room chair,
that fit two of me, into a rickety jumble of wood.

Cantor Ratner was the old guard, an eighty-year-old teacher
of teachers. If the principal of my school or the rabbi of my

synagogue had a problem, I imagined they went to him for guidance. When he entered a room, people stood up. He was a community member who actually deserved the title "Man of the Year," when it was bestowed upon him at the annual synagogue fund-raiser. It seemed as though God personally had the Cantor's back, which made my wandering eyes burn even hotter.

"How is your father?" he boomed at me.

"He's okay," I whispered. With his wife in the kitchen, I was more at ease with the Cantor's magnanimity; as if he could not tap into the full wrath of his larger-than-life persona with his woman in the next room over.

"Your father does very good things for the Jewish people."

Yeah, but not always, I thought to myself. My father's role in the American Jewish world was often mentioned by teachers or parents of classmates. *One time he took me out for fried chicken and forgot to order for me*, I wanted to tell them. *That's not very good for the Jews.*

Unfortunately, though, the Cantor's seal of approval overshadowed whatever issues I had with my dad. They became necessary even, as though my father was so busy being important that sometimes his children had to sacrifice meals. In front of the Cantor, I felt sorry for all the screaming and arguing and childish behavior that I directed at my father.

This was a problem because for the past few months the Cantor had been helping me prepare to become a man. Once a week after school, he taught me to read the musical notes that annotate the Old Testament. These notes would help me sing by heart my *parsha*, a seven-chapter section of the Torah, while standing on a platform in front of our fifteen-hundred-person synagogue congregation. All this was for my bar mitzvah and I was dreading it like a needle at the doctor's office.

Some friends of mine were getting away with reading one chapter, not by heart, followed by a party at a roller-skating rink. Others were celebrating their bar mitzvah in Israel, where they would read the Torah only in front of immediate family members and maybe a couple of Western Wall stragglers looking for a quick pickup prayer service. Everything about mine, from the seating chart I was supposed to rank my friends by, to the seemingly incredible amount of Bible that I had to memorize, said, *This is a big deal.*

"Have you been practicing?" the Cantor asked me that afternoon in his apartment.

The Cantor may have been inspiring of awe and legitimate honcho-ness, but there was nobody who could motivate me to do consistent homework.

"I didn't . . . really . . . get . . . a chance to go over it this week," I said, slowing my speech sympathetically and letting him down easy as to what a disappointment I was.

"You won't learn your bar mitzvah portion if you don't practice at home," the Cantor responded.

Under normal circumstances, after telling a teacher that I had not done my homework, a negotiation would ensue.

"What is so much more important to you, Mr. Bayme, than the quiz I assigned last night?" my no-nonsense science teacher, Mr. Gorfinkle, once asked me.

"I'm really sorry. I'll definitely, definitely have it by tomorrow," I said to him, spouting the lines I had rehearsed while not doing his quiz the previous night. "If you want, I could sit outside the door and do it right now," I continued, laying some bait to get out of class.

With Cantor Ratner, though, it was different. He stated facts without tone or threat of consequence.

"Yes, you are right," I told him soberly. "I should really practice more."

The truth was I was terrified of showing up to my bar mitzvah unprepared. I would be singing a very long, very particular passage from the Torah in front of my friends, my family, my families' friends, and hundreds of synagogue congregants. Everyone in attendance would have an easy-to-read Bible complete with vowels and musical notes to follow along in. I, on the other hand, would be reading straight from the Torah scroll; a hundred-foot-long, punctuation-less lamb-skin parchment.

The physical Torah is written by a certified Torah writer with a quill. He uses no vowels and skips all the musical notes in a personal affront to bar mitzvah students. Attempting to read from the Torah without practice wld b lt lk rdng ths hlf sntnc. To make matters worse, I would be corrected. If I made a mistake, any one of the synagogue attendees with their vowel-laden texts could and would halt my song and scream out the correct way to pronounce whatever word I was trying to speak. This was what my bar mitzvah all came down to: mistakes. How many I would make and how I would react to the pressure of surly adult men who wanted to hear their weekly Torah portion error-free.

Mistakes were something that I had a long history with. We had known each other well, ever since the first grade, when I realized that doing poorly in school was a lot easier than succeeding.

"Eytan scored a twenty-two on my exam," my fourth-grade Hebrew studies teacher Giveret Korach, or *Ms.* Korach in English, said to my father after I opted not to study for her big test. "And this was the easy test," she continued in a thick, hoarse Israeli accent, "the test I designed especially for Eytan and the other students who are falling behind."

Korach, my dad, and I were deep in the recesses of the teachers' lounge. There were exposed pipes on the ceiling and a bank of lockers behind my short, orange-haired teacher.

"Do you know what score Eytan received on the regular test?" Korach prodded as she brought a long black clove cigarette to her dry lips.

My dad looked down at me as I was trying to count the butts in the ashtray behind my teacher. I could see five brown stubs sitting in a comfortable-looking pile of cinder. No one ever smoked around me, and I was curious as to how soft the ash would feel under my finger.

"No, I don't know," he said impatiently, sensing that he was being set up for a punch line.

"Eytan got a four," said the *giveret*.

"Four out of what?"

"Four out of *one hundred*!" She raised her voice, indicating that her time was now being wasted. "It would be one thing if he scored a twenty-two on the regular test, Dr. Bayme, then I think that we would have something to work with. But this was a special test, the *eeeasy* test that I gave to only a few students."

Giveret Korach took a drag from her clove cigarette and allowed us a moment to absorb the news. "Dr. Bayme," she finally continued, "the score is *extreeemely* low. Your son will not pass my class if he does not shape up."

"How could you, Eytan?" asked my father as I tried to keep up with him walking to our car in the parking lot. I had to admit, a four was completely horrible, even by my standards. Yet I knew that my score would be poor because I didn't study. I had better things to do, like use every single Lego that I owned to build a house on wheels, or sculpt myself a Mohawk with the entire can of my sister's mousse. Activities like these were far more interesting to me than getting good grades, and in exchange, all I had to endure was an uncomfortable meeting with a teacher and the disappointment of my parents.

My bar mitzvah was different, though. If there was a bar mitzvah scoring system and I received a four or a twenty-two or anything other than a passable seventy-five and above, it would be posted to the door of the synagogue. Congregants, eager to get out of prayer service fast, would attack each of my mistakes and then discuss my poor performance over Shabbat lunch with their congregant friends.

*That Bayme kid clearly did not put the time into his bar mitzvah par-*sha *this afternoon,* I imagined Dr. Eisenman, an ophthalmologist who sat toward the rear of sanctuary, would tell his guests over a chopped liver appetizer. *He must not be very bright.*

Well, it certainly does reflect on his family, his wife might reply. *I would hate to be the parents of his parents. How embarrassing for everyone related to him!*

The implications for messing up my bar mitzvah *parsha* were far greater than any single exam or homework assignment. This was a public stage in front of a community jury. These were people whom my parents invited over for Shabbat meals, people allowed to sit on my mother's expensive living room couch, people to whom my father gave tours of his 4,500-book library. Screwing up my bar mitzvah would kill my parents, I thought. They would have to come clean to their community about how horrible a student I was.

It's not really Eytan's fault that he messed up his Torah portion, my mother might say. *He has a lot of problems*—emotional *problems.*

My poor work habits would no longer remain hidden. Adults would probably avoid direct eye contact with me and speak very loudly and slowly if they ever had to address me.

Mr. Bayme, a friend's mother might call out to me as we

played in his backyard, *remember not to eat anything you find on the ground, please.*

And so, there was a lot riding on this bar mitzvah. It wasn't simply about becoming a man and adhering to all the laws of the Torah. It was about maintaining appearances and not letting my community see how uninterested in schoolwork and Jewish ritual I truly was.

Cantor Ratner placed a black tape recorder on the table and hit the "record" button. "From the top," he said.

"Vayehee bayom hashemini," I began singing the Torah portion. My pace was fast and, with all the vowels and musical notes in place, relatively accurate.

The Hebrew alphabet is fairly easy to master, with twenty-two consonants and five vowels. In the Torah, the musical notes can take letters higher or lower in pitch and elongate or shorten the way they are sung.

The Cantor stopped me every so often and made me repeat a word until I pronounced it correctly. "Go back, Eytan," he said and I would try the word again until I got it right. Forty-five minutes later he pushed a button on the tape recorder and it snapped off.

"Take this home and listen to yourself."

"Really?" I asked.

"Record yourself practicing and then listen to how it sounds."

Cool! The device was about the size of a Walkman and had an internal microphone and speaker to record and play without any wires. It wasn't exactly a Super Nintendo, but free stuff was better than no free stuff. I couldn't wait to bring it home and play my Weird Al Yankovic tapes on it.

"Thank you!"

"Good evening, ladies and gentlemen," I spoke into the microphone later that evening, "my name is Tom Brokaw and this is *NBC Nightly News.* Our top story tonight is about a young boy named Yehuda Bayme. Yehuda is the fattest nine-year-old boy in New York City, and he is in our studio this evening. Yehuda, how are you doing?"

I put the tape recorder to my little brother's face for his response.

"Eytan," he said with a wry smile, "screw you," and then began swinging his heavy, log-like arms at me as I retreated to my bed for protection.

"Sorry!" I screamed. "I was kidding!"

"You jackass," he muttered before leaving the room.

Maybe I had crossed a line. My brother had only been sitting on the floor browsing a *Mad* magazine when I provoked him. There was no reason to call him fat on record, aside from alleviating my own boredom. I hit "rewind" and played back the events. My newscaster impression bookended on both sides by my bar mitzvah rehearsal showed how obnoxious I could be in a way I had never heard before. One side of me sounded vulnerable and small, but working toward something in earnest. The other was a self-absorbed, unwelcome intruder, bursting onto the tape like the Kool-Aid man through a wall. *Do I really sound like that much of a jerk?* I shuddered.

"Meet me at shul tomorrow night," the Cantor told me over the phone a few weeks later. I figured that he had business at the synagogue and meeting there was more convenient than his apartment, but as we walked into the empty sanctuary, I realized this was a surprise dress rehearsal.

The massive, main prayer hall was as big as a football field. I had been inside the room countless times but never when it was this empty. Normally amid the throngs of worshippers shaking back and forth and reading fervently from their prayer books, it was easy to feel small and hidden. Among all those people clamoring for God's attention as though it were an outdoor fish market, I could keep my head low and feel confident that God had His hands full handling the requests and prayers of my fellow congregants.

God, over here! I imagined a community member shouting in his mind on Shabbat. *Pete Blumenthal from 246th Street. I'm cheating on my wife. Can you forgive me?*

Lord! Sir! I accidentally turned on the bathroom light last Shabbat! What shall I do? cried another.

Got any stock tips for me, Almighty One? Send me a sign! Moshie Tietelbaum. Fieldstone Road. You know me!

But here, with just the Cantor and me, God had nothing but me and my dirty thoughts to keep Him busy. As I trod into the court of the King of Kings and He sat on His throne waiting to be entertained, my thoughts immediately betrayed me. Images of obese naked men and women flooded my mind. The Cantor's bulge seemed to be wriggling itself at me from between his legs. Neon silhouettes of reclining women flashed on and off inside my brain.

Well well well, what do we have here? I imagined God saying sarcastically as He eyed me walking up His aisle.

The Cantor headed toward the front of the room, where the *Aron Kodesh*, or Holy Ark, took over most of the eastern-facing wall. These two, ten-foot-high gold and marble tablets inscribed with the Ten Commandments were the doors to the most sacred property in the synagogue: the Torah inventory. The Ark was lit from the back and spilled light from each side. Even the massive rock doors couldn't contain the powers within.

I hung back while the Cantor ascended the platform before the Ark. If the synagogue was God's house, then the *Aron Kodesh* was like God's bedroom closet, filled with things that were none of my business. Would I ever go into a friend of my parents' home and start rummaging through his personal items? It felt wrong and I wondered if the rabbi knew we were here.

"Come," said the Cantor.

I looked at the empty hall behind me for someone to speak up and defend me. *No, Cantor,* they would say, *synagogue regulation forbids you from proceeding any further.* But I was on my own. It was like this was all part of the bar mitzvah. If I was to become a man, I would have to face God and walk up to His Holy Ark.

The Cantor slid the doors of the Ark open to reveal a gallery of ten Torah scrolls shining like royal jewels. He went down the row, lifting a flap on each of the Torahs' felt coverings, as though peeking up the skirts in a line of women and trying to choose the one he liked best. It was all so professional. To me, these forty-thousand-dollar scrolls with their intricate silver crowns and heavy breastplates were the holiest physical articles on earth. The Torahs were alive—thirty-pound representatives of God, whose home the Cantor was sorting through, trying to pick out a fresh one like it was a butcher's meat case.

"This one." He pointed to a medium-sized Torah covered in smooth blue velvet. There were two silver crowns and bells on the top with a large breastplate hanging on a silver chain around them. It looked sharp, perpetually dressed for Shabbat.

"Come on," the Cantor said, "take it."

"Me?" I looked at him incredulously.

"Let's go. We don't have all night."

Besides bending over deep into God's personal armoire and yanking out His scroll, I was worried that the Torah would be too heavy for me to hold. According to a Talmudic ruling, if a Torah was dropped, everyone in the room would have to fast for forty days. Was that even physically possible?

The Cantor was old, though, and in no shape to be lifting so many pounds of Bible, and as he waited impatiently, I sucked this up as another part of the bar mitzvah test.

At the Ark, I leaned in and lodged my arms around both sides of the scroll, jostling two adjacent Torahs in the process. As I pulled up, the silver around the Torah started jangling.

Am I doing it right? Is it falling from my hands? Is my whole body tilting backward onto the stairs below? Are you spotting me? This is it. I hope you don't like food, Cantor Ratner.

But no voices were raised, and when my body came to a rest, I seemed to be standing upright. I looked at the Cantor and he was calm. It must be in my hands, I deduced. Yes, it was heavy, but I had it. It was not going to drop. And with that, a confidence began to build.

I got you, Torah. Don't you worry.

The Cantor shut the Ark and I laid the scroll on a wide wooden podium in the middle of the sanctuary, where, in two months' time, I would be reading before my whole community.

"Let's go," he said. "Take it off."

I stared at him blankly and my heart dropped into my stomach. This was why I was so nervous around adults. Because of their size and reputations, they could force me into situations that I had no control over. All he had to do was ask and I had to give. He was a professional and had probably thought this all out beforehand. If I tried to run, he would hit a button and all the doors to the sanctuary would lock. Then he would sniff me out as I hid under one of the pews. After he had his way, if I cried to the authorities, no one would believe that a poor student who hated prayer services had been taken advantage of by the Cantor himself.

The Cantor widened his eyes at me and put his palms in the air as if to say, *Well?* And I realized that he was talking about undressing the Torah, not me.

As I pulled off the crowns and breastplate and laid them carefully on a chair, an embarrassed sweat formed under my clothes. Did he know what I was thinking about? I wondered while removing the velvet covering. Beneath the garment, a soft strap with a metal clasp held the scrolls together, and as I unhinged it, I began to imagine that this was what removing a bra felt like.

The words on the open Torah were mind-numbing. Gone were the vowels, the punctuation, and the musical notes, and in their place was one very long sentence in yard-high columns. The Cantor pointed to an area in the middle of the parchment. There was no paragraph indentation, it was not even at the beginning of a line, but after examining it closely, I realized that the word he pointed to had the same letters as the first word of my *parsha*. *Vayehee*, it said, "And it was."

"Commence," said the Cantor.

It began easily enough. We had practiced it from the top so often that I knew the first few sentences by heart, but around five lines in I got stumped.

"*Leez . . . Leezb.*" The sounds were there on the parchment in front of me, but I couldn't remember how to put them together. Sweat dripped from my hairless armpits. The Cantor waited for me; God waited for me. If I glossed over the tune part and pretended to be tone deaf, no one could blame me, but the pronunciation was the part that everyone has to get right. *This is the* eeeasy *part,* said Giveret Korach in my head.

I stopped pretending and said, "This is kind of hard for me."

"Have you been practicing?" the Cantor asked.

"Not so much."

"Are you using the tape recorder?"

"Sometimes."

"Give it here."

I took the recorder out from my jacket and looked at it wide-eyed, turning it over in my hand as though I had never seen such a contraption before. I was stalling, of course, because I thought he could sense that I was using his gift for forces of evil and was going to listen to my newscast.

So this is what you are doing while you are supposed to be preparing to become a man, I imagined him saying. *You know what, maybe you're not ready, maybe your little brother should get bar mitzvahed first and then we'll check back with you. Oh, your poor father.*

There was no avoiding it, though. I placed the recorder on the table and watched as he reached out toward the plastic buttons on the side. He ran his finger along the long black "play" button as though he were savoring my dread, but he kept going until he reached the small red "record" button, and pushed down.

"Continue," he said.

I slogged through the next half hour with the Cantor stopping to correct my pronunciation every third or fourth word. When my time was through, we packed the Torah back up and returned it to the Ark. I was humiliated, embarrassed for God and for the Cantor that they had to witness such a poor performance. Letting people down was something familiar to me, but this felt grave.

Twelve years earlier, in that sanctuary, at that very podium,

Cantor Ratner had clutched a pillow that my eight-day-old frame lay upon. With the entire congregation in attendance, the Cantor sliced my foreskin and made me Jewish. He then passed me to my father, who held me up and shouted my name for the first time.

"Eytan Tzvi," he said, meaning "strength of a deer."

Who was this Eytan who was now obsessed with crotches and people much heavier than he? Certainly not the same person who held fast through a circumcision and then filled the sanctuary hall with his wails, demanding that his congregation acknowledge him as a Jew. This was a fake—someone with the strength of maybe an overweight cat or sloth trying to pass himself off as the real Eytan Tzvi.

I felt bad for the Cantor, as if he were contractually stuck with me. Would he have agreed to circumcise me if he had known how I would turn out?

"Same place next week," the Cantor said to me as we walked out of the synagogue.

That evening, in a locked bathroom, I played back my performance on a pair of headphones. It sounded poor. I was screwing up the tune and the pronunciation often. My voice sounded weak and unsure of itself. Before bed, I pushed the record button and went to sleep. When I woke, empty white noise interspersed with sounds of Yehuda purring had replaced the newscast and the previous evening's practice. The void on the tape felt like a statement. It was not enough to simply start practicing more often. My behavior needed to be stricken from the record, like emptying a plate of bad food directly into the incinerator instead of the trash can.

The next night I asked my father to sit with me while I practiced.

"Sure. You know I used to be a *shaliach tzibur* myself," he said, referring to his days as the house Torah reader at his college synagogue.

"Yes, I know." I was acutely aware of this because each night, he sang the weekly Torah portions to himself in the kitchen as he happily cleaned the dinner plates. His memorization of almost the entire Torah was a point he didn't let any of us fail to acknowledge most nights of the week.

"Beautiful voice," he'd proclaim when I came into the kitchen for a glass of juice, "don't you think?"

"Sure, Daddy," I'd say, rolling my eyes.

"You know my bar mitzvah portion was a double, fourteen chapters long. No mistakes. Did I ever tell you that?"

"Yes, Daddy."

That evening I recorded myself singing the final four, most difficult chapters of my portion. My father hummed along throughout. He stopped to correct me less frequently than the Cantor and I wondered if he was paying close enough attention to me.

"Not bad, Eytan," he said after we finished.

We did it again the following night and most nights thereafter.

A few weeks later, Gilad had his bar mitzvah. He too had studied with the Cantor and was singing the full Torah portion in front of the entire congregation. The difference between Gilad and me was that studying came easy to him.

"The Cantor's balls are huge!" he exclaimed one day at

school. He must have been killing his Torah portion if he could afford to make such an audacious claim.

On his bar mitzvah day, the rabbi called Gilad up in front of the Ark and publicly presented him with a set of Bibles. He called him a "true *Talmid chacham*," meaning one who has an unusually strong understanding of the Torah, and said that there was a "bright future for this bar mitzvah boy."

During his Torah portion, Gilad messed up exactly three times and was abruptly corrected at each instance by Dr. Eisenman, the ophthalmologist who sat in the back of the sanctuary shouting "ah!" whenever an "eh" or "ooh" should have been uttered.

"'Ah'! 'Ah'! Not 'eh'!" he screamed.

After the reading, as the congregation pelted Gilad with candies, he ducked under the wide podium. I scrambled below and found him laughing as though he had won the lottery.

"You messed up only three times," I told him.

"Yeah. So what?" he said.

"Weren't you nervous?"

"A little, I guess. If only Eisenman would shut up and let me finish."

That week, at the empty synagogue with the Cantor, I felt more relaxed as I wrapped my arms around the scroll and carried it to the podium. God was still there, but He seemed distracted, as though He were busy reading the newspaper, cross-legged in a side pew, only half-listening to my performance.

I read at a loud and steady clip, mispronouncing words often. The Cantor told me to repeat myself over and over again until each mistake I made was more infuriating than the last. It was like trying to pass a thread that became more tattered and unwound each time it missed the eye of a needle. I had to stop.

"Continue," the Cantor said without missing a beat.

I took a breath and began reading again, slower this time and not pretending that I could barrel through it. It was sluggish, yet it gave me some extra time to think about the words before singing them. There was no way to decipher the correct pronunciation based on the vowel-less letters, but the slower I went, the less likely I was to carelessly mispronounce words that I had memorized. I added extra curls and twists to the words that preceded ones I was not sure of. An extra moment like this could save me from repetitious frustration, but it also showed me how to savor each word and push the musical notes to greater potentials. It was the difference between tapping on one piano key after another and holding a note, bending it up, supplementing it with a nearby key before letting it down gently. "Beautiful voice!" I heard my father say in my head and I realized that it was fun for him to see where the song led, how high the tune could go, and how long each word could billow out. Now I understood why he never complained about washing the dishes.

On the day of my bar mitzvah, my father and I got to synagogue before services had begun. At a break in the prayers, the rabbi stood up in front of the Ark and began his speech. My stomach began to tighten as I wondered what he would say about me. I wasn't a Bible genius like Gilad. Would he tell the congregation how poor a student I was, or how often I fought with my family? He didn't have much to work with. If only he would have consulted me beforehand, I could have told him about my decent baseball card collection or that I had memorized all of Winston's lines from *Ghostbusters 1* and *2*.

When he called me up and presented me with the same Bibles he gave to Gilad, I was too nervous to say thank you. Even good old reliable manners eluded me. Instead I smiled mechanically and sweated through my new hunter green suit. The rabbi put his arm around me and spoke out to the sea of congregants before us about how important this day was to me as a Jew. This was it, I thought, I was done for. It didn't matter that I had memorized the *parsha*, the rabbi was going to out me as a fool. He had an obligation to his congregants to be truthful.

I clutched the Bibles high up in my armpit as if they were the greatest gift I had ever received—as though the tighter I grasped them, the more studious I would appear in the eyes of the community. I wanted the synagogue to see that I loved learning Torah. Even if the rabbi was going to call me stupid, I could deny everything.

Nonsense, I would say, *I love Bibles! Just look at me. I could eat these crazy books. I'm so happy to have them.*

I looked down at the front row where Gilad was sitting. Maybe he could save me from this somehow, but when he caught my eye all he did was open his mouth and move a fist back and forth in front of it.

"I have witnessed Eytan grow into the impressive young man he becomes today," said the rabbi.

Huh?

"At services, each Friday night, he along with other children much younger than him come to the base of this lectern to receive a cup of grape juice during the kiddush," he said, referring to the ritual blessing over the wine.

"Eytan is always the last person to take a cup of juice. Each night, this *tzadik* will not take for himself until each and every other child has gotten their share."

Whoa, I thought. *Tzadik* was the Hebrew word for "righteous one." My grip on the Bibles loosened and I took in liberal breaths of air. It was true, I always let the little kids drink before me because I was older, like a grandpa in line at the playground slide. But the rabbi justified it. I was supposed to be up there and I was acting righteously, exemplary, even, while doing it. Take that, community! I thought, as I shook his hand.

A few minutes later, I stood in front of the open Torah at the wooden podium in the center of the room. On my left, the Cantor stood with an annotated Bible. To my right my dad followed along as well.

"Go slow," said the Cantor.

"No rush," said my dad.

"Vayehi bayom hashmini," I began to sing, *"karah Moshe LeAhron oole banav oole zikeney Yisra'el."* "And it was on the eighth day that Moses called to his brother Aaron and his sons and the nation of Israel."

The rest of my *parsha* was a list of animals and plants that are kosher to eat. The species go on and on and at some point, as I was harmonizing to the congregation about avoiding anything that swarms upon the earth, I said, "Sss," when I should have said, "Shh."

"'Shh'! 'SHH'!" screamed Eisenman, like clockwork from the rear.

"Pshh," my father whispered as he looked up and to the back, shaking his head. "Some people."

I knew where the mistake was and easily corrected myself before continuing along. Eisenman barely fazed me, but it felt good to know that my dad allowed me to feel hurt if I was so inclined.

"Try it once more," my father said.

Before it was over, I mispronounced words two more times.

At each instance, I paused and reread the word correctly, over-emphasizing the accurate vowel intonation as though responding directly to Eisenman. He's right, I thought, I should be more careful.

When I finished the final chapter, candy started flying at me from behind. As Gilad and my other friends scrambled to gather the booty, my father provided a little cover with his prayer shawl.

"Well done, Eytan," the Cantor said, offering me a congratulatory handshake.

"Thanks," I said confidently, looking at my dad for a moment. I was a man now, and I thought I should respond to the Cantor as an adult would. "Very much appreciated," I corrected myself.

CHAPTER 8

DIAGNOSIS: STUPID

"How do I know that I'm not stupid?" I asked Dr. Schneider. "That's what's really bothering me."

I was in the plush ground floor office at my weekly psychologist appointment. Dr. Schneider sat across from me, squinting and nodding at the same time.

"Why would you think that you're stupid?" he responded while writing something down on the legal pad resting in his lap.

I raised my eyebrows and mentally patted myself on the shoulder. Writing things meant that I was saying interesting stuff—doing therapy the right way.

"Because my grades are really bad and my parents sent me here."

I had been seeing Dr. Schneider since the beginning of sixth grade. Each week we would sit for an hour and not say much to each other. I would try to talk about not being popular enough or not knowing how to talk to girls, but most of the time I was at a loss for words and stared at the colorful wooden toys and picture books he stored in a corner. Usually the doctor would doze off for a moment or two in the middle of our epic lulls before snapping back awake and shaking off the sleeps like a wet dog. It bothered me slightly, but talking about myself for an hour felt like trying to fill a swimming pool with saliva; I couldn't blame him for getting drowsy.

Dr. Schneider wasn't the first professional that my parents had sent me to. There had been about a dozen since I was six.

In the third grade there was Morah Gilah, who helped me focus on the Hebrew language subjects that I struggled with. Each week, I would spend an hour with her after school and review the homework I was having difficulty with.

"You need to stop that nonsense this second and sit down," Gilah would demand, as I rocked against the desk where she was trying to teach me the weekly Torah portion.

I pulled my chest off the desktop and stood straight up on the tips of my toes, still leaning my nether regions against the edge of the white laminate table.

Morah Gilah, Hebrew for "Gilah the Female Teacher," was a short, thin woman with a thick Israeli accent and leathery, aged, steak-like skin.

"Enough! Bayme!" she said, refusing to refer to me by my first name. I was comfortable performing one of the most intimate acts in front of her, yet she would have called me by my Social Security number had it been available to her.

"Okay, I stopped," I said, still rocking in the standing position against the table not sixteen inches away from her.

"You are not stopped!" she screamed. "I will not continue while you do that . . . thing."

We didn't last very long.

In the fifth grade, I worked with Mrs. Trudeau in the school resource center. She was a sympathetic woman who covered her hair in the traditional Orthodox manner and tried to help me through the higher-level Bible subjects we were moving into. The resource center was a series of very small cubicles, each roughly eight feet by eight feet, with sliding glass doors and vertical blinds. They were the most private spaces in the entire school building and, with the doors locked and shades drawn, perfect for secret meetings with the girls in my grade. While I barely spoke to any girls besides those immediately related to me, it didn't keep me from fantasizing about using the tutoring area as our secret love getaway.

I imagined the twins in my grade, Sasha and Danielle, knocking on the door while I diligently studied.

Would you mind giving us some privacy, Mrs. Trudeau? red-haired Sasha would ask.

Sure, I'll go finish this take-home quiz for you, Eytan.

We'd then draw the blinds and the girls would take off their shirts and sandwich my head between them before flooding the cubicle with baby oil.

As Mrs. Trudeau translated Hebrew passages for me, I devised pornographic scenarios like these while nodding and saying things like "hmmm" and "sure" to give her the impression that I was listening. Unfortunately, her hard work didn't improve my grades very much.

My struggles with school came to a turning point later that year when my parents returned from a book fair with a gift for me.

"We got you a Bible with the English translation right next to the Hebrew words," my mom told me that night. "We thought it might help with some of the problems you're having."

I lifted the hard cover of the navy blue volume with my thumb before letting it fall back closed onto the dining room table.

"Why would I need such a dumb book?" I screamed.

"We just thought it might help," she said.

"I don't need any help. I'm not stupid!"

"No one is saying you're stupid, Eytan," my dad chimed in.

"Then why buy me this book for stupid people?" I countered.

The book was a reminder that I wasn't the same as the rest of the kids in my class. Everyone else used a standard Hebrew-only Bible. Having English on the opposite page was like putting training wheels back on a bike I had already learned to ride. I didn't want to be regarded as needing extra help in Hebrew language simply because I had a difficult time understanding it.

My father didn't own an English-Hebrew Bible, and none of the book titles in his vast library began with the words "How to," or ended with "for Dummies," which I thought would be an appropriate suffix for a Bible with the English translation so readily available. My dad's books all assumed their readers were familiar with the basics of the topics they explored. The book *Reactions of French Artists during World War 2,* for instance, didn't explain that Hitler was a very bad man, because that information was covered in the most fundamental Holocaust education. If my father didn't need supplementary texts to understand his work, then I didn't want them either.

"I hate you!" I told my parents as I started to cry.

"We didn't think—" my mother began to say.

"Exactly! You didn't think!" I cut her off.

Having heard the screams, Ilana and Yehuda had joined us in the room as well.

"It's just a book," my sister said. "Take a chill pill."

"Stop, Ilana," Yehuda said. "Not cool."

"Shut up," I pleaded with everyone while sobbing uncontrollably.

"Look, Eytan," my father said sternly, "it's just a present. You can use it or not. We didn't think it would cause you so much stress."

"I'm not using it!"

"Fine," he said.

I stood up and walked back to my room still crying but with my head up in the air, trying to maintain whatever dignity not using a Hebrew-English Bible held.

Later that evening, my brother carefully approached me.

"Why were you so angry?" he asked. "It was just a present."

"Because it means they think I'm stupid," I said. My siblings didn't struggle at school the way I did. Ilana was at the top of her class and would be attending a rigorous Jewish prep school in Manhattan the following year. Yehuda, though young, was already showing great academic promise by drilling his teachers and parents with all sorts of thoughtful questions.

"I'm not dumb," I told my brother angrily. "Okay?"

"Okay, I didn't say you were. Jeez."

The following day I came home from school and the book was still out on the dining room table.

"Get that fucking thing out of this house!" I screamed at my parents.

It was promptly moved to the back of my father's closet, and my parents began to think that maybe I needed a different type of help. So they began sending me to people with titles before their names.

First, they made me visit with a friend of theirs named Dr. Hal Lutwak. Dr. Hal and his family had been over to our house countless times for Shabbat afternoon meals, just as my family had been to his. I knew that he was a psychiatrist and discussed confusing things with my dad, like people at synagogue who were to the "left" and to the "right" of them. And

Hal knew that I was my parents' quiet, second child who sometimes pleasured himself on his staircase while everyone else finished their gefilte fish.

"I don't want to go," I screamed at my mother as she stopped the car in front of the Lutwaks' large home one day after school. "There's nothing wrong with me."

"Please just try it once," she said. "For me?"

"It's embarrassing, though. He knows me."

"But maybe he can help you to understand some things about yourself."

"I don't want to understand anything. I don't need his shrinking!"

"Why would you send him to someone he's going have to see in shul or at Shabbat lunch?" my sister piped in from the front seat. Finally, her obnoxious sniffling was working for me. "It's bad parenting," she further opined.

"Ilana," my mother shot back, "you're twelve years old. Keep your child-rearing tips to yourself, please."

"She's right!" I said.

"Eytan," my mother turned back to me, "go talk with him once and if you don't want to go again, I won't make you."

I slammed the car door and slowly made my way up to his front entrance. The house was set back from the street, and plants with large palm fronds hung over the stepped pathway. When I rang his doorbell, I was surprised how loud it was and that it actually made a *ding-dong* sound, just like in cartoons. Each time I had been to his house before, it had been Shabbat, when ringing a bell was forbidden, and I had never heard the satisfying chime.

"Hello, Eytan," Dr. Hal said to me when he answered the door. "Come inside."

Hal was old and he looked smaller than he did on Shabbat.

I frowned as he led me down a sun-filled corridor toward a study in a part of his home I had never seen before.

"Would you like something to drink?" he asked.

I was still fuming that my mother had made me come here. I didn't want to open up to someone who knew people I knew and might go tell them what was on my mind.

Hey, little Eytan Bayme, Dr. Eisenman, the ophthalmologist from shul might call out to me in the middle of prayers next week. *I heard that you've been seeing a shrink! What are you so sad about!*

"I'm not thirsty," I said to Hal.

"All right, then why don't you have a seat." He gestured toward a modern leather sofa with no armrests. I sat down without removing my jacket and glared at the floor.

"So," he began, taking a chair opposite me, "why do you think you're here today?"

"I don't want to be here today, and I don't want to talk to you."

"Okay," he continued, "but why do you think your parents sent you here?"

"I think my mom sent me here because she wants to get inside my head or something, but like I said, I don't want to talk to you about it."

"Why don't you want to talk to me about it?"

"Because I know you and I don't need a shrink!"

Hal looked uncomfortable. He hadn't anticipated me standing off this way, and he now seemed more embarrassed than I was. Good, I thought while watching him, I'd made a strong case for not being here. What if the next time we had lunch the adults decided to discuss my emotional well-being? Would my parents ask Hal how I was doing instead of addressing me directly, farther down the table at the kids' end?

"This is so stupid," I said to Hal, continuing the temper tantrum I had started back in the car.

"Okay," he finally said, "if you don't want to talk, we don't have to."

There were other people with master's and doctoral degrees mounted on their walls whom I met with only once or twice for evaluations. Sometimes I would enter the back door of a nice-looking home, and the person inside would watch me play with a set of blocks or a toy boat for a few hours. Other times I had to take tests with no right or wrong answers.

"Very good, Eytan," one woman said to me sympathetically while watching me shove a plastic triangle into a similarly shaped hole.

I never cared as much about these visits as I did about the Hebrew-English Bible because no one saw me at these meetings. The Bible would have sat out on my desk at school or home on display, like all the other books in our house, for everyone to see and discuss. The doctors' appointments were private.

Ultimately these meetings ended with prescriptions for things such as Adderall and Wellbutrin that I gleefully washed down as per the instructions detailed on the sides of the bottles. I liked the idea that whatever was wrong with me wasn't my fault and couldn't be fixed through working harder or thinking differently. Rather, all I needed to do was pop a pill or two at a designated time and watch the academic success roll in with the tide. But the medications didn't do very much for my grades, and I continued receiving 40s, 50s, and 60s on tests. In fact, the only thing that did help me at school was when my mother sat me down and helped me work through the subject matter.

"We're not leaving this room until we finish this chapter," she said to me one long Sunday afternoon spent studying for a biology exam.

"Oh God, okay," I said, bouncing off the walls of my bedroom before returning to the textbook.

Every hour or so we would take a short break for a drink of water or a bite of fruit and I would silently wish that my mother would forget to come back or say something like, *Why don't you take it from here now, Eytan.* I could then retreat to my room alone and fiddle with my brother's Pog collection or browse *Uncle John's Bathroom Reader* while pretending to study. But like clockwork, after ten minutes she was always ready to continue.

"Let's get to it," she said, pointing back toward my bedroom with her chin.

Six hours later we had hammered into my head every bit of knowledge about pistils and stamens and photosynthesis that I needed to know for my test. And that Tuesday, I scored a 100 percent on the exam, the highest grade I had ever received. But my mother had been on a mission that day and couldn't keep up the effort each time I had an exam to prepare for.

Someone had referred my mother to Dr. Schneider and I visited him one afternoon after school. His ground-floor office was filled with colorful children's games that I never touched and a stack of the magazine *Scholastic Parent and Child*. While our talk didn't result in better grades, the doctor was easygoing enough and I would never see him outside of our sessions, so I agreed to visit him once a week. After a while, I even wore my visits with him like a badge of honor.

"My therapist says that I should write an inventory of the

things that make me happy," I told Gilad one afternoon, as though I were a character in a Woody Allen film.

"Weird." He shrugged before lining up his half-sized pool cue on the mini-billiards tabletop he had set up in his den and knocking a shot in.

"Let me ask you something, Eytan," Dr. Schneider said, after looking up from his legal pad. "Do you consider your friends to be smart?"

I looked at him suspiciously and wondered if there was a right answer to his question. I thought about Gilad and the political conversations he had with his parents. I thought about other friends who were in the fast math track and one who had won a regional spelling contest and went to compete at Madison Square Garden. My instincts told me these friends of mine were smart, but maybe it was just the stupid in me talking.

"Yes," I said hesitantly.

"Then you aren't stupid."

"But how do you know for sure?"

"Because," the doctor said, "smart people don't hang out with stupid people. So if your friends are smart, then that means you can't be stupid."

I thought about his logic for a few moments before nodding. I was skeptical, because a smart person might not always realize that his friends are stupid, but it did make me feel a little better. A doctor had officially diagnosed me as not stupid.

CHAPTER 9
TANGLED

THERE WERE ONLY two high schools that I wanted to attend. One was a sixty-minute bus ride away in Sussex County, New Jersey, while the other was on the Upper East Side of Manhattan, where my sister was studying. At both schools, Hebrew and English courses were taught in coed classrooms, and the competition among eighth graders to gain entrance was fierce. The problem was that I was at the bottom of my class and had already been rejected by both schools.

The situation was upsetting, but my hopes were high because I was sure that my father would be able to pull a few strings. He was a well-known leader of the Jewish community, someone who did important work that was written about and discussed. How could a school claiming to care about the Jewish people not accept the son of such an esteemed figurehead?

"Why don't you try Manhattan," the principal of the New Jersey school told my dad after his appeal. "It was good enough for your daughter," he said, referring to my sister's pass on his offer three years earlier.

Though it stung, his recommendation seemed promising.

The principal wouldn't have suggested Manhattan, I reasoned, if he didn't think it was possible for me to get in.

Of course my dad would come through. He specialized in coming through. If I ever needed a folder for school, I could ask him the night before and he would bring me one from his office the following day. Usually it was the somewhat useless off-white kind with no pockets inside, but it was a folder nonetheless.

And so, eager to start enjoying my new status as a Manhattan high school student and despite not even gaining a spot on the waiting list, I spread the news before receiving an acceptance letter. Everything would work itself out, I was sure.

"Congratulations, Eytan," Gary Meier, my locker neighbor said to me the day that I told a few classmates of my acceptance to the Manhattan school. "Or should I say, 'Congratulations, Eytan's dad'?"

It was obvious to most people in our grade of eighty students that I could not have gotten in based on merit. Since the third grade, I had been in slow-track classes of eight or ten students that met in smaller sections off to the side of everyone else. Our little band of dreamers and notebook-margin artists and kids whose first language wasn't English had to be separated from the rest of the grade because we needed extra attention and less distraction than the normal classes could offer. So when news of my acceptance to the top-tier high school spread, students in the regular classes who had been placed on the waiting list were suspect.

"'Cause there's no way that you could've gotten in on your own," my neighbor continued his rant.

I stood at my square red locker, thinking about my father's role as the director of a nonprofit and an Ivy League–educated professor of Jewish history, and hoped Gary was right.

"Do you think he could help me get in?" Talia Bestmen asked me a little while later, after she heard my news.

"I don't know." I hesitated. It was an actual girl, a popular and pretty one, no less, talking to me. "I guess I can ask."

It felt as though I were a member of some rich legacy—a privileged class where women wanted me and men envied me. It was a status that I deserved after years of sitting through boring Shabbat afternoon meals where my father and his intellectual friends discussed Jewish community issues. This was my reward for all the times my dad said, "Look, Eytan, your father is quoted in *The Jewish Week*." Or another adult would tell me, "Your dad is the best teacher I've ever had." I was Jewish Communal royalty.

"Life isn't fair," my mother would always say after she refused to let me watch more than my allotted half hour of TV per night.

"It can be if you want it to," I would shoot back, missing the larger meaning of her comment. But now, as Gary, the locker neighbor, took jealous stabs at me, I understood my mother's motto. Some people in this world could work as hard as they wanted and they would never get ahead in life, while others only had to tip their hat or flick their wrist to make things happen. Life was not fair, so I didn't take offense at Gary's brash comments. They came from a deep hurt, like a broken heart, and judging him would have been cruel.

The following week, the headmaster of the Manhattan school told my father that my grades were "simply too poor" to allow me to attend.

"I'm sorry, Eytan," my father explained. "It's out of my hands now."

I was devastated. The magic button that could make

something incredible happen without having to work for it never existed in the first place.

"So you didn't actually get in?" Talia Bestmen asked when she heard the news.

"No."

"Oh," she said, shaking her head and slamming her locker shut. She looked disgusted in herself for believing in me.

"That sucks, dude," Gary said later that day. "Sorry to hear." He despised me no more. In fact, he didn't even care that I had lied. He was just so happy that I wasn't taking one of the scarce spots left on the admissions list.

This was the opposite of privileged, I thought. My father had laid himself out, practically begged for me to get accepted, and was turned away at the door.

"Can we move?" I asked my parents that night. They looked at each other knowingly as I plunged a fork and steak knife into the leg of the broiled chicken my mother had prepared for dinner.

"What about public school?" I asked, relishing the thought. A neighbor down the hall had once explained to me that everyone got oral sex at the city high school he attended.

"Like, it's mandatory?" I asked, wide-eyed.

"Basically." He shrugged. His days ended at 3:00 p.m. and there were no Hebrew courses at all.

"Out of the question," my father said firmly. There was no way my dad would agree to a school without a dual curriculum. A Jewish day school education was one of the key components to a strong Jewish identity, according to his Shabbat lunch discussions.

"Besides," he continued, "you got accepted to Beyt Shamai."

Beyt Shamai, meaning House of Shamai, and referred to

lovingly as B.S., was another school in New Jersey, not far from the second-most-desirable Modern Orthodox academy. The difference was that B.S. accepted boys only, and of those who enrolled there, many were known to have problems.

"Everyone's a loser there," I said, while picturing packs of yarmulke-clad boys roaming paint-chipped hallways under flickering fluorescent lights. They talked with thick Brooklyn accents and wore stained blue pants over generic black nurse's sneakers.

"It's gotten better in the past few years," my mother chimed in.

The truth was that it had. Gilad was the valedictorian of our eighth grade class and could have gotten into the high school of his choice, yet through the urging of his parents, he would be attending B.S. Other, more popular classmates were enrolling there as well, yet I couldn't get the thought of padded classroom walls out of my head. I pictured being handcuffed to a dusty volume of the Talmud while a Chasidic man droned on in Yiddish about an ancient argument between two rabbis over a mule.

At my sister's school, I imagined clean-shaven, modern-urbanite, Porsche-driving Talmudic instructors.

"I don't wanna go there," I cried while lifting my chin to the sky.

"Why?" asked my mother.

"There are no girls," I mumbled.

My parents looked at each other as though they too had thought about this point.

"Well, I don't know what other choice you have," my father finally said.

———

Beyt Shamai was a one-story building on a block in the middle of Morris County, New Jersey. In another lifetime it must have been a warehouse because there were loading docks in the gym. Once again, I found myself in the slow-track classes with a new mix of boys who buttoned their shirts wrong and stuffed their knapsacks with loose, crumpled papers in no particularly organized fashion. At B.S., though, our class didn't meet off to the side of the regular class as it had in elementary school. We had our own room with as many students, if not more, than the standard tracks. We were no less inept and awkward, but there were thirty of us packed into a room now.

Each morning, we would sit through a ninety-minute lesson on the Talmudic tractate *Gittin*, a three-hundred-page volume all about divorce. *Gittin* addressed questions such as when a man could ask for a divorce, when he couldn't ask for a divorce, and when he wasn't required to grant his wife a divorce. Why the school chose to educate a bunch of fourteen-year-old boys on this subject was never completely outlined. Could it be one big cynical joke about the lack of girls at our school? I wondered. Did they think that equipping us with all the arguments about how to leave a woman would make us want one less? By the middle of the year, I thought the answer became a bit clearer: Rabbi Slonin, the instructor teaching our class, had recently split with his wife, and *Gittin* was a subject matter he was personally invested in.

I had been in beginner Talmud classes before. Usually we pored over the medieval Aramaic text, trying to decipher an argument over the correct blessing to say before slaughtering a lamb. But at B.S., Talmud was different. It was more . . . erotic.

"It's the pubis," the rabbi said one morning, explaining a particularly foreign word in the text.

I was in the middle of drawing an intricate profile of a hideous, wart-infested old man in the margin of my Talmud when the rest of the class and I popped our heads up in a collective, "Huh?"

"Like pubes?" Allen Fisher exclaimed, creating a riot of laughter across the room.

"No," said Rabbi Slonin, "that's the next word, which would literally translate to 'hair.' This is the pubic region, or area, where the hair would be found."

The class was in tears. Students were high-fiving each other. If they had regrets about not getting into the high school of their choice, as I had, it seemed the rabbi had just erased them. No way an instructor could talk this way if girls were in the room.

"Does everyone understand the Rabbi Gamliel's argument?" the rabbi shouted over the howling class.

"No," I said from my chair closest to the exit. I had always thought the Talmud was the story of the rules, like keeping kosher, or the laws of Shabbat. I had no idea that it could get into such exotic detail.

"Gamliel says," Slonin bellowed, "that a husband has the right to ask his wife to trim the hair that she grows in the pubis region." The giggling ceased and a hush fell over the classroom, as though we were watching a tragedy unfold live on television.

"What?" Allen Fisher asked incredulously.

"Eytan, please read the next verse," the rabbi said at a normal volume.

The page was dizzying. There was a long column of

vowel-less, punctuation-less Aramaic in the center of the page, with rabbinical commentaries surrounding it at each point. It was as if the Talmud were being submerged into the commentary.

"Can you point to where I should start from?"

He looked at me with a wry smile, annoyed that I didn't know where we were but perhaps appreciating my honesty, before holding his volume high in the air and sticking his thick finger on the word *kacha*, meaning "this," in the middle of the page.

I struggled through each word, raising the pitch of my voice every so often to ask if my pronunciation was correct.

"Please translate," the rabbi said abruptly.

I shook my head. Maybe one or two words looked familiar, but I wasn't going to bother trying. There was no one in the room to impress, and I was eager to hear what was going to happen next.

"If," the rabbi said in a singsongy voice and began to move back and forth in his seat as though he were praying, "the hair that a woman has on her pubis region—as Eytan read so beautifully—grows to such a length that it becomes painful for her husband, the rabbis say that he has the right to ask her to shave it off."

A few students giggled, but as a whole the class remained still. Crazy words were coming out of the rabbi's mouth, though it wasn't entirely clear what they meant.

"How could it be painful?" I asked boldly.

"It can get tangled with the man," the rabbi said without missing a beat, "and make rips in the skin."

For a moment no one spoke, but you could almost hear the brains of thirty fourteen-year-old boys processing what they had learned. "Tangled," "shaved," "pubes," "he has the right," "rips"? Terms were being scanned a second time for accuracy and joined together for a more complete understanding.

Allen stood up from his chair and put his hands in the air. "Yes!" he screamed as though he had just won a lengthy court battle. The class broke into howling laughter; high-fives were apportioned; crotches were grabbed; Gershon Lipshiftz, a large, smiley member of our class, waved a bunch of Twizzlers in the air like a celebratory torch.

As I sat there off to the left, watching my classmates rejoice over their newfound appreciation for the Talmud, the word "tangled" hung in my mind. There was only one way for a man's pubic hair to get tangled with a woman's: Sex had to be taking place.

I pictured a group of medieval rabbis with long black beards and black fur *shtreimels* sitting around an oak conference table in a room full of leather-bound books. In the middle of the table, a sweaty man with a mustache and curly brown hair lay naked under a heavily made-up woman with a perm and triangular tan lines over her breasts. As she rode on top of him, the rabbis ducked and squinted at the hairy private parts rubbing against each other. "There is a *bissel* yanking," said one while rubbing his beard.

I looked at my holy text in front of me and tried to shake the fantasy. It was wrong to be thinking this way. God would excuse it or at least understand when it was done in the privacy of my own bed with the lights off, but while we were studying His holy text was an abomination, an act of defiance in the face of the Lord.

But the fantasy was too vivid to simply push out of my head, and my trousers were now sloping up at the crotch like an elevated highway exit ramp. I lifted the Talmud off the desk and pressed the bottom edge down hard on my pants. It felt good to grind the book against me, and I was glad no girls were in the room.

As I sat through the rest of the lecture trying to ignore the thought of God punishing me, I realized that I had just absorbed more Talmud than I had ever studied in all my years of school combined.

CHAPTER 10

TECHNICALLY CHEATING

"Eytan Bayme?" my ancient history teacher, Rabbi Sharrett, asked as he started on the attendance list.

"Here," I called, my head hanging low, but glad, at least, that I knew the correct answer.

"Are you related to Steve Bayme?" he replied, instead of moving on to the next name on the list.

Some of my classmates looked up from their doodles or paused their muted conversations with one another, eager to see where this personal question would lead.

"Yeah, he's my dad," I said with my eyes closed and a wave of my hand as if it were no big deal.

"Your father was the best teacher I ever had."

Yes, I thought sinisterly. Like so many others, the rabbi held my father in esteem and acknowledged my birthright. I was a special case, to be handled with care and dignity, not a gruff afterthought like the rest of my class. Perhaps I wouldn't have to do the homework that he assigned or take any exams, as it would be difficult to teach anything new to the son of the best teacher he had ever had.

"Oooooh," several of my classmates teased in unison.

Oh, don't be jealous, I thought.

"Please send him my regards," said the rabbi.

"Of course." I nodded.

Later that evening, at the dinner table, I told my father about Rabbi Sharrett and imagined that he wouldn't remember him. Over the years, my dad had had hundreds of students, and I didn't think that one who ended up teaching history at a second-tier school in Jersey would have made a lasting impression.

After some prodding, my father would often tell us a story of how, during an exam, a student of his kept blowing his nose from a neat pile of napkins on his desk. There was something so peculiar about the way he used the napkins that my father asked to borrow one.

"No," the student insisted, "they're mine!"

"Oh, interesting," my father would say while telling the tale, before snatching up a pretend napkin and showing my sister and brother the crib notes written all over it.

I wondered if Rabbi Sharrett was that cheating student. Not only would my dad and I be able to share a laugh over it, but it would offer the perfect chance for Sharrett to right his wrong: What better way to make up for cheating in my dad's class than by giving his son an easy *A*?

"Very nice," my father said to me at the dinner table. "Sharrett was one of my best students."

"Really? Are you sure?"

"Yes," he said. "Really talented guy."

In fact, Rabbi Sharrett's father had also taught my dad Medieval European history in college. Not only had it been a privilege to study with the elder Sharrett, as my dad explained, but his lessons had been "critical to his own success."

This changed things entirely. If my father was Sharrett's best teacher, Sharrett was his best student, and it was some special honor to take Sharrett's dad's class, then they all shared a meaningful relationship. They all held each other in esteem, and if I performed as poorly as I usually did, then I wouldn't fit into that dynamic.

The following day, I approached Rabbi Sharrett before class.

"My father says hello," I said, with a little more desperation in my voice than the aw-shucks response I had delivered yesterday.

"Oh, great," he said in earnest, nodding fast and hard as though he was processing a lot of other information at the same time.

"Please, uh, have a seat," he continued, gesturing to the many desks scattered about the room. I was hoping for further banter—some indication that I would "do just fine" in his class—but as he combed through a stack of handwritten notes on fading lined papers, he gave nothing else away.

Once all the students filed in, the rabbi began shifting his eyes back and forth between the clock on the wall and his papers. When the second hand was ten clicks away from three o'clock, Sharrett said, "We're just about ready here," and began talking loud and swift like a sprinter off the start line.

From behind the desk, he lectured about Hammurabi and important dates that would be on an exam at some point. He spoke faster than it was possible to write, and when asked for a minute to catch up, he would pause momentarily and say, "Okay, but I really need to get through this." It was as though he were worried about missing a flight scheduled immediately after class.

After forty minutes, five minutes before the official end of class, he dismissed us and scrambled out of the room before anyone else. It had become apparent rather quickly that he would not be one of the best teachers I ever had.

But this made little difference to me. It mattered not that he was bad at what he did. I needed to elbow my way into the "best teacher-best student" love triangle.

I imagined the four of us—Sharrett, his father, my father, and me—enjoying glasses of sweet tea together on a gabled porch somewhere on a clear spring day in the distant future. Four generations of the best teachers and students reminiscing about their times in each other's classes. Perhaps a newspaper-man would be on hand to write up a human-interest story about the bond. Could it be just a coincidence that our lives were so meaningfully intertwined? the article would ponder.

If I was to sit back and ride through Rabbi Sharrett's course the way I did in every other class, this legacy would never come to fruition. I would be like a square wheel on an other-wise normal cart. If the rabbi and my dad ever ran into each other again, they would avoid any conversation about me. What could Sharrett say if I performed so awfully in his course?

Yes, he's in my class, he might mention. *He's a very good . . . dresser.*

There's a chance that he's not really mine, my father might reply.

I wanted this to be meaningful, though. More than any-thing, I wanted to show my father that I could impress the same people he impressed.

So, the following day in class, I pushed my desk flush against Rabbi Sharrett's to listen to his lecture face-to-face. As he sped through the fall of Mesopotamia, I wrote feverishly everything I could. I had never actually taken notes in a class, and so, not knowing how to organize the relevant information, I tried writing each and every word that came out of his mouth. It was like taking dictation and I often had to cross out the letter *u* after realizing I was writing the word "um."

I forgot about my fellow classmates behind me. Normally, I would be enthralled by the way they gripped their pens or whether they kept their knapsacks beside them or underneath their desks, as though there was more to learn about the world through studying these details than whatever the teacher was spewing. In Sharrett's class, though, I was so busy trying to catch every word that I barely remembered there were other people in the room.

A few weeks later, I looked at the history section of my notebook. Like Sharrett's fading lecture notes, I had taken up almost every available writing area on the page. My paragraph indentations were conservative. I ignored margins and used dashes to continue words on the next line when they threatened to fall off the page. I didn't dare double space and felt embarrassingly wasteful when the back of a page was accidentally skipped.

In contrast, my Jewish history notes were airy and sparse. One page contained only a mysterious date written on the top line without any explanation beneath it. Another had the unhelpful reminder: "Theodore Herzl-Beardguy" in barely legible penmanship. Entire pages were devoted to cartoon sketches of birdlike creatures with potbellies and spikes running along their backs like stegosaurs. My ancient history notes felt heavy and valuable compared with them.

As the first history exam loomed in the distance, I read over my notes in preparation. They had a simple narrative arc that was easy to follow. I studied them thoroughly and scored an uncharacteristic 87 out of 100 on the exam. It was cause for celebration. My parents took the whole family out for dinner.

"*Mazel tov*, Eytany," my mother said. "I'm so proud of you."

"Thanks!"

"I don't get it," my sister snapped. "Why don't we go out to dinner when I do well on an exam?"

"Ilana, shut up," said my mother.

My sister always did well. This was my night. My father leaned over and lightly patted me on the back, as though I were a house of cards he was trying not to disturb.

"Good job, Eytan," he said quietly. "Good job."

I wondered why I couldn't take the same approach to my other classes. Just pay attention, I told myself.

"Bayme, what are you doing?" asked my Jewish history teacher, Mr. Barak, when I pushed my desk up against his one afternoon, like I did every day in Sharrett's class.

"I just want a front-row seat for class today," I explained. Barak liked an orderly classroom. Behind me, my classmates were lined up in three neatly arranged rows of desks that I had once witnessed Barak organize through the window in the door before class had begun.

"I like my space, Bayme," he continued with a plastic smile. He then waved the back of his hand at me, indicating that I should scoot.

It was no secret that Barak didn't find our slow class amusing. I had overheard him tell an English teacher that our collective IQ was the same as an eight-year-old's. So, without getting up from my seat, I held fast to the desk and pushed back on the floor with my feet, propelling myself and the desk a foot away from Barak and putting the bare minimum of breathing room between us.

Yet my proximity didn't result in a renewed interest in Jewish history, and I zoned out to fantasyland only a few moments after his lesson began. By the end of the class, my notes resembled a highly detailed depiction of a stick-figure army regiment storming the castle wall of a tyrant stick-figure monarch. They were easily within Barak's sight and most likely reinforced his views on our class's intelligence.

Paying attention in classes like Barak's didn't have the same payoff as it did in Sharrett's. My dad didn't know my other teachers or hold them in the same regard as Sharrett. So doing the work necessary to get good grades wasn't worth the effort. It was simpler to space out and relax. Besides, I needed to use the time to rest after my feverish note-taking in Sharrett's class.

"Are you ready for the exam?" Shimon Deustcher asked me one day before class, about three-quarters into the term. Shimon was a redheaded classmate who also took incessant notes in Sharrett's class. He, too, didn't seem to spend as much effort in our other classes, and I took pride in thinking that he was following my lead.

"Uh, yeah, of course," I said. "Which one?"

"Sharrett, duh," he said.

I looked at Shimon blankly, trying to find a hint in his face that he was joking with me.

"Ho! Ho!" he read my face and excitedly pronounced. "You forgot!"

"No, I didn't forget," I said defensively and rifled through my bag for my datebook. He must be screwing with me, I thought. This was just a competition to him. He didn't understand the tradition I was trying to uphold or the depth of my study. Did he even know who my father was?

SHARRETT! MID-TERM! 2DAY! was written in big block letters on the day's page in my planner. It felt as though my stomach were being prodded with a ruler. If this was any other class, I wouldn't care at all since I wouldn't have anything to study from in the first place, but I intended to do well for my dad. I was supposed to be prepared. How could I have betrayed myself like this?

When Sharrett entered the room, I pushed my desk over to the window, against the far wall of the class, before approaching him.

"Is there any way I could take the exam tomorrow?" I asked, nodding my head solemnly, trying to convey the difficulty I felt in making this request. "I'm really not feeling so well."

He pulled a thick stack of white papers from his frail leather bag and spoke without looking at me. "I can't give you the test tomorrow," he said. "Besides, *I'm sure you'll do just fine.*"

I remembered how I wished that he had said those words at the beginning of the term. Now he spoke them not because of who I was related to, but because I had proven myself to be a good student. He was actually sure that I would do just fine.

"Please?" I asked, as though asking God for forgiveness on Yom Kippur.

"I'm sorry," he said a little impatiently. "Please take your seat."

I felt as though a cruel trick had been played on me. Like I had been pushed over onto someone kneeling behind me and my legs were unreasonably coming out from under me. I had no control over the damage that would follow. *Life isn't fair*, I heard my mother say in my head.

I placed my notebook beside me on the windowsill and scanned through it as fast as I could, trying to retain any bits of information in the few minutes I had. It was useless, though, and the rabbi was already handing out the exams.

"All notes away, please," Sharrett announced once we all had the test.

"Are you sure?" needled Shimon before giving me a quick wink.

"Uh, yes, I'm sure. Now begin," said the rabbi.

I gave Shimon a sarcastic smirk and turned to the exam. There were five essay questions, each drawing on something Sharrett had lectured upon. I knew exactly where the answers were scribbled in my notes, yet there were too many details and specific points to recall without having properly reviewed them.

Across the room, my classmates were in the midst of vastly different activities. Some were heatedly writing on the exam; others were staring up at the ceiling, lost in thought. Gershon Lipshiftz, who had either given up on the test or never committed to it in the first place, was playing with a Game Boy at the other end of the room, his test papers sitting high atop his knapsack on the desk in front of him.

Meanwhile, at the head of the classroom, Sharrett was working through a stack of reports with an intense focus. He blocked everything out, directing all his concentration onto the page in front of him. While giggles and stage whispers came from the gallery of students before him, Sharrett rested a palm on his forehead and didn't look up. It was like he wasn't in the room with us.

My choice was pretty clear. I could answer a few parts of each question and hope that the rest of the class did just as poorly, forcing Sharrett to grade the test on a curve. Or I could quietly look for the answers in my notes, respond to the questions completely, and receive the score I deserved.

I thought about how this whole situation was one big misunderstanding. It wasn't as if I had not learned the answers, I simply had not been ready with them on this particular day. Unlike my father's cheating student, this was not an elaborately planned production with premade crib notes. I was supposed to do well on this exam. If I had never paid attention in the first place and was trying to read the answers off a fellow student, then I would be being dishonest.

This was a technicality, I thought as I easily scanned my notebook out of Sharrett's view. I was simply referencing information that I had already learned. Was I supposed to sit back and watch myself fail knowing that I knew better? After twenty minutes I sat still in my seat, waiting for a few other classmates to finish their tests before handing mine in.

"Nicely done," Sharrett said the following week as he returned my exam with a red "97/100" scribbled on the top. My hands shook as I reviewed his brief comments and check marks throughout the test.

"Yes," "Good," "Right," were written all over the pages. It was more than I deserved, better than I would have scored if I had studied. I had gone too far.

Shimon was happy with his 91, but when I told him my score, he grew quiet.

"You did great, man," I said, trying to cheer him up. He was the true winner. I felt like I had impulsively tripped him in the middle of a footrace and guiltily held the trophy in the winner's circle. All I wanted was what I deserved—an 85 with maybe a few points shaved off for technically cheating. My 97 was the highest mark in the class. It was too much.

"I'm so proud of you," my mother said when she found out. "You're on a roll!"

"Yeah, it's whatever." I shrugged it off. I imagined my dad

physically recoiling from me, like a slug from salt, if he ever found out how I had achieved my score.

How could you, Eytan? he would say before melting into a pile of steamy clothes.

"Well done, Eytan," he said instead. "Well done."

As class continued, I grew lazy and uninterested. Doing well in Sharrett's class didn't matter to me any longer. I would never be like him and my father. If the article on the four of us were ever written, the piece would be a sham. I sat in the back of class, sometimes reading a newspaper circular or falling asleep with my cheek on the desk and waking up in a puddle of drool.

Something had changed in me. I no longer found it funny when Gershon Lipshiftz sat at the far side of the classroom, out of Mrs. Feingold's line of sight, and translated her entire forty-five-minute lecture on Shakespeare into fake sign language. When Jonathan Murray emptied out his knapsack and wore it over his head in Barak's Jewish history class to better keep out the light, I just found it sad.

I started throwing back handfuls at a time of the Wellbutrin that Dr. Schneider prescribed, thinking that it might pull me out of the funk. Tilting the little pill canister into my mouth and shaking a few out like they were Tic Tacs felt cool. But after three days, I was experiencing short, uncontrollable spasms on the bus ride home or in the middle of the street, like a spontaneous orgasm, and decided that it wasn't helping me through anything.

As the next exam rolled around, there were glaring omissions from my notes. Rome was an underlined heading at the top of a blank page, the Peloponnesian War described in two quick bullet points. I photocopied Shimon's notes and tried to learn what I could from them, but they weren't enough. I scored a 58 out of 100. My little experiment in success was officially over.

Not long after, when my parents were at a parent-teacher conference, I was worried that they would come back livid and insist that I stay in my room until the entire ninth-grade curriculum had been memorized. But instead, they were concerned about my grades and returned home with a new plan of action for my struggle.

While I continued with Dr. Schneider once a week, I also began weekly tutorial sessions with a young and personable child psychologist who helped me organize my schoolwork and study for exams. In addition, I checked in with the on-site school psychologist every two weeks to update her on my progress. Finally, I also met with a child psychiatrist once every two months to follow up on a new medication that I was trying out. The new attention was great and I basked in the eagerness of these specialists to try to determine what, exactly, was keeping me from academic achievement. Secretly, though, I felt like I had gotten away with a robbery. Everyone was so determined not to blame me for my failures. It was as though they were all waiting for a certain drug to kick in or for a serious mental health issue to reveal itself.

Oh, I might say in a moment of clarity, *I had to fail the Jewish history exam because a toilet paper dispenser told me to.*

I thought so, they would respond triumphantly and tick the schizophrenic box on my chart.

But in reality, I was simply not interested in schoolwork. It was boring. Academic success was my father's identity, not mine. I needed to stand apart from him and figure out who I was for myself.

The night after receiving my failing mark on Sharrett's

exam, I removed $40 from my mother's purse. In a mall that weekend, at a store called Screeem! I spent the money on a tight-fitting black sweater with racing stripes running down the sleeves. When I got home, I locked myself in the bathroom, pulled it over my head, and flexed my nonexistent muscles in the mirror. The sweater made me look like I worked in an Israeli nightclub. I may not have been the hippest-dressed kid, but I thought I looked like someone you'd think twice before insulting.

With no appropriate affair on the horizon to wear my new garment, I took it off and folded it neatly back into the tissue paper that the store clerk had packed it in. I carefully laid it at the bottom of the underwear drawer that Yehuda and I shared and waited for the right time to bring it out and show people just who Eytan Bayme really was.

CHAPTER 11

COFFEE, CIGARETTES, NON—KOSHER PIZZA

"Eytan and I are trying to get tickets to the Nine Inch Nails concert next week," Shimon explained to our Talmud teacher, Rabbi Slonin, in the middle of class. "Do you have any extras?"

I stared at the exit in embarrassment and pretended not to hear. Outside a narrow glass window in the door, a developmentally challenged student peered into our class as if we were fish in a bowl. He caught my eye before quickly looking elsewhere in the classroom.

The rabbi shook his head and laughed. "Shimon, I don't even know what a Nine Inch Nail concert means, but I wish you and Eytan luck in your search."

As the rest of the class giggled, I rolled my eyes. I didn't understand why Shimon had to bring this up here. Yes, I wanted to go, but was this the best place to be looking for scalpers? The kid outside the door looked at me one more time before running off down the hall, his sneakers squeaking on the laminate tile floors.

"Let's get back to the matter at hand, shall we?" announced Rabbi Slonin while shaking his volume of the Talmud in the air.

Later that day, during phys-ed, Shimon and I were pelting the basketball rim in the B.S. gym with basketballs. At the other end of the room, next to a bank of mat-covered walls, the disabled student from outside class, along with a group of six other kids, sat in a circle of folding chairs. Their backpacks lay haphazardly on the floor around them, while an attentive-looking woman in a long skirt leaned forward in her seat and nodded. As the rest of our class practiced layups and played H-O-R-S-E, the group stared stone-faced at our games. This was the Atid program. A school within B.S. for children who needed even more help than the bottom class that I was in could afford.

Meaning "future" in Hebrew, Atid had seven students enrolled in its program. Two of them suffered from Down's syndrome, but the only problem I could see with the other five was their preference for chain wallets and military boots. Sometimes I wished that their sympathetic, pen- and pad-holding psychologist was my teacher, but for the most part I found Atid mysterious and disturbing. Why were some of them so obviously disabled, while others were just poorly dressed?

The most frightening part was that there was nothing between Atid and my class. If I messed up big-time and failed enough of my slow-track classes at B.S., the next and only step down was Atid. I had never been so close to being mentally challenged.

"Take a shot," I told Ben, a wallet-chain-and-flannel-shirt-wearing Atid-er, who left his circle to shoot around with Shimon and me.

The Atid boys didn't keep the same schedule as the rest of the school. Their blackboard-less learning area was more like a holding station for their book bags, as they could get up and join our games or roam about the school, peering into class-rooms, whenever they liked.

I tossed Ben the rebound and he shot again.

"What up, Shimon?" he said.

"Hey, man." Shimon and Ben were from the same neigh-borhood in North Jersey and attended the same synagogue.

"Did you get the new Slayer album?" asked Ben.

"Yeah, pretty sweet."

I didn't share their enthusiasm for death metal, but I paid special attention to their conversation. It was the first time I had heard any member of Atid speak and I wanted to catch the differences between us. Perhaps he would have an untam-able stutter or a strange odor following him around wherever he went.

They're nothing like me! I would be able to say to the principal if I was ever forced to join their class.

"Not as good as *Reign in Blood*, though," Ben said to Shimon.

"That's a classic."

Their choice in music was a little intense, but nothing in the conversation struck me as particularly special-ed.

"Nice shot," Ben said to me after I hit a foul throw.

He seemed like a decent guy, not a loose cannon without control over his body or the words coming out of his mouth.

"We're going to the Nine Inch Nails show on Saturday night," he continued. "Do you guys wanna come?"

Shimon and I looked at each other in disbelief.

"Seriously?" asked Shimon.

"Seriously."

I was nervous. No one could deny that the Nails live onstage was cool and added to the street-smart-yet-laid-back attitude

I was trying to cultivate, but this would be my first arena concert. A new Goth act called Marilyn Manson who sang about necrophilia and sodomy would be opening. There could be drug addicts in attendance. Or anti-Semites. It would be an extreme introduction into the world of live music.

That night, after dinner, I asked my mom if I could go to the concert. At the kitchen counter, she looked up from her copy of *The New Yorker*, a little confused and not really sure what to answer as she set down a cup of decaffeinated coffee. At fifteen years old, I usually just did the things that I wanted to do, the details of which she would piece together afterward.

"I'm going to the city!" I'd scream on Sunday afternoons with my coat already on and the door open.

"Wait," she'd come running, "where in the city? Why? When are you coming home?"

"West Side. Just because. Later," I'd call back, already inside the elevator and on my way to a day spent browsing the stores and street merchants on the Upper West Side.

Now she seemed suspicious, as if there must be a larger implication to this concert that I was choosing not to mention. Perhaps the show was in another country or at a strip club somewhere.

"When is it?" she asked.

"Saturday night."

"Where?"

"Madison Square Garden."

"Who are you going with?"

"My friend Shimon and some other people from school."

"Who's Shimon?"

"He's in my class. He lives in New Jersey."

She scrutinized my face.

"What kind of music is . . . Nine Inch Nails?"

"You know, like rock."

"Uh-huh."

In reality, as much as I wanted to be at the show, part of me wanted her to forbid me from going. It would be downtown in the city on a Saturday night with people I did not really know, and a potentially dangerous event. What if the crowd was so loud that my eardrums popped and I became deaf? What if there were no concert tickets at all and the Atid kids just needed some extra people to help hold up a convenience store? There were too many risks and unknowns involved, so I secretly wanted my mom to bail me out.

"Will there be drug dealers at the show?"

"I don't think so."

"Maybe it's not a good idea," she said. Yet the moment she began to show any reluctance, I felt that I couldn't miss it.

"But I want to!" I whined.

She let her palm slap onto the counter and rolled her eyes, as if to say, *Well, why did you even ask?*

Sitting on the express bus that Saturday night, after a couple more days of prodding my mother to let me go, I pulled my black sweater out from my knapsack and put it on. I also wore my vintage-looking New Balance sneakers, quad-pocket cargo pants, and a red baseball cap. I had never understood why my sister cared so much about new clothes and looking good, but recently it had started to make sense.

A year earlier, someone had said that my mother dressed me. At the time, I scoffed and laughed at how wrong he was. But only now did it begin to occur to me that the insult didn't necessarily mean that my mom pulled the shirt over my head and helped me roll my socks onto my feet, which she had stopped doing several years before. It really meant that she chose the clothes I wore. That the way I looked was a reflection on how she wanted me to appear. If I was truly trying to toughen my image, this was something that I could not allow to continue. On the bus I may have looked like some kind of jogging, club kid with pocket space for four overstuffed deli sandwiches, but at least it was on my own terms.

"Eytan, this is Freddy," Shimon said when I met up with them on a corner outside of Madison Square Garden.

"Yo," I said.

"What's up, man?" said Ben, swinging his arm out to slap me five. He held a cigarette between his lips and a paper cup of coffee in his left hand. There was something sweet yet grizzled about Ben, who wore the same outfit he had on the day we shot hoops at school. Aside from my mom, I didn't know anyone who drank coffee, and the cup that he held by its white plastic lid made him appear older than his years.

"S'up?" I said, our hands coming together solidly.

"So this is the guy?" Freddy asked Shimon after barely acknowledging me. I recognized him from school. He wore black Levi's over combat boots and an extra-long, heavy-duty chain wallet suitable for locking up a fast food deliveryman's bicycle.

"Eytan's cool," said Shimon after taking an awkward puff from a cigarette too large for his fingers. He and Freddy wore the same black and orange Nine Inch Nails long-sleeve T-shirt.

"Oh, okay," said Freddy, unconvinced. "You wanna smoke?" He held out a pack of Marlboro Lights.

I looked at the slightly crumpled open package and shrugged. Freddy was testing my character. Poking at it a little to see where it was soft enough to shimmy inside and get a clear read on how cool I was.

"I'm good," I said, waving my hand. "Thanks."

"Well, all right then," he said in a mock singsong voice to Shimon.

"How ya doin'?" Shimon asked me, ignoring Freddy.

"Pretty good. What's with the *kippah*?" I said, gesturing to the gray yarmulke in his left hand.

Ben was distracted by a group of people eating pizza nearby, but Freddy stuck his head close to our conversation as though he couldn't believe the words coming out of our mouths.

"It's just in case I run into someone I know," Shimon said. I understood the instinct. If somehow a friend of my parents happened to show up at this exact time and find me without a head covering, I would worry about it for weeks.

Eytan isn't wearing a yarmulke these days, Ilene or Yocheved or another of my mother's friends might say to her.

Yes, he is, my mother would reply.

Well, not when I saw him with a group of hoodlums out on the street in Manhattan, he wasn't.

I would have to lie and tell my mother that the wind blew it off my head and into a gutter or a McDonald's that I didn't feel comfortable entering. It was simpler to wear a baseball cap and avoid the issue entirely.

"You really think you are going to run into someone?" I asked Shimon, sensing an opportunity to look cool at his expense.

"I told you, man," Freddy piped up, "nobody is gonna see you."

Shimon glumly looked to the sidewalk and slid the head covering into his pocket.

"Yo, let's get something to eat before heading in," said Ben, and we started down the block.

City buses and taxis honked at the concertgoers smoking

along the sidewalk. They wore black tutus and combat boots that came up past their knees. I wondered how someone with a permanent drawing of a naked lady on his neck explained his decision to his parents and teachers.

In the middle of the block, Shimon, Ben, and Freddy casually strolled into a Sbarro's pizza as if it were their own bedroom. Sbarro's was not kosher and, since I had never eaten non-kosher food, I never had a reason to go inside one. I thought about Shimon's yarmulke while scanning the streets for anyone who looked familiar before ducking in.

On the long countertop lay circles of pizza with mini-meatballs and shrimps poking from cheesy surfaces. There were entire servings of baked ziti on slices and polka-dot patterns of pepperoni that glistened under heat lamps. The choices at the kosher pizza store in Riverdale included cheese and cheeseless with a side of french fries or falafel. Here the creativity was astounding. What could have inspired them to put a full salad on top of a slice of pizza?

Shimon, Ben, and Freddy, each holding a different level of non-kosher, found seats at a table.

"You're not getting anything?" Freddy asked accusingly as he took a bite of a chicken and barbecue-sauce-covered slice.

"I'm good," I said, trying to ignore the tone in his voice that asked, *Do you actually keep the laws of kosher?*

"Lemme see yours?" I asked him.

He handed me the green-and-red-ringed, specially printed paper plate with the once-bitten slice on it. As I lifted up the edge of the pizza to reveal the Sbarro's logo underneath, I felt like an aboriginal tribesman meeting contemporary man for the first time.

"It's just a pizza," Freddy said, sitting with one leg bent under his butt, his wallet chain clanking against the steel chair.

"I know," I said defensively, returning the plate and wiping my hand on a napkin.

"So what's the problem?"

"Nothing," I said, turning to Ben and his pepperoni slice with a side of something I'd never seen before. Freddy and his non-kosherness weighed on the back of my neck as I studied the shiny mess of dough on Ben's plate.

"What is that?" I asked, pointing to a reddish leak sneaking out from the beige baked crevasses.

"It's pizza crust rolled around a bunch of meats," Ben said with a mouth full of cured pork.

"Try it, man!" Freddy said.

"Yo, if he doesn't want it, don't force him," said Ben as he plunged a plastic knife into the top of his evil pizza roll, forcing it into two chunks.

"*Does* he not want it?" Freddy asked.

"I don't know!" Ben said, stuffing one of the pieces into his gaping mouth. "Ursk im."

While I had always been intrigued and interested in eating non-kosher food, it had never been so readily available to me as it was right now. I didn't like Freddy's pushy tone, but part of me wanted to take his entire slice and shove it all in my mouth at once.

See! I eat whatever I want! I'd scream through the tomato sauce and cheese dripping down my mouth and shirt. *Lay off.*

"Do you eat this pizza, man?" Freddy taunted.

Across the table, Shimon furiously scarfed down a cheese slice. His eyes nervously darted this way and that, as if this were his last meal and an executioner would soon drag him off to the electric chair. Laying next to him absentmindedly on the table, his yarmulke was back out of his pocket.

"Lemme see yours," I said to Shimon as I pulled the plate and pizza away from his face. It looked a little more vibrant than regular kosher pizza; the whites in the cheeses were whiter and the reds in the sauce, redder. It was like an artist's rendition of what pizza should look like.

"Hullo, dude? What's your deal?" Freddy continued jabbing.

I felt their eyes all over my face as I sniffed the edge. Just do it, I told myself, and shut this guy up. I placed a half-inch of the slice in my mouth and bit down.

It tasted more rubbery than kosher pizza and I felt a mixture of regret and maturity. In the course of those few millimeters of sauce and cheese, I grew up a little. A piece of my innocence was gone. It wasn't the most amazing food in the world, and I didn't feel the immediate urge to burn a Torah or smash a rabbi in the face. It was a piece of food like any other, with no chance of killing me or turning me into something awful. Tasting it was like learning the rather boring explanation to a particularly astounding magic trick.

"Well, I guess that's not it," Freddy said, unsatisfied. As though had I not eaten the pizza, all the suspicions and questions he had about me would have been answered. *So that's why you're dressed the way the you are,* he might have said, *and seem nervous about the concert, and keep watching me smoke my cigarette like you've never seen one before, and look like you need to go to the bathroom really badly. Because you don't eat non-kosher pizza!*

I stared blankly into space while chewing. There were no high-fives or slaps on the back the way there would have been if I had survived a ritual hazing and was now a member of a tight-knit gang. I took a second and third, larger bite one after another without stopping to chew before tossing what remained back on Shimon's plate.

"I do what I want," I announced with a full mouth, to no one in particular.

After the meal was finished, Shimon and I slipped out of the restaurant and briskly speed-walked toward the Garden, worried that someone we knew might see us coming out of the non-kosher establishment.

NINE INCH NAILS: LIVE, read the ticket stub that Ben sold me. It was printed proof that I was in attendance. The usher at the front gate tried to examine it closely before allowing me in, but I wouldn't hand it over.

"See?" I said to him, grasping the printed stub with two hands and holding it up at eye level for him to confirm that I was here on the right day and time. This wasn't just a pass for letting me into the show; this was a historical document that would prove how cool I was, and no one could take that away from me or rip it in half like it was a ticket for a PG-rated movie.

As the four of us made our way into the arena, the crowd grew dense and more sinister. Men with shaved heads and muscles bulging from the sides of tight black tank-top shirts pumped their fists in the air and walked with conviction up the stadium ramps.

Once inside and in our upper-deck seats, I noticed people drinking brown liquor out of small glass bottles. The yellow- or rose-colored wine that my family and I took delicate sips of before Shabbat meals sat on the bottom shelf of our refrigerator door during the week. Sometimes, after the blessings were made and we all had a tiny taste, my father would pour the mostly full cup of wine back into the bottle for use the following week. The healthy-looking swigs people were taking in our section came from a deep thirst. Bottles were passed around and drained quickly before being shoved underneath seats and forgotten about.

Down on the floor below, the standing-room-only crowd swayed against itself to the angry music that played over the speakers. Here and there a pocket opened up in the full-court mosh pit, where one or two people got knocked around like frenzied pinballs.

"You see that?" Shimon said as he bent over into my seat and pointed to a bulky guy in the row ahead of us wearing a black *Pretty Hate Machine* T-shirt. The man held a small vial with a metal fitting on the top and a plastic straw coming out of the side. He pulled something out of a tiny bag and stuffed it into the metal piece. "That's weed," said Shimon.

All I knew about drugs was what I had heard on TV. They ruined lives, got people into car accidents, and turned users into zombies. Pot, coke, heroin, whatever, there was no difference to me. Storekeepers didn't sell them from behind countertops, and they weren't packaged in brightly colored wrappers. They were dangerous, unknown substances with unexplainable, perhaps magical effects. I thought about the smoke wafting up into the joints of the exposed ceiling beams and loosening them up. There would be no place to hide once the pieces of building came crashing down on us.

Yet one thing I felt more strongly about than the impending doom we would all experience was Shimon knowing more about something than I did. This was the kid who tried to outshine me in Rabbi Sharrett's class, the little sack of nerves from Jersey who lured me into academic and now social competition.

"I know what it is," I snapped at Shimon. "Freddy, give me a cigarette, will you?"

After my un-kosher pizza snack, Freddy had ceased taunting me and he handed over the pack without irony.

"Sure, man," he said.

I lit the cigarette between my thumb and forefinger and took a drag the way I had seen Matt Dillon do in *Drugstore Cowboy*. It tasted like a campfire in my mouth, but made me feel more relaxed around all the drug addicts and alcoholics, so I kept it lit in my hands and flicked the ashes from the tip every so often. Now there could be no mistaking how cool I was. I even took a sip from the giant cup of coffee that Ben had purchased from the concession stand.

We had been sitting in our seats for over an hour and the lights had yet to go down. The arena was packed with howling fans pushing into each other, and a haze of pot and cigarette smoke hung over center court, yet nothing had stirred on the dark stage.

What was the delay? I wondered. Marylin Manson had not even come out yet. Were they all taking drugs backstage? Were they trying to start a riot by delaying the show? Finally, after sitting for an hour and fifteen minutes, three men in tight-fitting black clothes and long black hair emerged from the back of the stage.

"Arrrhha," chanted the crowd. "Arrrhha." After a few moments, they died down slightly, only to decide seconds later that they weren't through. "Arrrha! Arrrha!" they cried louder.

All at once, everyone stood and began banging on the seats in front of them—twenty thousand people clanking in unison—as if we were at a Roman gladiator battle. This was it, I thought, the drumroll before the main event. I crossed my arms and gritted my teeth.

Onstage, one of the men raised his hand to calm the audience.

"It's been a crazy night so far," he spoke over the PA. "Our bus had a little accident on the way over and our bassist broke his finger."

"Ahhhh," the crowd responded sympathetically.

"I know, it sucks," the man continued, "and unfortunately, we gotta cancel the show tonight."

"Booo!" screamed the crowd.

"We'll be doing it tomorrow, though! Your tickets will be honored!"

As they walked off the stage, I looked to Shimon and Ben. The crowd was growing louder; the chair smacking became angrier and faster. I wondered if I, too, should start slamming the seat in front of me and try to tear it from its hinges. I didn't want to stick around and possibly get crushed by an angry Goth mob, but maybe that's what cool people like me did at times like these.

"Let's get the hell out of here," Ben said before I had to decide. "There's gonna be a riot."

"Good thinking," I announced and wasted no time in leading the group out of the row toward the exit. We weaved down the stairs, past adults wearing sunglasses who were in no rush to get as far away from their seats as possible.

"Excuse me," I said confidently as I sidled past a couple of women with a metal chain connecting their nose rings to each other. "Pardon me."

I speed-walked down the ramp, passing muscular skinheads and women with pink hair. Every few seconds I checked behind me to make sure my friends were still in sight. "C'mon," I waved at them to keep up.

When we got back down to street level, I told them that I wouldn't be able to make it tomorrow night.

"Why, man?" asked Shimon.

I paused momentarily, trying to come up with a feasible lie that made me look so cool that it would be Nine Inch Nails who would be missing out on me not being at their show. Something like a base-jumping appointment or a surgery involving prosthetics that I was to perform or a ménage à trois, but the only thing that came to mind was, "My mom won't let me," which wasn't even true.

"What?" asked Shimon, smiling and looking around the street as though my excuse were so ludicrous that a crowd would start to form. Freddy looked elsewhere, at the sides of the buildings next to him or the dirt under his cuticles or anywhere else except me. My reason was so lame it wasn't even worth his dissection and ball busting.

"Yeah, man," I said. "Totally sucks."

"Hey, that's too bad," Ben said.

"Anyway, I'll see you guys in school on Monday." I excused myself to catch a bus.

At home that night, my mother was waiting for me.

"I thought you'd be home later," she said as I walked in the door, my sweater balled up in my hand.

"The show got cancelled."

"I'm sorry about that. You were really looking forward to it."

It felt good to be home. The temperature in the apartment was just right. The leather of our green sofa looked sumptuous and inviting.

"It's whatever," I told her. I went to the kitchen and opened the fridge door. Inside, the shelves were packed with Tropicana orange juice, an assortment of nice cheeses, barbecued-chicken pieces from the day before, and a multitude of other options. I chose a jar of bread and butter pickles, grabbed a fork, and moved to the couch. "They postponed it until tomorrow," I continued, holding eye contact.

I was acting strange, friendlier, and less confrontational than I normally was. She knew something was wrong.

"You don't want to go," she asked, "do you?"

Earlier that evening I had eaten non-kosher pizza and smoked a cigarette for the first time. I had seen people take drugs and get drunk. I had sipped very sweet coffee while sitting near someone with a tattoo that read, "unfucked," and I had a ticket stub to prove my attendance at the show. This rock-and-roll lifestyle felt right, like tucking into a freshly laundered set of jersey bedsheets, but I knew that I couldn't sustain it for two nights in a row. I needed to decompress after a night of firsts, let the non-kosher food pass through my digestive track, and allow my lungs to recover from the drags I'd inhaled.

"I don't think so," I said, before bringing some sweet pickle chips to my mouth.

CHAPTER 12

FAT GERSHON

A FEW MONTHS BEFORE the end of my first year, I was loitering in the aisles at Raoul's, the convenience shop a few blocks from school, eating half a buttered onion bagel and flipping through an issue of *Juggs*. *Juggs* was a magazine that specialized in photographs of women with unusually large breasts. This particular edition listed the results from a contest called "Slut of the Year," as well as a profile of a group called Amateur Pregos. The models in *Juggs* seemed happier than those in, say, *Penthouse* or *Hustler*. They looked like students eager to please a charming school photographer with the biggest smile they could muster, except they were naked and one woman had a penis in her mouth. These mothers and very-soon-to-be mothers appeared almost as excited to be working for the publication as I was to be browsing it.

With only five minutes before class started, I needed to pull myself away from the dirty magazine and head back to school, yet there was still so much more to discover. If only I could bring *Juggs* home with me and take my time perusing its pages without any distractions. Unfortunately, Raoul had a policy of not selling porn to high school students. Gilad had negotiated a deal on a bulk purchase from Raoul's wife once, but Raoul himself took a hard-line stance on minors and smut. He had no problem taking our allowances for packs of cigarettes and Skoal, but for some reason nudie magazines were off-limits to those of us who could not yet vote.

I popped the last hunk of my bagel into my mouth and looked up at Jonathan Taylor Thomas on the rack in front of me. His auburn hair fell easily down the sides of his face as I jealously rubbed down one of my many stubborn cowlicks. JTT smiled warmly and tilted his head thirty degrees. *You can do anything!* he seemed to be saying from the cover of *Teen Beat.* So I pulled the issue out and slipped *Juggs* inside of it, next to a full-page photo of Jodie Sweetin, the middle child from *Full House. Juggs* fit perfectly inside *Teen Beat.* The pages were flush with each other and the porn stayed inside even when *Teen Beat* was held vertically. The age-appropriate magazine did appear fatter than usual, but maybe I could pass it off as a special double Jonathan Taylor Thomas issue. I tucked it under my arm and pulled a ten- and a one-dollar bill from my pocket, enough cash to cover the cost of both magazines.

My heartbeat ramped up as I approached Raoul's counter. Aside from absentmindedly taking a hard candy from a Ronald McDonald charity box without leaving a quarter, I had never intentionally deceived a shop clerk. This would be my first premeditated crime that broke both biblical and New Jersey state law, yet I was excited to get away with it and add a racketeering badge to my expanding sash of disobedience.

Raoul was waiting for me at the front with suspicious eyes. He followed me up the long counter, the way a guard dog would track an intruder along a fence, and met me at the cash register.

"Just this," I said, holding the *Teen Beat* in my arms and plopping the money down before him. "You can keep the change," I continued and turned towards the door.

"Wait, please, mister," said Raoul in an Indian accent.

I about-faced and gave the man an impatient look. "Why? I need to get back to class."

"Please to give me," he explained. "I need to scan."

Shit, I thought. This was it. I rolled my eyes wide and dramatically, as though this were the most inconvenient request ever asked of me.

"Uchhhhhh," I said. With two hands holding the magazines together, I presented the bar code of *Teen Beat* to Raoul in an easy-to-scan manner that didn't require him to touch it. "Here," I said. "Scan."

"Please, mister," he responded, grasping the issues and trying to pry them out of my hands.

"What?" I said, holding strong. "I really need to get back."

"You must let go."

A moment before we were in full-blown struggle, I released my grip and made a big show of my arms while saying, "Jeez." As though Raoul were simply the rudest store owner I had ever done business with.

"You must not do that," he told me, my money still sitting untouched on the counter. He laid the magazines down, the *Juggs* still squarely hidden away, and took a hard look at Jonathan Taylor Thomas. *Is this boy trying to fool me?* Raoul seemed to be asking the young star. He ran his hand along the cover and opened the magazine to a page in the middle of *Juggs*. Before him a woman named Coco Puffs squatted in front of a yellow background. Her vast chest spilled over her tiny arms like parade workers trying to gather their deflating Thanksgiving balloons. Coco was *Juggs*' first-runner-up in the 1994 "Slut of the Year" contest.

Raoul's eyes widened. He flipped through some more pages, past the second- and third-runner-ups and past several other equally endowed boob queens I would have bowed to. He flipped and flipped until finally the two issues were together no more and *Juggs* fell away from *Teen Beat* like the peel of an orange. Raoul held the two magazines side by side and absorbed the full extent of my deception.

"You try to steal from me!" he shouted.

"No, I didn't," I protested. "Look, the money is right there."

"You are thief," he continued. "This magazine is not for you."

"I paid you for it!" I tried explaining. He might be able to call the police on me for this, I thought. I didn't know the law and there might be a special clause in it for people who try to pay for porn without the store owners realizing. I felt a very urgent need to get the hell out of there.

"Fine," I said, throwing my hands up. "I'm sorry. Forget it." I turned again to walk out the door, but Raoul called back.

"Wait," he said, "not yet." And he scanned the *Teen Beat* and made change for my eleven dollars. "Do not try again," he warned while handing me six dollars and Jonathan Taylor Thomas.

"I don't want to stay in B.S. next year," I told my parents that night, while we all ate dinner around the granite kitchen countertop, as we did most evenings.

All at once, everyone looked up from their broiled chicken and eyed each other awkwardly—my mother and father exchanging glances, my sister and brother studying our parents' response. Rarely did I speak my mind in front of my whole family. Sometimes I would open my mouth to berate Yehuda or Ilana for trying to steal my designated seat next to my dad, but usually I just slumped in the chair, brooding over the hot meal that my mother always prepared, and answered questions with one-syllable answers.

"How was your day today, Eytany?"

"Eh."

"Did you learn anything interesting?"

"No."

"Would you like some lemon on your broccoli?"

"Fine."

Unlike grades, which my parents always caught wind of, and my obsession with sex and girls, which I was not very good at trying to hide, my thoughts were the one thing that belonged solely to me. When school or a sleepover at a friend's house didn't go exactly the way I hoped it would, I didn't give my family the satisfaction of opening up to them about it. Those were my secrets, my information. There were five of us in the three-bedroom apartment, and remaining silent was a form of power that could keep them guessing whether or not I was happy or upset, or if I planned on showering more than twice in a week.

If my parents continually prodded me at dinnertime about how my day at school was, I would usually scream, "It was *just* fine! Jesus!" and leave an uncomfortable silence over the table that could only be soothed by Tom Brokaw's reading of the nightly news.

By my starting the conversation, though, and about my own future, no less, everyone in the household was interested to see where it would go.

"Why do you want to transfer?" my father asked from the head of the counter. "You're doing well at B.S."

It was true. On paper I had been scoring the best I ever had in my academic career. *B*'s and *C*'s, a *B*-plus in Sharrett's class. Most of my classmates in the slow track performed worse than me. Several of them wouldn't hand in exams in the hope that the teacher would assume they misplaced their test papers, as though it would help them pass. Yerachmiel, a stocky, mumbling classmate who was never without his hockey stick, had the nerve to submit an eight-page term paper on *Macbeth* with one giant letter spelling out the name of the play on each page.

"There you go," he said with a smile to our English instructor before mashing the paper into the middle of a stack of essays on her desk. The final page of his report was a period.

And so, I benefitted from my classmates' even poorer performances than my own. Teachers appreciated the quiet, preoccupied spectator role I played in their classes. I may not have been paying attention, but I wasn't dancing on the tables or shouting obscenities the way some of my classmates were.

Yet an increased grade point average did little to distract me from failed porno heists and other messed-up ways that days at B.S. could sometimes unfold. Only a few weeks earlier, while standing by the school vending machines, trying to trade a crumpled dollar for a Barq's root beer, Yom Tov Silverman, a senior classman, confronted me.

"Hey you," he barked, as I ironed out the bill's wrinkles on the corner of the soda machine. Yom Tov was a muscular guy whose *tzitzit* hung out from under a formfitting polo shirt. Each morning, he led the school in prayer services or recited the weekday Torah portions using the traditional musical notes. Teachers and administrators held Yom Tov in high regard for continually performing these skill-based rituals, and he contrasted starkly with students like me, who often needed to be told to "stop talking," or "put that bagel away now," during the services.

"What?" I cried, turning my back against the humming soda dispenser, instinctively shielding my face.

"This," he responded and bashed his fist into my pretzel stick of an upper arm. When teachers weren't looking and there wasn't a volume of Talmud in front of him, "this" was the other Yom Tov, a righteous bully who regularly preyed on a few, select weaklings. One of his lucky victims was Si Friedman, a junior class member who rode the same bus home as I did. Yom Tov shook Si down embarrassingly, perhaps because his hair was too curly or because he had an unfortunate lisp. Once I witnessed Yom Tov wrap his forearms around Si's neck and kick his feet out in front of him. Friedman's arms flayed above his head and he fell back helplessly into his attacker's arms, as though he were drowning and Yom Tov was a dutiful lifeguard dragging him to shore. That evening, on the bus ride home, the normally chattering Si stuck his head out the window while we were driving over the Henry Hudson Bridge and threw up.

Yom Tov also had a special place in his chiseled heart for Shimon, who maybe smiled too much or had hair that was too red or perhaps wore his yarmulke too far to the side.

"She-Moan!" Yom Tov would sometimes call out when he passed Shimon in the hallway before punching him hard in the arm, or snatching at the back of his thigh in a jarring move called the "shark bite." Yom Tov acted collegial, as though he were just saying "What's up?" to his good buddy, but the force behind his attacks was in no way affable and left Shimon with fading marks on his legs and arms that looked like old stains.

When Yom Tov hit me, I fell back into the soda machine

and dented the plastic outer frame. He wasn't smiling and he didn't call out my name, if he even knew it.

"Fuck!" I screamed, clutching my arm.

This was the first time Yom Tov had ever touched me or even spoken to me. We had nothing to do with each other aside from knowing the same people he liked to beat up. Why now? I thought.

"Don't curse," he said and hit me with another right hook to the forearm. It was a classic Yom Tov move, known as a dead arm, that resulted in a dull, throbbing pain and a hand rendered useless for at least a minute and a half.

"Godda—" I cut myself off before swearing a second time. "What is your problem?"

"What's my problem? What's your problem, Bayme?" It was nice to know that at least he knew my last name, and this wasn't some serial act of violence.

"I heard you've been calling me a bully," he said seriously.

"What?" I said incredulously, looking around while holding my lame arm, as though the words with which to respond had been dropped somewhere on the floor around us. While Yom Tov was a bully—the biggest and only real bully in school—I had never, as far as I could recall, gone around proclaiming him one.

"I'm not a bully," he continued without irony. "I'm a *Talmud chacham*," meaning he had a very strong grasp of the lessons in the Torah.

"Yeah, totally," I said. "I know that, but I swear that I never called you a bully."

"Don't swear, Bayme," he warned, referring to the Talmudic debate discouraging Jews from taking oaths or vows lest they might break them in the face of the Lord at a later point.

Yom Tov reiterated the decree by looming a balled-up fist between us.

"Sorry," I corrected myself. "I *promise* I never said that."

"Well, that's not what I heard," he said with a slightly softened tone.

"Believe me, Yom Tov," I continued, "it wasn't me."

"Yeah, well, you gotta be more careful," he said. "In martial arts you attack first, when you see the whites of your enemy's eyes. Then ask questions later." This was somehow supposed to make me feel better, or put his attack into perspective, but I was pretty sure that he was just combining a Revolutionary War quote with an Arnold Schwarzenegger line.

"Yeah, well, maybe you should rethink your approach," I told him. "We're not in a karate match."

"Ha-ha." Yom Tov smiled, as if my suggestion were playful sarcasm. "Anyway, watch that arm." He pointed at me and walked off.

I spent the rest of the day in a sour state, wondering who sold me out to Yom Tov and applying cold soda cans to my tender limb. On the bus ride home, as we sped up the northbound lanes of the Henry Hudson Parkway, I stuck my head out the window and threw up.

"B.S. sucks," I said to my father, back at the dinner table, explaining why I wanted to transfer out.

"You'll have to give me a better reason than that," he said as he cut a piece of steamed broccoli with a steak knife. "I pay good money for you to attend that school."

"Ma?" I whined to her across the counter.

"What?" she responded, hands out, deflecting my pleas.

"You haven't given us a good enough reason to switch,

Eytan," my father said pointedly, "and until you can, this isn't even a discussion."

I looked down at my chicken, covered in burned barbecue sauce the way I liked it, and pursed my lips. If I looked angry enough, maybe my parents would begin to understand.

"Can you even get into another school?" my sister asked.

"Ilana, that's enough," my mother cut her off.

"I'm gonna go to Harvard!" Yehuda piped in, extending his fingers out at the name of the school in an incorrect use of air quotations, as though the university were sarcastic code for some high school alternative.

"There's no reason to put that in quotes!" Ilana exclaimed.

"That's not even a high school!" I screamed simultaneously.

"Enough!" my father said. "Don't raise your voice at the table."

This was not going the way I planned. B.S. obviously sucked, but all I could think about was my episode with Raoul that morning and Yom Tov punching me. I needed something appropriate and more substantial to make the case for my parents to help me transfer out. I needed something that spoke to their concerns.

While walking through a busy hallway one afternoon on his way to a science lesson, Gershon, a heavyset, well-dressed classmate of mine, lifted his leg to fart the way a dog would to pee on a fire hydrant. The accurate, crude impression was standard behavior for the student body, yet Gershon made the grave error of performing it in front of an adult.

"That's repulsive!" screamed Mr. Barak, our equally portly Jewish history teacher, upon witnessing the prank in front of his classroom door. "You're not coming into my class, you fat punk."

The bustling hallway traffic froze. It was no secret that Gershon was heavy. He embraced his weight like a status symbol.

"I need the size large," he'd explain before partially breaking a desk so it could fit his frame. Most of the stick figure–like student body would have flattened under him, but Gershon used his extra pounds responsibly and always laughed generously at jokes told by even our nerdiest classmates. He took pride in being called "big man." But coming from a teacher's mouth, "fat" was hostile.

"What?" Gershon shrugged in the hallway. "I farted. It was an accident."

"I saw what you did," Barak called out. "Get to the principal's office now."

"No!" he protested. "I didn't do anything."

"Now, fatso!"

The word hung in the air. If it had come from a student, even a senior classman, Gershon would have cheerfully thrown his book bag at the name-caller and bear-hugged him down to the floor before sitting on his chest and rendering him helpless. This was coming from a teacher, though, someone who was supposed to defuse situations like these.

Gershon eyed Barak suspiciously, weighing his options. After a moment, he dropped his books in the middle of the hallway and turned toward the principal's office.

"Look who's talking," he shouted with his back to Barak.

"Oh no," our teacher set the record straight, "I'm not as big as you."

There was something inherently wrong at B.S., like a tub of cream cheese with a fungus inside that everyone eats around instead of throwing away. After the incident, Gershon was unfairly expelled from school.

"B.S. doesn't pay enough attention to the lower class," I said to my father at the table, in a moment of inspiration.

"What do you mean?" he asked, surprised.

"Look, I'm not the best student, but I'm doing a little better and they haven't offered to move me up to the next track."

"Interesting," my dad said before sticking a spear of broccoli into his mouth.

"They don't care about the students who need extra help," I continued. "They're trying to raise their ranking in the Jewish high school ratings and us kids who aren't as smart as the top-track classes are getting the shi . . . crap end of the stick. Gershon wasn't expelled because he farted. They kicked him out because he was a poor student and wasn't worth the effort." It was one of the finest yarns of bullshit I had ever spun.

"So you don't think they are giving you the opportunities necessary to succeed?"

"Not at all," I said.

Over the past ten months, my parents caught me with more pornography than all my years combined. I had racked up hundreds of dollars in pay-per-view charges, knowing full well that my parents would see the adult channel listed on the monthly bill. I had cheated on exams and nearly overdosed on antidepressants. I needed to get a girlfriend, or make out with a girl, or at least hold one's hand. Something had to change and I couldn't see that happening at a place like B.S.

"Fine, Eytan, you've made *a* point," my father finally said. "Where do you think you would perform better?"

I told him either my sister's school in Manhattan or Beth Hebrew, the coed school in Jersey.

"Okay, good luck," he said. "Those are fine institutions and you are welcome to apply there."

Later that evening, I sat up in bed unable to sleep. Staring at the *Teen Beat* centerfold of Jonathan Taylor Thomas that I had hung on the wall, I knew it was time to make a change.

CHAPTER 13

HEMOPHILIAC COWBOY

EACH SUMMER SINCE the fourth grade, I spent two months at a camp deep in the Lehigh Valley in Pennsylvania. The thirty-acre coed religious getaway was a long hundred miles from my parents and school, and it provided a place to recuperate after an often tumultuous year of angst and frustration. That summer after ninth grade, when I was still unsure of where I would be attending school in September, was no different.

"Summer camp is an integral component to a proper Jewish education," my father had said once to his guests at our Shabbat lunch table. Normally I tuned out their talk of modern Jewish thought and fidgeted in my seat until my mother allowed me to go play, but this remark jolted me from the barley and chicken I was scarfing down.

"I like camp," I blurted from the kids' end of the table. My father and the two couples sitting to each side of him and dressed in their synagogue best craned their necks to see what their hosts' normally silent son had to say.

"That's very good, Eytan," he encouraged. "Why?"

A cold sweat formed over my skin as I realized that these

adults with their pressed shirts and pickle-sized fingers were waiting for me to say something intelligent to reinforce whatever it was they were discussing.

"Because it's . . . awesome," I heard myself speak while searching their faces for approval. "And I get to meet new people," I added, thinking that it sounded more mature.

"I like that, Eytan," said my dad, smiling.

Camp *was* really awesome. With an entirely different group of friends than back home, I was free to try out new roles and personas. That summer, after a difficult year at Beyt Shamai, I was sick and tired of being Eytan, the awkward and frustrated kid in the dumb class. I needed something edgy and new to make me stand out and attract women, so I put gel in my hair, started wearing an oversized Corona beer T-shirt, and told people to call me Bayme.

"Your name is Babe?" an older female counselor named Miriam asked during dinner one evening.

"No," I shouted, trying to speak clearly over the voices of the two hundred people in the expansive dining hall. "Baymuh," I emphasized.

"What's a Baymuh?" she said, covering her mouth while chewing.

"It's Bayme, without the 'uh' at the end. And it means 'tree' in Polish, but that's not really important. Do you know my sister?"

Miriam looked at me quizzically. "Why would I know your sister?"

This was becoming more complicated than it needed to be. I only wanted to see if maybe the two of them had gone to the same school or met at a party once. I hoped this girl thought Ilana was cool and she would then introduce me to the girls in the bunk she was responsible for, who were my age.

Hey, everyone, put down your forks! She might interrupt their meals from the head of the table. *This is Bayme. His sister is a close friend of mine, so you should all make an effort to talk to him.*

"I think that maybe you guys are the same age," I explained to Miriam.

"Who's your sister?"

"Ilana," I said.

"Ilana who?"

"Bayme!" I said, exasperated.

She shook her head and shrugged her shoulders. "Why do you want me to call you by your last name?"

"That's what everyone calls me," I lied.

"It's just that people usually introduce themselves to me with their first name," she explained. This girl didn't get it. Eytan sounded lame, like a really religious kid who always wore his yarmulke and folded his clothes before putting them away. That wasn't me, or at least not who I wanted to be in camp. Cool people had nicknames like Stack or Birds, who were both in my bunk. I thought about using Hot Shot or Killer or even just Jonesy, but none of them fully communicated the depth of my character. So I went with my last name. Bayme was simple and rolled off the tongue, and I never felt strange asking people to call me by it, until now.

"I don't know, Miriam. It's just what people call me around here. What do you want me to say?" I brushed her off before turning to my bunk table and finishing dinner with my back to her.

"Yo, Bayme," said Jack Lewinstein, a bunk mate from New Jersey, in our cabin one afternoon.

"S'up?"

"I saw your name on a garbage can this morning."

A bad streak, I thought, would certainly make me cooler, so the night before, I had taken a black marker to some of the metal trash cans spread across campus. *BAYME, BAYME 95,* and *BAYME WUZ HERE* were written in capital letters that sloped down unevenly.

"Cool," I said to Jack.

"Marnie was spilling hot water over it," he said, referring to the camp director. "I think she's pissed."

A small pit formed in my stomach. All I wanted was for people to see my name written on the side of the cans and think I was a graffiti artist from the streets.

Did you ever do a subway car? I hoped a fellow camper from Staten Island or Boston would ask upon seeing my work.

No, but I've been on one, I'd say with a half smile and cocked eyebrows, impressing him with my urban smarts.

When Jack told me that the camp administration might be angry with me, though, I got worried. *What if Marnie takes away some of my canteen money? Or worse: calls my parents?*

"Eytan Bayme," the camp director called over the loudspeaker later that day. "EYTAN. BAYME. Come to the front office. Now."

"What baffles me about this, Bayme," Marnie smirked at me from behind her cluttered desk in the air-conditioned director's office, "is that you thought you would get away with it. What did you think would happen?"

From beneath the curved brim of my baseball hat, I looked worriedly at Marnie. I was relieved that she wasn't taking my offense so personally, but troubled at the same time. I wasn't very good at being bad.

"You are Bayme," she said with her palms up. "Who else would have done this?"

"I'm not sure." I shrugged.

As I spent that evening on my knees, glumly scrubbing the sides of trash cans with steel wool, I took a little satisfaction knowing that all five hundred campers had heard my name being called in such an annoyed, forceful tone over the loud-speaker that day.

I wonder what he's in trouble for? I hoped girls were saying. *Maybe he got caught stealing the hubcaps off Marnie's car.*

The following Shabbat morning, in the middle of prayers, I walked up to the front of the synagogue where my bunk mate Jack was in charge of services for the entire camp.

"Yo," I whispered to him during a short break in his duties. "Let me get the first blessing on the Torah."

Jack wore a white prayer shawl over his shoulders and an oversized multicolored yarmulke on his head. He gave me a confused smile.

"Ha-ha," he said. "Good one, Bayme."

"I'm serious, man," I reiterated. "Give it to me."

"Dude, you know I can't do that. You're not a *cohen*." I did know this. The first blessing on the Torah always had to go to a descendant of the ancient high priests of Israel, or a *cohen*, which I was not. But I didn't care. Of the handful of *cohens* at camp, none was so different than me. They weren't any better at sports and they weren't any holier. In fact, one *cohen*, aptly named Ralph Cohen, who slept on the bunk below me, loved pro wrestling and had a subscription to *Hustler* magazine that his parents purchased for him on his fifteenth birthday. I always thought it unfair that only certain people could receive the first Torah blessing simply because of some centuries-old birthright that I doubt could have been verified. So with my buddy Jack in charge of services, now was my chance to challenge that tradition.

"So what?" I goaded Jack.

"So I'm not allowed to give it to you if you're not a *cohen*."

"That rule is archaic," I told him. "Ralph jerks off on the bottom bunk every night. You think he is more godly than you and I?"

Jack laughed and looked around the room to see if people were paying attention to us. "That doesn't make a difference."

"You're in charge here, Jack. You can rule over this service any way you like." I was trying to boost his confidence. "If you want the entire congregation to stand on one leg and salute, they have to listen to you."

Jack smiled but hardened his tone. He needed to get back to the service. "Man, I'd love to, but I really can't."

"Oh, so we're not good enough friends," I said, now hoping to guilt him into the blessing.

"That's not it," he said defensively.

"You give it to Ralph. I guess you two are best friends."

"Bayme, you know that's not why he gets it." A few people around us were now looking up from their prayer books, interested or distracted by our hushed argument. "You're just being a jerk now."

"Oh, I'm the jerk?" I said. "I'm not the one hoarding Torah blessings."

Jack giggled, but remained firm. "Get out of here. We can talk about this after services."

"Nah, man," I said, holding back the giggles myself. "You're a sheep, just like everyone else." To my surprise, I then pulled back and punched Jack in the cheek. He didn't lose his balance, but it was just hard enough to cause a little pain.

"Shit, sorry," I said.

Jack put his hand to his cheek. "Are you crazy?" he asked, rubbing his face and flexing his jaw. "You can't punch me in the middle of services."

A few older campers had witnessed the jab and were understatedly holding me back with a palm on my chest. They kept their eyes glued to their prayer books, trying to put an end to my antics as quickly and quietly as possible.

"Time for you to leave, Bayme," one of them whispered, and gently shoved me in the direction of the door. I walked backward, my eyes trained on Jack, who shook his head and grinned in disbelief.

Outside, I didn't entirely believe what I had gotten away with either. I'd never even punched my brother in the face, let alone someone who was leading prayer services. I had never been escorted out of anywhere either. And I did it all without pissing off too many people. There were no stern words of advice, and Jack looked almost amused as I left him. I was like a thug who only knew how to react to his emotions through brute strength and rage, yet was also beloved for his simplistic understanding of right and wrong. *Don't cross Eytan,* people would understand. *He wears his heart on his sleeve.*

That night I asked a bunk mate named Hillel Allon to shave my head for me.

"What number?" he asked, referring to the size of the clipper he should use.

"A one," I said coolly, which would leave my hair only a millimeter or two in length, the most extreme hairstyle without actually looking like a skinhead. "Can you stencil the word 'Bayme' into the side?" I added.

"Uh, okay." Hillel was from South Jersey. He had long hair that he pulled back into a ponytail and then shaved the underside off, which was then only visible when his hair was up. Late at night, when the bunk lights were off and we all stayed up in bed cracking "yo' mama" jokes or referencing our favorite Beastie Boys albums, Hillel had a quiet coolness about him and chuckled lightheartedly when the jokes were addressed to his mama.

I took my shirt off and sat down on a steel folding chair in the recesses of the bunk, by the bathrooms and rear entrance. Hillel plugged the clippers in and turned them on with a sharp click and a deep hum. He started shearing off my hair from the back of my head forward. Soon, a few of our bunk mates joined the party, like a regular barbershop hangout.

"Dude, that is short," said Ralph Cohen, *the* Cohen, smoking a cigarette out the back door behind us.

"You look like a racist," declared Mihkail Vidomlanski, our recently emigrated Russian bunk mate.

"You sure you want the 'Bayme'?" asked Hillel.

"Do it, man," I told him.

Hillel removed the number-one fitting on the clipper and took one of Ralph's smokes. He lit it up and let it dangle from his mouth before gently touching the vibrating, bare blades to the back of my head.

"Oh, shit," cried Ralph, leaning in for a closer look. "That's gonna look gnarly."

"You are a crazy man, Bayme," Mihkail admitted.

Hillel squinted so his eyes wouldn't burn from the smoke, and he held his head sideways to get a better look at the detailing. I wondered if gnarly was a good or bad thing. Surfers on TV sometimes used the term to describe waves, as in "Gnarly waves, my man. What a great day for surfing." But the word could also refer to something crooked or distorted, as in "That old lady's got some gnarly fingers." Which one did Ralph mean? Did I have the hair of a laid-back beach bro in board

shorts or something resembling the twisted claws of a septu-
agenarian?

All of a sudden someone shouted my name from the front
of the bunk. "Bayme!" the voice cried. "Bayme, where the hell
are you?"

I looked back at my barber and the Cohen and the Russian
as though they might know who was searching for me, but
everyone just shrugged. Feet stamped on the cabin floor in
the direction of our salon and a moment later Jack stood
before us.

"You son of a bitch," he blasted at me.

"What?" I said. This was not the smiling Jack from earlier; this was Grudge Jack, Angry Jack, Jack with a Score to
Settle. He breathed heavily and sweated as though he had
been running all over camp looking for me.

"Are you allowed to be smoking in the bunk?" he demanded
of Hillel.

Hillel lurched his shoulders and looked away, not wishing
to get involved in fights that weren't his own.

"What's your problem, man?" I asked Jack stupidly. "I
thought we were cool."

Jack wound up and drilled me in my left eye.

"Oh shit!" Ralph shouted.

"Damn!" said Hillel.

"*Na kaleni, suka,*" cried Mihkail in his native tongue.

"Fuck!" I screamed before sliding to the floor and grabbing
my face. His bash was more serious than the one I had plugged
him with. It probably wasn't the hardest he could deliver, but
it stung no less. As I dropped to the ground, my head grazed
past the buzzing clipper in Hillel's hands, leaving a healthy tuft
with it.

"Whoa!" called Hillel as he pulled it away.

"Crap, I'm sorry," Jack pronounced, urgently bending to his knees to help me up. "I didn't mean to do it so hard."

"You got me right in the eye!" I wailed.

"I know," he said. "But we're even now. Okay?"

"Shit! Okay," I said as he lifted me up. "No more fighting."

"Sounds good."

"Ohhhh!" everyone hollered together when I was back on my feet.

"What? What's wrong?"

"Look in the mirror, bro," advised Ralph.

I shuffled around Hillel to the vanity over the sink and examined the damage. The area under my eye was a deep red, like a blister full of blood that had yet to burst. There were some yellow streaks where the bruise faded into my natural skin tone, and a blueish-reddish mess on my upper eyelid where it met my eyebrow.

"I totally didn't mean to do that, man," said Jack. "Really. I'm sorry."

In real time, my face began to swell around my left eye. It grew and grew, and within moments, I could barely see out of it. It was as though two fingers were being held in front of it, leaving only a tiny slit to peer between. Other than being tender, my eye didn't hurt much. I almost grinned at myself in the mirror.

"Are you all right?" whispered Jack, breaking the silence.

"That's gonna be black in the morning," said Hillel.

I turned to my friends and paused, before raising my hands in the air and declaring, "I got a black eye!" as though I had just won the Stanley Cup.

"Awesome!" howled Ralph.

"So cool!" shouted Jack.

"Congratulations!" said Mihkail.

I held my hand up in the air for a thorough round of high-fives.

Never in my life had I seen a black eye, let alone received one myself. They could have been a myth, for all I knew, something that only occurred in the movies like *The Sandlot,* where they were treated with a beef bandage that a lovable dog was bound to get his teeth on. But this actual shiner was a badge of honor, like a temporary face tattoo that told everyone, *Yeah, I get into fights. Does that make you uncomfortable?* It was the perfect affect for the urban hustler I was trying to model myself as.

"What a clocker!" said my counselor when he saw me that night.

"No biggie," I told him.

"Ouch!" cracked my swimming instructor the following day as I practiced my crawl alongside the wall at the deep end.

"You should see the other guy," I said between breaths.

"Who's he?"

"Jack Lewinstein."

"He doesn't look so bad," he said, looking across the pool at Jack drying himself off.

"Eytan Bayme. Eytan Bayme. Please come to Marnie's office right now," the loudspeaker broadcast.

With my towel wrapped around my waist and what was left of my hair dripping wet from the pool, I sat across from the camp director once again.

"Bayme, is someone hurting you? You can tell me anything."

"No. What do you mean?" My teeth chattered in her freezing-cold office.

"Your eye! Where did it come from?"

"Oh, this is nothing. Jack did it, but we're cool."

Marnie held her fingers to each side of her head, looking

unsure of where to begin with a line of questioning. "And what about your hair! Why would you do that to yourself?"

My hair did look pretty bad. It was short all over, like an army cadet's, but there was an uneven triangle of scalp visible on the side where I had fallen into the razor. In the back, a single large *B* had been carved out that, Hillel felt, we should leave as it was after all the commotion the previous evening.

"It looks gnarly," I offered.

"That's one way of describing it," she said. "Do I need to let your parents know about this before visiting day?"

"No!" I insisted. "The bruise will be gone by then, and they let me style my hair however I wish."

Two weeks later, my whole family came to see me on visiting day. My hair had grown in somewhat, and only a shadow of black and blue surrounded my eye. Strangely, my parents said nothing.

"I brought food for a picnic!" My mother smiled after smothering me in hugs and kisses. "Where should we set up?"

"Um, let's go to the area behind the bunks," I suggested, not wanting my fellow campers to witness me lounging on a patterned bedsheet eating sandwiches with my wholesome-looking family. I had a reputation to uphold.

She had prepared barbecued chicken, my most favorite food, and as the five of us sat down on the grass, I couldn't help but feel warm and loved.

"Thanks, Ma," I said and laid my head down in her lap, like a dog wanting to be petted.

"It's my pleasure," she said, running her fingers along my scalp. "Your hair looks pretty ridiculous."

"I know. Sorry."

"The camp director warned us about it last week."

"What?"

"She called us," she said, while I bit my tongue. "And we said if that's the worst he's done, I'm sure we'd be able to handle it." My mother looked at my father for confirmation.

"Then what did she say?" I was worried that Marnie might have touched on the garbage can incident.

"She said, that's it."

I breathed easy once again. I was right that my parents didn't care about my hair or the bruise, but who knows how they would have reacted to the vandalism charge?

"Are you even going to school next year?" Ilana chided.

"Yes, obviously," I shot back.

"We just haven't figured out where," my father said diplomatically. The New Jersey coed school that I wanted to attend had placed me on a non-merit-based waiting list, and they still had not given me an answer.

"Just so you know," my sister added, "your hair looks stupid."

"I would have gotten the *Ghostbusters* logo," Yehuda said.

Later that afternoon, my dad came into my cabin to use the bathroom.

"Why is my name on the inside of that stall?" he asked when he came out drying his hands. "It says, 'Bayme's Office.' You know how I feel about defacing property?"

Using a pen, I had declared the stall mine on its particleboard walls. Marnie didn't know since she never used the rest room in our bunkhouse.

"They're cool about that stuff here," I said with a quick wave of my hand.

"Really?" asked my dad, thick with sarcasm.

"Really," I told him in all seriousness, hoping this would put the matter to rest. "It's no big deal."

"Eytan, I'm not a fool," he said firmly. "I'm certain that this camp doesn't want you drawing all over their walls, so I would appreciate a little honesty from you."

I looked over at my bed. It was covered in Yodels and Ring Dings and homemade chocolate chip cookies. There were new undershirts that my parents had brought and a pair of sports sandals that I had specifically requested.

"Sorry, Daddy," I said. "I'll try to clean it off later today."

A few weeks later, after my hair grew back and my black eye had healed completely, my face swelled up again, this time more dramatically, and I checked myself into the infirmary for an extended stay.

"Bayme? Is that you?" It was Hillel Allon, my laidback hairdressing bunk mate. He had come into the infirmary each night I was there. Every evening, he stood in front of the mirror a few feet from my bed and injected clotting factor into his butt.

"Yeah, man," I said, "I've been here for the past week. You've said hi to me."

"Sorry, I thought you were some kind of elephant boy."

A week earlier, during a camp-wide game of Manhunter, I had sat in a patch of poison ivy. A rash formed on my legs and quickly spread all over my body, swelling my entire face to the point that my eyes could barely open.

"I didn't realize it was you," Hillel said. "I was just being friendly."

Aside from an extremely fat, sideshow-worthy face and an itchy red rash all over my body, there was nothing wrong with me. I could breathe, speak, eat, and play like any other camper, yet I was utterly embarrassed to leave the four-room infirmary.

While my camp mates were outside canoeing, shooting guns, and throwing rocks into the cesspool, I was reading Archie comic books and taking oatmeal baths. It was the opposite of badass.

Each night as I lay on my cot, trying not to scratch myself, I imagined Rachelie, a camper I could not bring myself to talk to, outside my window visiting me as though I were an inmate in the local jailhouse.

Things are gonna be all right for the two of us when I get out of here, I would say as she fought back tears. From the bed, behind the drawn curtains so she couldn't see my face, I would reach up and place my palm upon the glass. *I promise,* I'd tell her, and she would press her hand against her side of the window.

You're so strong, she'd say.

But I was too embarrassed to use the poison ivy as a way to gain sympathy. Hillel, I found out, had the ideal disease: hemophilia. His face looked normal and all he had to endure was a syringe that he stuck in his own ass each night. My pediatrician had to concoct all sorts of diversions and bribes before giving me a shot, yet Hillel was doing it himself, barely flinching. No one could argue that he wasn't tough. As I applied cold compresses to my face and asked the nurse for apple juice refills, Hillel was sitting shirtless on the wooden porch railing in front of our cabin, his long hair, deep tan, and toned fifteen-year-old biceps glimmering under the powerful midday sun.

Yeah, I gotta take care of some things at the infirmary now, I imagined him saying to a group of girls standing the regulation ten feet away from the boys' bunks. *If I don't get this injection,* he'd continue, *I may not make it through the end of the day.*

If only I had hemophilia, I thought, then girls would see me as some kind of hero with a debilitating ailment.

You're so brave, they would tell me, as *I* jumped down from the porch and took one lucky girl to escort me to the first-aid cabin.

I'm just doing what I gotta do, I'd say, raising my hands in humble submission.

If I had hemophilia, male campers would look up to me as a legend who felt no pain. I wouldn't have to write my name on garbage cans, waiting for my bunk mates to start respecting me. I could go around with a well-worn leather satchel attached to my thigh, like a gun holster. If someone made fun of me, I would slowly, methodically pull a needle from the case and, without taking my eyes off him, shoot my arm full of replacement therapy before pushing a plastic cap back onto the syringe and properly disposing of the sharp needle in a red biohazard bag. I would be a hemophiliac cowboy, secreting macho-ness.

When the poison ivy swelling finally wore off and I felt confident enough to leave the safety of the infirmary, all I wanted to do was shoot a gun. I wanted to feel powerful over something, anything, and the paper bull's-eyes at the rifle range would do just fine.

"Do you have something in an automatic?" I asked Dror, the sports director, as he pulled a metal chain from the rifle triggers, securing the guns inside a cabinet in the sports shed.

"*Loh,*" he said curtly in Hebrew, no, before handing me an unloaded weapon and leading my bunk toward the range by the woods behind camp.

Riflery was an activity offered to the older campers in an effort to give us a taste of the Israeli army. By the range, my bunk mates and I sat cross-legged on the floor of the forest as Dror talked about safety precautions and the Israeli Defense

Forces' rules of engagement. Finally after an hour and a half of lectures, he allowed each of us to fire off a tiny nine-millimeter bullet or two.

As I lay down on the wooden platform with the butt of the gun up against my shoulder, I imagined spraying bullets at the targets fifty feet down the line.

Don't mess with this! I'd scream.

Zionist sleepaway camp was supposed to be a place where I could mold myself into whomever I wanted to be. Even though every Shabbat, all five hundred of us had to dress in blue and white and stand in neatly arranged rows, singing Theodore Herzl's official song of the Zionist youth organization, I felt free to express myself in ways that were difficult back home.

"The Bronx," I would say with conviction, whenever someone asked me where I was from. Technically speaking Riverdale was part of Bronx County, but it was a small, elevated section of the borough where John F. Kennedy and the heir to the Stella D'oro cookie fortune had once owned homes. We lived in a comfortable co-op apartment building, several miles from the closest open fire hydrant or inconsiderately loud car stereo. In my mind, though, in front of all these campers from suburbs in Long Island, New Jersey, and Cincinnati, I was from the 'hood. Someone had once stolen the airbag out of my mother's Mercury Sable, leaving a gaping hole in the center of the steering wheel. Another time I found the remains of illegal firecrackers scattered in a park.

"Da Bronx," I'd say, as though part of a hip-hop entourage, as the summer continued, "represent." When would people understand me? When would they see me as the thick-skinned roughneck who lived through the harsh realities of a violent world, yet had a sensitive side and knew what it meant to have good manners?

I pulled the trigger and the rifle cracked alive without a kickback. Down the range, the paper target was still attached to the plywood. It had not blasted off as I had imagined. Perhaps it needed an extra nudge before it burst into flames, I thought while reloading, but the second bullet fired off with the same result. Where was the charge of light from the tip of the barrel, the smoke, the destruction, the instinctual urge to scream, "Get some!"

"Is it working right?" I asked Dror.

"Go take your target so de rest of the bunk can go," he said, ignoring my question.

At the end of the range, I pulled my target off the plywood. There was a tiny hole by the top right corner of the eight-by-eleven-inch sheet, as though the tip of a fine pencil had stabbed it. I folded the paper twice and placed it carefully in the pocket of my jean shorts—more proof that danger existed in my life.

CHAPTER 14

HERE FOR THE CHICKS

BY SOME MIRACLE I was admitted to Beth Hebrew a day before classes began. No longer would I have to be embarrassed by the school I attended. I would be enrolled in an academy that didn't accept everyone who applied. By the standards of my friends and community, Beth Hebrew was a perfectly reasonable coed religious yeshiva high school, with two sexes of students bustling through the bright and colorful hallways. Finally, I felt like I was winning the battle of being a teenager.

The most exciting part about Beth Hebrew was the other sex: girls. There were tons of them everywhere and in every class I attended, and they seemed smarter and more attractive than I remembered them from junior high school. As I followed the lines of students through the packed hallways on our way to and from class, I passed girls in tight long-sleeve, crewneck T-shirts and even tighter black slinky skirts that came down to their ankles. They held their books close across their chests as if to protect their bosoms from my wandering eyes.

Classes were hopeless. Any minor headway I had made toward becoming a better and more focused student at B.S. was washed away by the waves of distractions—like Golda's freckles, Tovah's breasts, and Samantha's butt—flooding the school halls. I quickly established myself as one of the weakest students in the slow class when my new Bible teacher asked me to read aloud and the words would simply not come out of my mouth. Hebrew, the language I had been studying every semester for the past ten years, was all of a sudden foreign to me because I was too distracted by the back of Zahava's olive-skin neck in the desk immediately in front of me.

But these were minor concerns. I was used to such fumbles in elementary school, and as with a bitter friend to keep you company while depressed, there was comfort in sliding back down to the bottom rung of academic achievement. Besides, I didn't transfer to this new school to improve my grades; I was here for the chicks. And this seemingly normal, bully- and wrestling-fanatic-free school zone, where the gym teacher made us change before class so we didn't sweat through our dress-code-compliant collared shirts, was overflowing with them. The only problem was that I had no idea how to talk to them.

"Eytan!" a girl named Tamar called out to me as I passed by her and her friends one afternoon.

"Uh, oh, hi," I said, not quite understanding why she was speaking to me. Had she caught me ogling her? Did she somehow know that I was thinking about her at night?

I stood dumbly in front of the group of three girls as they sat by their lockers, twirling pens and clutching binders.

"Who's your best friend?" Tamar asked me with a devilish smile, her thick brown hair falling richly over her shoulders, probably providing an extra layer of warmth in the colder months.

While trying not to stare at her chest, I wondered what she meant. Was this some kind of trick question or inside joke that

I was not hip to? I needed to channel Bayme, my cool alter ego from camp who didn't get nervous in front of girls.

I don't have best friends or second-best friends, little lady, I'd say. *I'm what you call a loner.*

"Um, well. His name is Gilad," I said instead.

"Who?" she asked incredulously, her eyes tightening at me.

"Gilad. He doesn't go to this school. Do you know him?" I tried to keep the conversation going.

"Uh, no," she said. "Whatever."

Something was wrong. She seemed upset. I began to sweat.

"Well, I gotta go," I said, "over there," as I pointed across the hall and fled, leaving Tamar and her friends as confused as I was.

I didn't understand. She had asked me who my best friend was and I answered her truthfully. Should I have said, *You, Tamar! You are my best friend?* These were the first words we ever really spoke. I couldn't lie to her like that. Besides, best friends didn't imagine shrinking down to the size of a gerbil and nestling inside each other's cleavage.

Two years earlier, in the eighth grade, Gilad himself had tried to teach me how to talk to girls. He wasn't exactly Richard Gere and had never had a girlfriend, but I was in no position to turn down free advice.

"Take this mirror," he explained one afternoon before his advanced-level Talmud class began, "and try to reflect the light onto the girl's face." The mirror was about the size of a cereal bowl, and he used it to bounce sunlight coming through the overhead windows straight across the room.

"See?" he said, maneuvering a bright shard of light over the blackboard and onto a large color map of Israel.

"Not really," I said. "How is that going to help me talk to girls?"

"Look," he said, agitated. "You want girls to think you're a good-looking guy, right?"

"Yeah, I guess."

"Then first you have to get their attention."

"Right," I said, losing patience. "And how is your mirror trick gonna do that?"

"When a girl first sees you, what do you think she's thinking?"

"There's Eytan."

"Good, but if she's looking your way, and light is glaring into her face, then what is she going to think?"

"Um, that she's blind?"

"No. She's going to think that Eytan is a ray of light. That Eytan is so pretty, that she can't even see him without shielding her eyes and she needs to talk to him right now because he is basically God." Gilad was in his zone, spouting sleek, well-packaged bullshit. I admired him for it.

"There's no way that's gonna work."

"Try it," he said, handing me the mirror.

"Not a chance." I backed off. I thought girls were angry at me for the lewd situations I subjected them to in my head. I didn't want to piss them off further with Gilad's cheap tricks. "Why don't you demonstrate for me, ladies' man?" I taunted.

"Fine," he said, as though it were something he did all the time. "Watch."

Gilad's class was filling up. Students were taking off their knapsacks and unloading their contents onto their desks. Across the room, Talia Bestman, a brown-haired, studious classmate, who rarely ever smiled, let her volume of Talmud fall from her hands and onto the table in front of her with a slap. Gilad took his mirror and aimed the sunlight into her face. Talia squinted and, like a soldier deserting his troop, I slipped away and stood by the exit to easily run off in case things got heated.

Talia frowned and tried to block out the light with her palm.

"What the heck?" she exclaimed, trying to decipher the source of the flash. "Gilad, is that you?"

"Maybe," he called across the room.

"Will you please stop!" She was annoyed, exactly how I had imagined. Gilad was in for it.

"Yeah, sorry," he said finally and calmly put the mirror down.

"Why did you do that?" she asked him.

"I was just playing around. Relax." Talia shook her head and took a seat, all rather anticlimactically, I thought. Gilad then looked my way and gave me a thumbs-up. It was true, she had spoken to him.

Gilad may have been on to something, so I tried a variation on his technique at Beth Hebrew. One afternoon, in the back row of math class, I played with a small square of aluminum foil while trying to decide what to say to Devorah, the tall, black-haired girl sitting next to me in Mrs. Eshkol's trigonometry class.

"Devorah," I whispered, as she slouched down in her chair, legs up against the seat in front of her. I could tell that she was as bored as I was by the way she ripped apart her split ends, a natural class distraction that I was always jealous of girls for having.

"What?" she whispered back.

"Do you have fillings in your teeth?"

She shook her head and gave me a funny look.

"Fillings," I whispered before opening my mouth and

pointing to the silver splotches that covered my rear teeth, "Do you have 'em?"

She nodded, still confused.

"Bite down on this," I urged softly as I handed her the square of silver foil.

I figured everyone knew about the sharp, screaming pain felt when metal came in contact with cavity fillings. I thought Devorah would laugh at my idiotic suggestion, and my sarcasm would break the ice and allow us to become fast friends.

Good one! she'd exclaim and then stop by my house the following Sunday unannounced in a Jeep Wrangler with the top down.

C'mon, Eytan! she would shout up to my kitchen window, as I was busy polishing my mother's silverware. *There's a secluded crater right over the George Washington Bridge. Let's go check it out!*

Devorah examined the wrapper as I stared on, smiling and waiting for her to get the joke. When she brought the foil to her mouth, I felt a fleeting moment of terror that she might actually bite down on it, but I figured she was bluffing. Then the wrapper crossed her lips and I realized this was no joke. Devorah was clueless. She was about to chew the foil.

"No! Stop!" I cried loudly for the rest of the class to hear, too late.

"Aaaah!" Devorah shrieked high and loud, as though someone were stabbing her.

"What is going on?" demanded Mrs. Eshkol.

"Nothing! It's okay," I stammered.

"That kills!" Devorah screamed, tears flowing from her eyes.

"I'm sorry," I swore, wishing I could take it back.

"Why would you tell me to do that?"

"I don't know. It was stupid."

"What's wrong?" Mrs. Eshkol asked.

"Eytan made me bite on this!" Devorah held the aluminum foil high in the air.

"Okay, just please go to the nurse!"

She grabbed her jaw and squeezed between our desks toward the exit.

"I'm really sorry," I said as she passed me without looking.

"That was dumb, Eytan," the teacher said.

"I know."

Later that day, I peeked in the nurse's station and saw Devorah lying on a cot with a damp washcloth on her head. I felt hopeless and unable to do anything right. Other boys were able to ask a girl, "What's going on?" and take the conversation from there. Not me, though. Nothing was going on, obviously, so why would I ask such an idiotic question? I needed something that set me apart and showed girls how cool and interesting I was.

My dad had something like this, I believe. He always bragged about never being without a book. Even when he was in kindergarten, he carried around Golden Books, those thin children's storybooks with a gold spine. Not only was this a productive way to spend his time on trolleys and buses in the greater Boston area, where he grew up, but books also always gave him something to talk about with his female classmates.

I see you're reading The Little Red Hen, I imagined a five-year-old girl in his class striking up a conversation, *my mother read it to me last night.*

Interesting. What were your impressions? he would ask.

I loved the illustrations and it made me hungry.

It really is a classic, he would reply. *And a larger comment on our society's consuming, rather than contributing, culture.*

I decided to try something similar and asked my dad to

borrow his hardcover edition of *Truman*, by David McCullough, the week after I injured Devorah.

"Great book," my dad declared.

"Oh, good." I chose it because it had a colorful drawing of Harry Truman's head in a bright field of grass under a blue sky. There were also two separate sections, visible on the side of the book, that were printed on a shinier paper stock than the rest of the volume, and I knew that these were pictures. I did plan on reading the book, but I really just wanted it to make me appear intelligent and elicit conversation with those girls interested in smart guys. Most important, the book was long. Over a thousand pages. If I carried around a book of this size, I was sure to impress.

On the school bus the following morning, I tried to read some of it, but the words were dizzying and boring. Young Truman does stuff in Missouri. Young Truman meets a girl at a dance. McCullough meant for me to string the words together, one after another, and make sense of the work, but he wrote so many of them. Even trying to speed through the tome, flip book style, was overwhelming. I turned to the back of the book and looked up the word "Jew" in the index, hoping to find something, maybe even about my dad, to pull me into the story. It was referenced several times and I turned to one of the instances near the beginning. The passage talked about a visit Truman made to New York City as a young man. Afterward, in his diary, he wrote that "New York was full of Jews."

Whoa! I thought, that didn't sound very presidential. Truman was a total anti-Semite.

That day I sat in front of my locker, with my feet crossed, reading *Truman*. Rather, I was looking at *Truman*. Lots of people passed by as I examined McCullough's rounded serif font and the black-and-white pictures of the former president's memorable moments, yet no one stopped to discuss any of it or tell me how impressed she was that I was reading it. Mostly, my classmates frowned and avoided eye contact.

During lunch, my American history teacher, Ms. Dayan, stopped before me on her way to class.

"Whatta ya got there, Eytan?" she asked. Ms. Dayan was carrying four canvas totes, full of papers or books or anvils, and a tall traveling coffee mug.

"Oh, nothing, really," I said shyly. "Just the latest Truman biography." I held up the book to give her a good view of the dazzling artwork on the cover.

"Gosh," she said, readjusting a few of the bags over her shoulder. "Serious stuff. What year was he president again?"

"Um, you know, I'm not sure," I confessed. "It doesn't really get into that. But interestingly, he was a total anti-Semite. He thought New York was 'full of Jews.'" I added air quotes for effect.

"Really?" she said skeptically.

"Oh sure. It's all right here in the book."

"Interesting. Well, do you want to talk about it to the class?"

"No, that's okay," I insisted. "I'd want to finish it first."

"You could just say a few words about what you've read so far? Nothing too crazy." This woman was really trying to mess this up for me. I didn't want to get up in public and discuss what I learned, I just wanted a casual conversation starter that perhaps would lead to an after-hours study session in the bedroom of a female classmate whose parents were out of town. Was that so much to ask?

"Let me think about it and get back to you," I said. "But probably not."

"Okay. Let me know if you change your mind," she said and continued walking to her classroom.

A little while later Jack Lewinstein, my punching buddy from camp, stopped by.

"What are you doing, Eytan?" Jack attended Beth Hebrew and he, along with a few friends who had transferred out of the all-boys B.S., were the only people I knew during the first few weeks of class.

"Just reading my book on Harry S. Truman," I explained, emphasizing the dead president's middle initial.

"Is it good?" he asked.

"Yeah, man, totally," I assured him. "This is, like, a really famous book." I placed the publication in his hand so he could feel how heavy it was.

"Did you know," I continued, "that Truman was actually *vehemently* anti-Semitic?"

Jack shrugged.

"He absolutely despised us," I promised.

"Okay," he said uneasily.

"Anyway, if you wanna borrow it, it's no problem."

"I'm all right," he said. "Thanks, though."

Toward the end of the day, my locker neighbor Sam Drucker mentioned that he had "already read that, twice," before abruptly running off to perform a yo-yo demonstration, which appeared to garner more of a crowd than my choice of nonfiction reading. Nobody was interested in the stupid book. I would have gotten more people to talk to me had I brought a pop-up book or the Scholastic Book Club catalog from elementary school. At least then I could understand what it was they were writing about. I needed to try harder or get more creative if I wanted to be popular and get chicks. I needed something cooler than anything my dad could offer.

CHAPTER 15

POPULAR DRUGS

NEVER IN MY LIFE had I desired to take drugs. According to the baggy-clothed, plastic-wrist-banded teenage spokesgirl, they sucked. Her jingle, "Users are losers, and losers are users/ so don't use drugs, don't use drugs!" hit me soberly, since being a loser was the opposite of what I had been trying to achieve in my life so far. No need to mess around with drugs, I thought, there were already enough factors working against me.

But early in the first semester at my new school, rumors wafted through the halls that popular students were getting high, and overnight my position changed. If I were into drugs, I thought, I would be undeniably cool.

Since elementary school, I had tried everything to gain acceptance to the ever-shifting ranks of the popular crowd. I stayed up-to-date with the latest rock bands, memorized crude morning-radio-show jokes, and used excessive amounts of hair gel. Nothing worked.

"Ha-ha, Bayme! Good one," JJ Shamir, the star basketball player at my elementary school, once said to me after telling him a drawn-out sex joke that replaced the words "bossa nova" with "boss-a-favor." "Now get the fuck out of my face."

By the time I transferred to Beth Hebrew, the players had changed but the game was still the same. JJ Shamir was at another school, but Jared Ehrenreich was the goalie on our hockey team and star of the softball team. He could walk down hallways not searching the faces of every one of our classmates and not wondering if they thought his hair looked stupid or if his pants were too short. Jared could make a group of girls in our grade laugh, dole out high-fives like a camp counselor, and then confer privately with an upperclassman in a serious-looking manner. To Jared and his friends, being popular seemed to come easy, so when word got out that he was experimenting with drugs, I was ready to join the party. Drugs would be a simple antidote to my problem—a drug, if you will, to make me popular. I just had to become an addict.

"Hey, Jared!" I called out in the middle of a busy hallway one afternoon. "Can you get me some crack?"

A girl walking ahead of me in a long black skirt and bright blue top turned around and glared.

"Ha-ha, Bayme, good one," said Jared. With his broad shoulders and six-foot frame, he appeared larger than life. A drab, pattern-less button-down shirt hung upon him loosely in a stylish lack of style.

When he realized I wasn't joking, though, he blushed. "I don't know, man," he said wearily, his eyes looking around the hallway. "I'll see."

As he walked away, I felt ridiculous. What did I know from crack or marijuana or meth or magic LSD? Drugs were drugs. I didn't realize that it mattered which one I was supposed to take. In fact, I thought it would be better to start off big. The more hard-core I presented myself, the cooler I would become.

At a tobacco shop in the West Village that weekend, I made some progress. I browsed through seven-foot-tall bongs with smoking aliens stenciled on them and three-hundred-dollar glass-blown "pieces," sold with fluffy carrying cases made of corduroy. There were cute nitrous oxide canisters that looked like mini gasoline tankers and all sorts of "legal weed" in brightly packaged pouches. I enjoyed learning about all these exciting new products and shopping opportunities, and I looked forward to impressing my peers with the options and prices available to them if they were ever in the market to purchase.

For legal reasons, I would explain, *shops that sold pipes like these had to state, on a sign behind the counter, that their products were "for tobacco use only." If not, they risked a court summons and maybe even a fine. It was all laid out in the law books*, I would add as they rubbed their chins and nodded intently.

That night, as I sat cross-legged in the tiny space under my desk while my parents and siblings slept, I disassembled the small steel "bowl" I had purchased from the tobacco shop. More fittings could be added to make it infinitely bigger, just like Legos. With my pipe purchased, I was ready to try to become a druggie.

Teaneck, New Jersey, is a clearinghouse for modern religious living. Dozens of synagogues, Jewish day schools, and kosher restaurants spackle the leafy terrain, serving the tens of thousands of Jewish families that call it home. Every autumn, on *Simchat Torah*, Orthodox teenagers from across the Eastern seaboard would descend upon the neighborhood for an airport terminal–sized social scene. So when Jack invited me to spend the holiday at his home, on a tree-lined street in the heart of this Jewish mecca, of course I accepted.

Simchat Torah, or the Celebration of the Torah, commemorates the Jewish people's acceptance of the Bible. Like on most High Holidays, Jews celebrate *Simchat Torah* by attending lengthy prayer services, eating large meals, and refraining from using electrical devices such as cars and electrolysis machines. But *Simchat Torah* is a true celebration. No temples were destroyed or plagues smitten; the Jews behaved themselves and finished reading the Bible that God had handed down to them. So we have a party. Whether that means singing and dancing with the Torah scrolls, throwing candy around a packed synagogue, or smoking a blunt laced with angel dust is a matter of personal preference.

Jack loved hockey. His closet brimmed with equipment and his walls were blanketed with autographed pictures of famous players. I didn't care much for the sport, but his collection impressed me nonetheless. When I arrived at his house the afternoon before the holiday, he stood on his driveway covered in gear. An oversized jersey held heavy Styrofoam pads over his chest, goalie pads covered his legs like giant slabs of tofu, and a cage helmet sat on his face and head. He looked like a five-foot marshmallow man on Rollerblades. All this equipment seemed a bit unnecessary since he was only playing against a garage door, but I was no expert on the sport.

"Did you bring your skates?" he asked as I walked up with my suit on a hanger and a knapsack on my back.

"No, I don't have any."

"Ah, it's cool, you can use my spares."

Jack and I had known each other since my earliest days at summer camp. He laughed at the right times, never told me to fuck off and, despite our barbershop scuffle, we became close friends. On my first day at Beth Hebrew, he gave me a tour of the school, and I was impressed by the way he handled himself.

"Hey, Babs!" he called out to a girl named Babbette, as we trawled the hallways.

"Ja-ack," she rang back, rolling the middle vowel.

Wow, I thought, I didn't call any girls by shortened versions of their names. I didn't call girls at all.

Jack was a good guy to keep close, but he was exemplary. He excelled in his schoolwork, never bad-mouthed his father, and, as far as I knew, kept no porn. I didn't think he would approve of the collection I had under my mattress, or that it was stolen from a homeless guy on the Upper West Side of Manhattan. So, on the eve of *Simchat Torah*, after I gave up trying to fit into his size-six Rollerblades, we put on our synagogue clothes and I neglected to tell him about the pipe in my suit pocket.

Whooosh! Something shot past my ear and slammed into the wooden pew behind me. I ducked down and looked at Jack to my right.

"Whoa!" I said.

Bang! It happened again, this time farther down the aisle. And again, before picking up like rain pounding a tin roof.

In our dark dress suits and yarmulkes, we bent down on the synagogue floor. All around us, children shrieked and ran, sliding on the carpet, while men lifted their heads and shouted prayers toward the ceiling. Behind us, past a nose-high wall, hundreds of women, the source of this barrage, looked on in glee.

I shielded my face with a prayer book and picked up a projectile from the bench. It was lime green and wrapped in cellophane.

"Yum, apple," I said to Jack.

We fled from our synagogue seats and joined the herd of

children bum-rushing the front of the sanctuary. At sixteen, we were about six years older than the average candy grabber, but hey, this stuff was free.

I was boxing out a nine-year-old over a Tootsie Roll when I felt my chest and realized something was wrong. I knelt down on the synagogue floor and began crawling. My fingers gripped at the beige carpet. Men wielding tuba-sized Torah scrolls danced around me. My eyes darted from their bearded faces, red with spiritual belief, to cackling children, high on Sugar Daddies. Sweat dripped from my brow. Somewhere in this celebratory jungle my coveted new drug pipe had fallen out of my pocket.

Bang! went a projectile directly into my temple. It was a soft, unwrapped jelly thing, the size of an apricot and covered in crystallized sugar.

"Fuck," I cried from my crouched position on the synagogue floor. A man with a Torah paused from his song to scowl at me.

The situation was dire. Drug paraphernalia wasn't allowed in synagogue. This was a holy place with Bibles and rabbis and God all over. If someone here found my pipe, I would probably get kicked out of my new school and sent away to an academy for disturbed boys. It would be the end. My parents would be shamed in their community. My father would lose his job and my mother would have to clean people's homes to support us.

Jack was on the other side of a wide pedestal that held dozens of prayer books. His arms were full of mini-chocolates and individually packaged wafers, and he had a smile the size of a shoehorn. I was about to explain that we had to leave when she caught my eye—a small girl about six years old in a flowing white dress curiously examining my shiny property. She put it up to her mouth and licked it before I scrambled over, snatched the bowl from her hand, and stuffed it in my pants pocket.

"Hey! That's mine," she screamed as I walked briskly away, like a gunman trying not to attract attention after a hit.

"I gotta get outta here," I told Jack without looking back.

Outside, the streets surrounding the synagogue were choked with Jewish day school students. Small circles of teenage boys in suits and ties sidled up close, like gears in a wristwatch, to circles of girls in ankle-length dresses. Here and there the cliques overlapped, spinning the hands of the teenage Modern Orthodox social network.

Jack led us down the synagogue stairs toward a group of five girls who went to our school.

"Hey, Tams," he said to a dark-haired girl named Tamar, who I had once embarrassed myself in front of in the school hallway, and now often thought about before falling asleep.

"Jack-o," she said, deepening her voice at *O*. "Hi, Eytan."

"Yo," I said quietly, as if acting too friendly would somehow reveal the fantasies I had about her at night.

Jack started talking about his favorite hockey player named something-or-other, and the girls teased him and took some of his candy. I stood a bit back from the circle, unsure of what to add to the conversation. I felt as though I were in Bible class and couldn't work with the foreign-language text in front of me. Soon, my mind began drifting off to more easily decipherable matters in the periphery—black tar street, lamp over synagogue door, breast of Tamar.

The conversation meandered across topics such as ugly teachers and driving tests. I wanted to participate, but I thought that my word choice would somehow create a scene or offend someone. *Fuck out of my face*, one of these tastefully dressed, giggling girls might inexplicably respond to me after I mentioned that I, too, wished I had a car.

I had to get out of there, but there was no stopping Jack. He was in his zone; he loved the teasing, the questions, the wisecracking. It was as though I were in a department store with my mother and she stopped at every rack, examining each article of clothing, while I tugged on her dress, trying to inch her toward the cashier.

Through the crowd, I spotted another camp friend sitting on the sidewalk curb. Good old Hillel Allon, my hemophiliac hairdresser from Cherry Hill, had his long hair tied in a rubber band under an oversized multicolored yarmulke. He wore a brown blazer with black pants and an untucked white dress shirt. Hillel was sixth man on our camp basketball team and once almost got kicked out for smoking a cigarette behind a bunk.

I stepped a bit closer into the circle and placed a hand on Jack's arm to indicate a pause in the conversation. "Would you excuse me?" I told the group as if I had a pressing business matter to attend to.

"Where ya going, Eytan?" Jack called.

"Uh, I just need to check on something," I said while skipping away.

As I made my way toward Hillel, I noticed a whitish stain on his black pants. How cool is that, I thought. He didn't even care that his holiday clothes were filthy. I had brought a lint remover with me to Jack's house to ensure that I looked as sharp as possible.

"Bayme! What's up?" said Hillel moments later.

"I'm cool," I said, looking down at Hillel sitting on the sidewalk curb. "Ya know."

I sat down next to him and slowly opened my jacket.

"Dude, check this out." I showed him the bowl in my blazer like it was a bootleg wristwatch.

"Sweet, man," he said. I expected he would then high-five me or put an arm around my neck and say something like, *You know, Bayme, I always knew you were a cool one.*

But instead, he asked, "You wanna smoke up?"

The question surprised me. I didn't anticipate actually smoking pot. It was illegal and had to be purchased from gun-wielding drug dealers. Furthermore, I didn't need to *do* drugs; I just wanted people to think I did drugs. This was about my reputation, not altered states of mind. Actually getting high scared the shit out of me.

But Hillel had called my bluff. I couldn't turn him down. Why would a stoner not want to get stoned?

"Uh, really?" I asked.

"Totally!" he said.

"Uh, okay."

We walked a few blocks away from the synagogue. Thoughts about living on the street, oncoming traffic, and Todd, that *Beverly Hills, 90210* character that shot himself, flashed through my mind.

I wanted the skies to open up and drench us with rain, snow, hail, anything that would force us to cancel our drug-ingesting play date.

Well, unfortunately it looks like we're going to have to reschedule, I'd say once I felt a couple of drops. *Why don't we touch base in the morning and see if we're still up for it then?*

But it was a beautiful evening, and when we could hear the crowd no more, we took a left into a densely wooded lot behind some homes. Dead leaves crunched under my feet and I felt a growing urge to use the bathroom.

"This is good," Hillel said, as we reached a clearing, about thirty feet back from the street.

We kneeled down on the ground and he took something out of his pocket.

"Can I see?" I asked, and he handed me a mini-zip-lock bag, unlike one I had ever held before. Do they make special tiny bags for drugs? I wondered while opening it up and sticking a finger inside. The weed felt like old leaves and dirt.

"Let me see that bowl," he asked.

"You know," I advised him, with my hand down my breast pocket, "legally speaking, it's for tobacco use only."

"He-he," he snickered, mistaking my counsel for sarcasm. "Guess we're breaking two laws then."

With my pipe stuffed tight with weed, Hillel lit a thick white candle and placed the bowl underneath the flame. He inhaled deeply and held the smoke in his chest before engaging in a loud coughing fit that sounded like a train crossing a track. I sat there wondering if he had just contracted lung cancer when he began taking more hits off the pipe. He worked hard, smoking the pipe like he was on a mission to get high. I wondered if it could aggravate his hemophilia.

As he sucked on the pipe I hoped that he would finish all the pot and leave nothing for me, and he soon did—but to my disappointment, he refilled it afterward.

"Okay, this one is for you," he said.

Nah, it's cool, man, more weed for you. Enjoy! I wanted to tell him, but I couldn't back out.

"This is my first time smoking," Hillel then confessed.

I was touched. If Hillel chose me to get high with for the first time, I must have been special. He wouldn't go to the woods to do drugs with any old loser. Becoming a stoner was the right decision. Such a significant bonding experience would be impossible without the magic of drugs.

But then I thought, He must think I am a seasoned pro at drugs. I mean, I had a marijuana pipe, after all. So instead of confiding in him that this, too, was my first time, I said, "Cool, man, you're doing great."

I put the pipe to my mouth and tilted the candle into the bowl; a line of wax began dripping on my leg. The pot tasted harsh, like a dentist rooting around my mouth with lit matches. I began my own industrial-strength cough and couldn't take another hit. It tasted gross and I was worried that I would become insane. Hillel turned away for a moment and I blew into the pipe, shooting the little ember of flaming drugs out onto the ground.

"I think it's cashed," I said, quoting *Dazed and Confused* while placing my foot over the lit weed on the floor and snuffing it out.

"That was quick. You want some more?" Hillel asked.

"Nah, man, I'm cool."

I put the filthy bowl in my pocket and we walked out of the forest. Back on the street, Hillel's eyes were red and his hair fell over his face.

"Let's go this way, man," I said, starting to walk in the direction of the crowd and feeling exactly the same as I had before smoking pot.

"Hold up . . . ," Hillel mumbled. "Let's just chill a sec."

"Chill" was a new term being used around school that related to acting cool or something that was cool, as in "Let's light some incense in here and chill out," or "That's a pretty chill yellow Walkman." I always associated it with an act that flirtatious boys and girls performed on each other at summer camp where they tickled the back of each other's neck, giving them a cool tingling sensation, or the "chills."

"You want me to give you the chills?" I asked Hillel jokingly.

But instead of laughing or saying no he just stared blankly.

I was fairly certain that Hillel didn't want me to give him the chills, since that seemed like a pretty gay thing, and I knew Hillel had dated Annie Meyerwitz in camp, so he wasn't homosexual. But then I thought about how Hillel was stoned, and perhaps the chills would feel good to him. Then I thought further that maybe Hillel *was* actually gay and this was his way of letting me know. I looked at my friend in his mismatched suit and oversized yarmulke and thought, If Hillel confided in me that he is gay, it would definitely mean that I am cool.

"All right," he said finally.

And so, on that cool September night, under a streetlamp on an empty suburban road in Teaneck, I stood behind Hillel in my wax-stained suit and tickled the back of his neck. For fifteen seconds neither of us spoke, and when he shuddered, I removed my hand.

I smoothed down my jacket and waited for him to say that he had something to tell me, but instead he simply mumbled, "That was weird."

I smiled crookedly and wiped my sweaty hands on the butt of my pants. I felt used. Hillel had no intention of coming out to me; he might not be gay at all. He didn't even offer to give me the chills in return.

"You know what," I said, "I gotta go." And before he could respond, I ran off toward the crowds, leaving Hillel and his chills behind.

As I rushed back into the scene in front of the synagogue, I saw Jack chatting up some other girls.

"Eyy-tan!" he howled as I passed by. "Where you been?"

"Hi, Jack," I shouted as I ran up the steps of the synagogue. "I gotta make!"

In the men's room, I slammed the door shut and locked it behind me. Was this cool? I wondered, as I sat picking at the textured mess of wax on my suit jacket. I couldn't tell.

CHAPTER 16

SUBTERRANEAN LOVE

A FEW MONTHS LATER, during morning prayers, Jack told me something strange.

"Hannah told me that Tamar told her that she likes you,"

"What the shit?" I said.

"I'm just repeating what I heard."

Jack was in the academically rigorous classes, so I didn't see him much during the day, but we sat next to each other at prayers and killed time by quoting lines from *The Simpsons*.

"That's so stupid," I said, feigning disgust.

"You're blushing."

"No, I'm not."

Aside from TV, telling jokes, and perhaps the effects of microwaving household objects, I didn't want my male friends to think I cared about anything, especially not girls. My intense longing for physical contact, which had led me to hoard the lingerie pages from Caldor catalogs, were known only by me. Even the simple act of liking a girl didn't fit into the cool persona I was trying to cultivate. I was a loner with a quick wit and a street sensibility, who tucked only the front of my oxford shirts into my pleated pants and slicked back my hair Pat Riley–style before covering it with a yarmulke. Needy women only held me back in my pursuit of being the coolest yeshiva high school student. So I let the subject of Tamar drop and moved onto Homer's more memorable lines from the previous night's *Simpsons*.

Secretly, though, I felt like there was magic in the air. An actual, physical girl was interested in me, a creepy public nose-picker, the former "rocker." In my head I saw Julie Andrews spinning on the side of a lush green mountain in the Alps. "Wonder of Wonders," the song that the lowly tailor in *Fiddler on the Roof* sings when Tevye grants him permission to marry his daughter, played on a loop in my mind.

Was Tamar desirable? Yes, of course. She was a cute girl with longish red hair who wore the same ankle-length black skirts that all the other girls in our grade wore. She was very pretty, but the point was that she liked me.

"What should I do?" I finally asked Jack after I felt as though enough time had passed to bring the matter up again.

"About what?"

"You know," I said evasively, "that chick. Whatsherface."

"I don't know? Talk to her, I guess."

Easier said than done. Tamar belonged to a pool of girls in my class who I thought about often and in compromising situations. I had imagined us as a jungle-dwelling couple swinging together from trees wearing only loincloths, and I had wondered what it would feel like to be an old king suffering from pneumonia with Tamar as a young maidservant warming me with her body heat. So vivid were these fantasies that I felt they might somehow leak out of my mind and into any conversation I attempted to have with her.

We should walk deep into a forest together, I might randomly blurt, or, *I want to die at the same exact moment that you die,* could come out of my mouth and Tamar would swiftly erase any interest she originally entertained. Instead, I took a deep breath and tried to talk to her about less-graphic and more administrative, easier-to-navigate topics.

"Can I borrow a pen?" I asked her one afternoon after taking a seat next to her in English class.

"Yes," she said and handed me an expensive-looking, fine-tipped implement with a window along the shaft displaying the ink inside. "Don't steal it," she added with a smile.

"I promise I'll give it back," I said soberly. "Thank you."

I pulled off the cap and marveled at the continuous black lines that the pen left on a piece of loose-leaf paper I had picked up off the floor. I felt honored that Tamar trusted me with such a fine writing utensil and doubted that she would lend it to just any schmo classmate who asked her for one.

As we sat next to each other in silence, I thought about keeping her pen safe. I would give it back to her right after class, maybe even before it ended so she wouldn't have to feel awkward asking for it. I wanted to make the transaction as easy as possible for her. In fact, since I barely ever took notes in class and spent my time sketching Smurf-like dwarves instead, I decided that I would save her ink and not draw anything. For the next forty-five minutes I would anticipate giving Tamar her pen back.

As I stared at it laying on my desk, Hannah, Tamar's friend, turned around from her seat in front of me.

"You guys are so cute!" she whisper-squealed at the two of us.

Immediately, I froze up.

Why would she say that? What is cute about us? What is "us"? I had barely ever spoken a word to Hannah, but now I wanted to scream at her. *What are you trying to do! I'm just here borrowing a pen. I'm not some psycho who sits next to girls to look cute beside them!*

"Shut up, Hannah," Tamar said through her perfectly spaced teeth and plump red lips. She was upset, too, and I wondered why. *Does she not think we are cute? Does she not want to be associated with me?* Oh God, I thought, that would be even worse than being called cute. Perhaps Jack's info was all wrong and Tamar didn't like me at all and was disgusted by being referred to as "guys" with me.

Hannah made her mouth crooked in a look that said, *Jesus, relax,* before turning back around to face the teacher.

For the rest of the class, I sat silently staring ahead at the back of Hannah's skinny neck, wondering if by sitting next to Tamar, I had made it too obvious that I was interested in her. Perhaps she had wanted to begin a secret love affair, and by sitting too close, I had come on stronger than she preferred and spoiled the mood.

Tamar and I had reached our end too soon. I imagined myself layered in the latest J. Crew designs near a New England pond on a blustery gray day. I knelt down and touched the damp earth as I thought about the love that could have been. A crow with no capacity to show emotion landed next to me and flitted his wings, and I heaved my breath and committed to attempting to go on with my solitary life.

I took the pen in my hand and held it as though I was going to take notes. If this was the end of Tamar liking me, I wanted to relish in the warmth of what her property meant in my possession. The pen had represented the closest attachment I had formed with a girl and it was a moment that I needed to remember vividly.

When the bell rang, Tamar turned to me. "Eytan?" she said.

"Yes?" I responded, feeling like a dog at an adoption center. Would she forgive the mess I had made, take me home, and make me hers? Or would she leave me here to get euthanized if nobody came around in the next week?

"Do you want to call me?" she asked.

It was like being asked if I wanted a winning lottery ticket. *Yes, goddamnit. I do want to call you. Just tell me when. I could leave school early so the phone rings the moment you step inside your house.* For fifteen years, girls had been interested in me only in my imagination. Over the years, I had married scores of classmates in my mind. I had fathered countless children with them, charmed each and every one of their parents, and weathered multiple complicated divorces. Sometimes, in bed with the lights out, I would live out two or three love affairs a night. It was a tumultuous and heart-wrenching era for me, and now I would finally be given a chance to live out a real, live relationship. I could barely speak.

"Okay," I whispered almost inaudibly.

"You don't have to," she said, sounding hurt.

"No, no, I do!" I cried. "I just don't have your phone number."

Tamar put her hand out toward me and I hesitated a moment before slapping her five.

"The pen," she said.

"Oh, sorry." I had been clutching it so hard that it was slimy from my sweat, so I put it under my armpit and wiped it off on my shirt before presenting it to her in an open palm, like a ring on a pillow.

"Ew," she said softly while clawing it between her thumb and forefinger and dropping it into her open knapsack.

"My bad," I said.

Tamar took a second pen from her bag and scribbled her

phone number down on a scrap of paper. As I glanced over the magical ten digits, the first phone number a girl had ever given me, I imagined they were a secret pass code to a treasure chest of riches. All I had to do was type them into a phone and I had direct access to a chick who wanted to hear from me.

"I should call you tonight?"

"Whenever," she said, before exiting the classroom.

That night, I was in a different world. Normally, during suppertime, around the kitchen table with my family, I was a horrible dinner guest.

How was school today? my father might ask.

It was retarded! Why are we even talking about it? I'd scream while scowling at a pot of steaming barley, ceasing any further dinner table conversation from anyone.

This night was different. I was chipper if not pleased to be eating a meal with my family.

"More broccoli, Ma!" I squealed while holding my plate out toward her across the table. My parents looked at each other, confused.

"How was school today, Eytan?" my dad asked.

"Fine," I said, suspiciously eyeing him and my mother, wondering if they somehow knew what had transpired that day.

"Did you want to tell us something?" asked my mother.

"Um, about what?"

"I don't know. It just seems like you had a good day."

"Jesus!" I cried. Could a kid have a decent day at school without getting grilled by his parents about it? "No, I didn't," I continued, and put an end to any further discussion they felt like having about me.

In my room after dinner, I studied the sheet of paper with

Tamar's number. Her penmanship was so consistent, I thought. The curves of her zeros matched those in the bottoms of her fives. It was refined. Entirely different from the sometimes choppy, sometimes swollen letters and numbers that I produced.

As I leaned over my bed with my knees on the floor, I thought about her sitting on my lap. My arms were around her stomach and I inhaled the mountain-fresh-detergent scent from her finely knit sweater. Suddenly we were naked and hungrily nibbling at each other's lips in a fully carpeted sewer. The plush, odor-free, well-lit tunnel offered complete comfort and privacy and was accessible only by ladders under my mattress and hers, in Morristown. I imagined some sort of high-speed golf cart allowed us easily to meet in the middle, perhaps beneath Patterson.

My mind wandered to things like nude piggyback rides and installing a Jacuzzi in the sewer. All of a sudden the 1986 Mets showed up through the ladder under my bed and a party was under way. "Bayme!" a smiling Darryl Strawberry shouted at me from down the tunnel. "You the man!" But I was indulging myself too fast and too soon. The more I had these strange and dirty thoughts, the harder it would be for me to talk to Tamar. I would be so focused on not blurting them out that I wouldn't be able to say anything.

I breathed deeply and shook the images from my mind. The party receded. I was back on my bed aboveground. Now what the hell was I going to talk about? My mind was blank.

Tamar would almost certainly ask, "What's up?" Technically, *I just had dinner with my family* was up, but why would I respond with such a lame, useless fact? It was 7:00 p.m., probably everybody just had dinner with their family. It was unoriginal and common.

School sucks was up as well, but that was more of an ongoing comment about life in general. Tamar was in the same slow-track classes as me, and I was fairly certain that she agreed with my sentiment, but what kind of conversation would that lead to? A deep exchange about how much we hated our day-to-day existence? It seemed like a downer of a topic and not something cool guys would mention.

Forget preparing, I thought. I'll wing it. Johnny Depp's character in *Cry Baby* wouldn't sit around all night deciding what to say. If the conversation came to a lull, he'd run his hands through his hair and squint his eyes a little before saying something like, *I can't play by anyone's rules except my own.* I punched her numbers into the keypad and the phone rang in my ear.

"Hello?" asked a female voice on the other end.

"What's up," I asked quietly.

"Hello?" she asked, louder this time.

"Hi," I said, nervously matching her pitch. "Is Tamar there?"

"This is she."

"Hi, Tamar," I continued. "This is Eytan Bayme. From school."

"I know who you are, Eytan," she said. "I asked you to call. Remember?"

"Yeah," I said, in an a-ha! moment, as if it had slipped my mind. "I remember."

"Ha-ha," said Tamar.

"So what's up?" I asked before she had the chance.

"Oh, not much. The usual, just had dinner with my parents. You know."

"Oh yeah, totally," I said.

"What's up with you?" she countered.

I paused and waited for something to pop into my head, some awesome anecdote that would magically slip from my lips with casual ease. I teased a curl out from the front of my hair, trying to conjure *Cry Baby*. It could have been *I was reminded of something you spoke of* or *Ain't you something special*, but nothing was coming out, not a single shred of what I imagined would be the perfect goddamn thing to be up.

"You know," I said at last, "school sucks."

"Uh-huh," Tamar said, imitating Butthead. "Yeah, school sucks."

"He-he," I responded Beavis-esquely. "Cool."

"I love that show!"

"Yeah!"

"It's so funny!"

"He-he."

Silence. I didn't know where to take it from there. I felt as though I had walked into a sprawling valley and now lacked the energy to hike out. I wasn't necessarily going to die, but I may have to figure out how to live here for a while.

"So . . . ," Tamar said, waiting for me to talk.

"So . . . yeah," I said. "You know, you, like, said I should call." I thought that since I didn't know what to say, I could fill the silence by summarizing the events that had led up to the call. "Thanks again for lending me the pen."

"You're welcome."

More silence. It was killing me. I feared she was losing interest in me with each wordless moment. I couldn't let her slip away, so I took a risk.

"So listen, Tamar," I said. "Jack mentioned to me that Hannah said to him that maybe you . . . liked me?" My voice rose at the end.

"She said that?" Tamar asked.

This was how grown-ups talked, I thought. They dumped everything out on the table and then sorted through their feelings like Rummikub tiles. There was no use hiding such things in plain sight.

"Well, Jack said that she said that." The words practically flowed out of my mouth.

"Hmm."

"So," I continued farther out on a limb that was sure to snap at any moment, "do you, like, wanna be my boyfriend?"

The question hung in the air. As entire civilizations seemed to flourish and die in the silence that followed, the reality of what I had asked began to sink in.

"I'm a girl!" Tamar spoke finally.

"I meant the other way around."

"Jeez."

"I'm sorry."

"You know, I really wish Hannah hadn't said that."

"Oh."

"You seem nice, but I don't know you." With every utterance, I felt as though the walls of my stomach were crumbling in on themselves. The words "seem" and "I don't" knocked chunks of gray matter out of place. Before I was reduced to nothing, I needed to hold back the damage and somehow make a solid point about why we were meant to be together.

"So?" I said.

"So what do we have in common?" she came back immediately.

"I don't know."

"Exactly," she said. "You don't know and I don't know."

"But why does it matter what we have in common?" I countered.

"Because it does."

"Oh," I said.

"You seem like a nice guy, Eytan," she continued. "Let's be friends."

"So you don't want to be my girlfriend?" I asked again.

"Let's be friends. Okay?"

I felt like crying. I was getting dumped without even having been in a relationship.

"Okay," I said, sounding extra sad, thinking that perhaps she would feel so bad for me that she would agree to be my girlfriend.

"Oh God," she sighed, "are you okay?"

"Yeah, I'm fine."

"Friends? Okay?" she asked one more time.

"Okay."

"Good. I'll see you tomorrow, Eytan. Right?"

"Yeah," I told her, slightly annoyed. She sounded as though she were trying to talk me off the ledge of a building.

"Bye," she said and waited for me to say good-bye before cutting the connection.

I hung up the phone and fell on my bed face-first. I felt like a complete loser. Once again I had exposed myself to someone else, laying my feelings out, only to be battered and torn apart by forces out of my control. No matter what I tried, nothing seemed to work for me. I would never get a girl.

CHAPTER 17

POOR MAN'S SMOKED SALMON

OVER THE NEXT FEW WEEKS I avoided sitting close to Tamar in class and resented her for making me like her so much. If Jack never told me what Hannah said, I never would have spoken to her. She would be just another girl I thought about with no expectation of making an honest woman of her. Yes, I would have imagined her in compromising and sexual situations, but I would never have thought they could become a reality.

Now, as I sat on the opposite side of the room, trying to get her out of my mind, I realized I was heading down a familiar path. Tamar and I were in almost every single class together. Ignoring her would be difficult. Our high school classrooms were nothing like the open-plan "learning areas" at my elementary school, where the mind of an easily distracted student could drift off into the thrum of the dozens of conversations within earshot throughout the giant room. The rooms at Beth Hebrew were well-designed boxes with heavy metal doors that made a *swoosh* sound as they sealed the fifteen students inside.

Unless I convinced myself that she didn't exist in the same dimension, there was no escaping Tamar.

I thought about the conversation we had and her painful "let's be friends" line that uninterested girls said to overeager guys. Comments like these were never spoken in earnest. They were stock phrases to use instead of the truth, which was, "I don't want to be in a relationship because weird things come out of your mouth," or "You're creepy." Yet, despite the hollowness of Tamar's speech, I wanted to take something tangible away from it.

I thought that having a friend who was a girl could teach me to be more comfortable around the opposite sex and perhaps help me to hold actual conversations with them. A girl who was a friend, I imagined, would let me use her leg as a pillow whenever we stretched out on the grass in a public park. People would walk by and see us in our sunglasses and layered autumn outfits, smiling and high-fiving each other like we lived in a Tommy Hilfiger advertisement.

Look at those two casual and unselfconscious friends, they would think jealously.

More important, becoming friends with a girl seemed easier than most of my other fantasies. While sneaking into a water park at night and receiving oral sex on the tube slide was incredibly alluring, it was literally a pipe dream. The desire to say "hey" to a girl who says "hey" back was more attainable than getting that same girl to take a shower in lubricant with me. I needed some easier goals.

One morning I tapped Tamar on the shoulder as she was packing up her bag after a history class.

"Hey," I said coolly, "what's up?"

"Oh," she said, glancing back at me momentarily before returning her focus to a book she wrestled into her knapsack.

"Hi, Eytan." Without warning she then stomped in a tight half circle away from me, leaving the desk as a buffer between us.

She was obviously uncomfortable that I was talking to her. Perhaps she thought that I was going to start crying and make a scene about how unfair it was that she had told Hannah that she liked me yet for some reason wouldn't be my girlfriend, and leaving a couple of extra feet and a heavy-duty classroom desk between us was her way of telling me so. It hurt a little knowing that someone didn't want me around, but I was determined to plow through it. She had said we should be friends, and I was going to make her stand by it.

"Did you hear what the homework assignment was?" I asked.

"Uh," she said, "there was none."

"Oh, my bad," I replied, inadvertently setting myself up for a joke. "I forgot to pay attention."

"Ha-ha," Tamar said, without laughing. "Very funny, Eytan."

I was winging it, not worrying so much about the perfect things to say and comfortable with what was coming out. Knowing that Tamar didn't want me removed the pressure of trying to impress her.

"Do you want to go to the bagel store with me?" I asked her.

She hesitated before responding, composing herself the way my mother did before having to remind me a second time that it was after my bedtime.

"Eytan," she explained, "we're just friends."

"I know, but friends can go to the bagel store together."

She squinted her eyes at me as though looking for a pore or tiny tattoo on my face that was asking her to be my girlfriend.

"What?" I asked with a twinge of impatience. "You said we should be friends."

"Okay, Eytan," she said finally, "but just as friends."

"Yeah," I told her. "Obviously."

That afternoon, as we walked beside the eastbound lanes of NJ Route 4, cars whizzed by us at four-lane-highway speeds. The sharply cut grass at the side of the road crunched under my feet and I felt anxious. Even though this wasn't a date, I still did not know what to say to Tamar. There was no way to be charming and witty at every lull in our conversation and it didn't feel right talking to her the same way my guy friends and I talked. Tamar wouldn't have the patience to listen to references from *The Simpsons* for a half hour straight, and she might think that the tricks I played on mail order record clubs to get free CDs were not so clever and cunning, but rather fraudulent and larcenous. And so, as we walked along the roadway, passing outlet malls and car dealerships on our way to the bagel store, I felt relief each time a car careened by us at fifty-five miles per hour. The sound they made barreling down the road was so loud that there was no point in trying to talk over them.

"I like lox spread," I said when we took seats across from each other at the bagel shop. "It's the poor man's smoked salmon."

"Eh, fish is kind of gross to me."

Tamar ordered a toasted raisin bagel with scallion cream cheese. She held half of the sandwich in front of her face and squeezed it so the cheese shot out of the edges, dripping onto the sides of the bread.

"Is yours good?" I asked as she licked the excess cream cheese.

"It's delicious."

"Cool, enjoy. I like Quik chocolate milk okay, but I think

the Hershey's kind is better," I explained while sipping from a carton of Quik.

I was back to square one of not knowing what to say. Each time I filled my mouth with a chunk of bagel, I took small solace knowing that I didn't have to talk for the few moments it took to chew and swallow.

"I guess," she said, "I'm not really down with all the different types of chocolate milk." She could have torn my heart out with her plastic knife right there, but I was determined to brave through the meal.

"Do you ever go to the record store next door?" I asked.

"Yeah, I love that place!"

"They're really into Kiss there," I said, referring to the excessive number of Kiss action figures they offered in addition to LPs.

"I know," she said, seeming truly interested. "Who even is Kiss?"

"I don't know, some lame band. They wear tons of makeup."

"Seriously, so weird."

Steam had picked up. Common ground was found. I was on a roll. This was what friends talked about.

"What music do you like?" I asked.

"Well, my favorite band is Fleetwood Mac."

Wow, I thought, Tamar was actually cool. I didn't know who Fleetwood Mac was except that they were from the 1970s and had long hair and beards.

"Cool," I said. "Have you heard of the Allman Brothers?"

"Well, I haven't listened to them so much, but they are my dad's favorite."

It was an actual conversation. There was a back-and-forth exchange, where one comment or question seemed to lead to the next and it was all happening with a girl!

"You should check them out," I said, lifting my chocolate milk for a hard-to-reach gulp through the straw. "They're the best. I'm actually going to go see them live next month."

Tamar's eyes widened and her mouth fell open. I must have been impressing her with my knowledge of music and rock concert attendance. In fact, by the look on her face she seemed almost too impressed.

"Oh my God," she said and let out a clipped laugh.

"Yeah, it's gonna be a cool show."

Her face had gone blank.

"What?" I asked, smiling.

"You just spilled all over yourself."

My smile turned slightly crooked, like that of a stricken child not quite realizing the pain he's about to feel. I was so elated that we were talking that I didn't believe her. Nothing could stop me, I thought, but when I looked down at my blue button-down shirt, it was completely soaked with chocolate milk.

"Oh no," I whispered.

"Yeah, it was pouring out as you were talking," she blurted.

I sat there dumbfounded.

"It was the straw," I said, thinking aloud. I was drinking from a straw while also tilting the carton, as though I needed to bring the liquid closer to my mouth. The straw screwed me.

"Oh no," I whispered again.

I looked at Tamar, searching her face for a solution to my soaking mess. *It's okay,* I wanted her to say. *No big deal.*

"I can't believe you just did that," she told me instead.

My chest stung. I wanted to run away, back to the deafening security of traffic on Route 4, where people were traveling too fast to notice what a mess I had become. But I had to suck this up, absorb the embarrassment, like deli napkins on chocolate milk, and toss them into the trash at the back of my mind before moving on.

"That was, like, kinda pretty klutzy," Tamar said.

Enough already! I thought, as I stood up and excused myself to go to the bathroom. *I was already down. I don't need your analysis.*

Behind the locked restroom door, I examined the extent of the damage. The entire front of my shirt was soaked through, and my nipple was visible through the blue fabric that clung to it. I wished I could stay in the bathroom for the rest of the afternoon and only head back to school during dismissal. The next day, I could go to school with clean clothes and pretend none of it had ever taken place. But I couldn't leave Tamar alone like that.

As I limboed myself under the hand blower, I wondered who would believe the situation. It was like a gag on a TV sitcom: Guy tries to impress a girl and makes a fool of himself instead. These types of things weren't supposed to happen in real life. It was so unbelievable that I felt a little relieved; the irony of the situation stood out almost as much as the mess on my shirt.

"Such a klutz," I said to myself in the mirror while buttoning my jacket up to my neck.

When I came back out, I sat down and continued eating.

"I'm retarded," I admitted to Tamar, who seemed unsure how to act, contemplating whether to stay or not.

"Are you okay?" she asked.

"It's fine, whatever," I assured her. "It just sucks that I don't have any more Quik left," I continued while trying to sip from the mostly empty carton.

"Yeah, sure," she said and smiled uneasily.

As I pushed forth and picked up where the conversation about 1970s rock bands had left off, I felt a little pride. Uneasy or not, a smile was a smile.

CHAPTER 18

JUGHEAD

OVER THE NEXT FEW WEEKS, hanging out with Tamar became easier. I had embarrassed myself so completely at the bagel store that there was no point in pretending I was a suave high school sophomore with all the right things to say. Like Jughead Jones from "Archie Comics," I was an absentminded and harmless goof, prone to daydreaming and "spacing out." It was a convenient characterization if I was ever lost in thought over an exposed sliver of her skin.

"What are you looking at?" she once asked me suspiciously as I stared blankly at the curvature of her right breast behind her shirt.

"Oh, sorry." I calmly lifted my eyes toward her face, as though she had woken me from a light slumber. "I just spaced."

At home, this distinction didn't serve me as well.

"Your teacher said that you need to stop coming to class stoned," my mother said to me from my bedroom doorway one evening after she and my dad returned from a parent-teacher conference. "What exactly does that mean?"

I looked up from the carpeted floor, where I was reorganizing my two-hundred-plus CDs according to race, in what I thought was a clever observation on world inequality. "I have no idea," I said.

"Then why would she say something like that?" my mother prodded.

"Because she's crazy," I said.

In truth I knew exactly why she said it. Ms. Dayan, my American history teacher, had said the same thing to me earlier in the week.

"You need to stop coming to class stoned, Eytan," she shouted at me from the door of her classroom as Tamar and I passed by in the hallway.

"I'm not!" I exclaimed in embarrassment. "I swear!"

"Is he on drugs, Tamar?" she asked.

Tamar looked back and forth at the two of us. "I really don't think so," she responded shyly.

I was simply playing cool, or maybe a better word for it was slow, but certainly not stoned. During the few times since *Simchat Torah* that I had tried weed and experienced the effects, I did it only in the safe confines of a locked bathroom with the sink running. The last place I wanted to be high was at school.

"Are you still doing pot?" my mother whispered to me from my doorway that evening, looking behind her to make sure no one else could hear.

"I never have," I lied.

"Then what is going on?" she demanded.

"Nothing." I raised my voice. "The teacher hates me."

I could hear my father's leather slippers brushing against the hardwood floor on their way toward us. "What's this stuff we heard about getting stoned up?" he demanded while cinching the waist belt on his green bathrobe, fresh out of a shower and ready for bed. He carried a large book on the history of the 1967 Red Sox pennant race under his armpit.

"Nothing!" I insisted, meeting his level of impatience.

"Seriously, Eytan. Drugs are no joking matter."

"I'm aware."

"Steve," my mother interjected, "let me handle this."

"Okay," he acquiesced. He held the book across his stomach and bowed slightly. "Good night," he said, through a bitten lip, before sweeping his slippers back across the apartment.

"Please don't lie to me again, Eytan," she said once we were alone.

"I'm not," I insisted.

A few months earlier, not long after *Simchat Torah*, I purchased a small plastic device about the size of a pack of gum. Running the length of it were two rollers inside a nylon belt.

"It's a joint-rolling machine," the tobacco shop owner clarified.

"But where do the batteries go?" I wondered.

"No batteries," he explained. "Just put everything inside and use your fingers."

That night I sat under my desk rolling Nerd candies, in place of weed, inside my new toy. I still didn't understand exactly how it would work, as I could find no papers inside the machine or any liquid to moisten their adhesive-stripped ends. In my mind, I pictured an all-in-one joint-rolling mechanism that, after pressing a button, spat out perfect sticks of weed to impress my friends, but this was some kind of archaic manual design, like a NordicTrack cross-country-skiing machine without instructions. Nonetheless, it was only a dollar and fun to play with, so there wasn't much to lose from buying it. Except when my mother walked into my room to check up on me, and

I hastily tossed the roller into my Boston Celtics steel trash can with a loud clank.

"What did you just throw out?" she asked. My mom had just come home from a conference and was wearing a straight-legged pants suit with a silk, collared white shirt.

"Nothing important," I assured her.

"Well then, what was it?"

As I slowly fished it out of the can, I stalled, hoping that a strong passable lie might come to me. Something like, I found this on the street, or, *It's used to polish small twigs,* or even, *It's a cigarette-rolling machine.* Yet I could not think of anything.

"Okay," I said, "this is a machine for rolling marijuana, but I've never used it, so there's no reason for you to get upset."

She took a seat on my bed and examined the machine. "Why do you have it, then?"

"Because maybe I was gonna roll some pot at some point, but I never did, so it doesn't even matter." I took the roller back and returned it to the garbage. "See, nothing to worry about."

"Have you ever done marijuana?" she asked.

"Of course not," I smiled. "I don't know from drugs."

She looked at me stone-faced. "Give that thing back to me."

"I've touched them, though," I divulged while again retrieving the evidence from my green bin. "Once, with some kids from my last school, and then they gave me this machine. Which I really just like to play with. Look, there's only candy inside."

She opened up the roller and neon orange Nerd pebbles fell out.

"It's cool," I continued. "Please don't punish me."

My mother looked like she was about to cry. Her hand was balled into a fist and covering her mouth. Finally she said, "I don't believe that you never tried pot, but if you promise to never do it again, I won't tell your father."

"I promise that I won't, but I also promise you that I haven't."

"I don't want to hear it," she said and walked out without returning my rolling machine.

I had lied to her that night, but I wasn't lying about Ms. Dayan's claim.

"I've never smoked pot in school," I said to my mom the night that she met with my teacher.

"Then why would she say that to us?" My mother had some papers in her hand, perhaps a detailed report on how poorly I was doing in school, that she rolled up into a baton and gently swatted into her other palm. She took a seat in my swiveling desk chair.

"Because," I looked down at my CDs in front of me. Hendrix was next to Snoop Doggy Dogg. I wasn't sure what to do with Cypress Hill. "Sometimes I space out, and I'm thinking about other things in her class."

"Like what?"

"Music, food . . . girls."

"You have a girlfriend?"

"No!" I shot back. My father's slippers were on the move again.

"But there's someone you like?" she inquired.

"What is this I hear about you having a girlfriend?" My dad poked his head in the doorway.

"I don't have one," I said.

"Your teacher mentioned that you were spending a lot of time with a girl," he said.

"I'm not!" I protested.

"There's nothing to be ashamed of," my father told me

before locking eyes and nodding to my mom. "We're okay with it."

"I don't have a girlfriend," I insisted.

Tamar wasn't my girlfriend, but we were spending more and more time together during school hours and on the phone a few nights a week. We had become actual friends.

About a month after the bagel store episode, she came to watch me compete in a grapefruit-juice-drinking competition.

"Go! Go! Go! Go! Go!" a group of four friends surrounding my opponent and I chanted while banging a steady beat on the lunch table. Barry Frommen, the challenger, kept bringing the ten-ounce can of juice away from his lips, breaking for air, his eye clearly not on the prize. I swallowed and poured all in one motion by holding the can slightly away from my lips and letting the nectar flow freely into my open mouth. In six seconds, it was all over. I slammed the empty can on the cafeteria table, high-fived some spectators, and stood up.

"Whoo!" I whooped triumphantly and winked at an impressed Tamar.

"Good effort, Frommen," I said sarcastically as he shook his can to see if anything was left.

I was in fine form. It might not have been varsity basketball or model UN, but I was a contender when it came to competitive juice drinking. *Let's get outta here*, I motioned to Tamar without actually saying a word, and we walked off toward the exit.

It was a sunny April day and the tall New Jersey suburban trees swayed lightly along the border of the grass outside of school. Tamar and I took a seat on the lawn and she asked me to punch her in the stomach.

"What?"

"Do it," she said. "I'm ripped!"

Over the past few weeks, Tamar had told me about the bandana her father wore while he pounded on his drum set each Sunday and she confessed to being embarrassed when he scrubbed his 1982 DeLorean wearing only cutoff shorts. I had told her that I often limped off the school bus when my leg fell asleep on the way home, and that I was secretly learning how to play guitar. A trust had formed between us, and it was ridiculous to think I would betray it by knocking the wind out of her.

But this request was different, as if she was asking me to do one thing, but meaning something else. *Punch me in the stomach* really meant *I want you to touch me.*

I sat up on my knees to meet Tamar at eye level and shuffled toward her so I wouldn't have to reach so far. In a quick motion, I pulled back my fist and brought it within millimeters of her stomach before stopping and giving her a muted stage punch with a little weight behind it; like pushing a stone into a pillow. I let my fist linger against her for a few extra moments afterward.

"You all right?" I asked.

"Yup! See how strong?"

Did she really believe that her muscles were so firm that she wouldn't feel me punch her? I didn't care. If she wanted to maintain the charade, it was fine. I got to touch her.

"I'll do you now, okay?"

"Yeah, but you're gonna hurt yourself, 'cause I got a six-pack," I said, flashing her a glimpse of my stomach and intensifying my face, trying to will some definition into my abdomen.

She socked me without holding back.

"Uh," I groaned.

"I told you I'm really strong."

I stared up at the sun, trying to catch my breath and not

minding the cramp beginning to form in my side. Our violent little game was like an inside joke we shared. She had let me feel her stomach and, in turn, had not hesitated to touch mine. Lying down in the fetal position on the grass near her, knowing that she knew that I was there, felt like an accomplishment. I had formed the casual relationship that I had so wanted.

"Are you going to ask me something, Eytan?"

It was clear that things were heading this way, but I almost didn't care. Hanging out and joking around with Tamar was fun. I didn't need anything more.

"I don't know," I said, sitting up.

"Well, you should ask me something."

"Okay," I said, embarrassed and proud at the same time. "Um, do you wanna, like, go out with me?"

"Sure," she agreed, smiling.

I smiled back and looked around awkwardly, waiting for something to happen. Perhaps a rainbow would suddenly appear in the sky or a small flock of sparrows would land beside us and whistle a tune. But nothing changed. Now what? I wondered.

"Should I give you a hug?" I asked.

"Yeah, that would be nice."

With my arms around the area above her waist, her body felt like a preheated foam mattress. I hugged her for a while, wanting her to know that this was a special embrace and not the same one that I gave my dad before he left on a business trip. I put my face in her scarlet hair and breathed in her perfume. When I pulled away, my clothes were rumpled and my face red.

"You're wearing cologne," I said.

"It's perfume. Do you like it?"

"It's nice."

For the rest of the day, I walked around school a little taller and stepped a little wider. I felt like my feet were making a deeper impression on the tiles in the school hallways. With a girlfriend, I was more significant than I had been just a few hours earlier, and the school would probably have to redo their floors a little sooner than they had planned.

CHAPTER 19

HAND JOB PILLS

"We were making out the whole time. And then . . ." Barry paused to catch his breath; he was giggling and talking at the same time and needed a moment to compose himself before continuing, ". . . and then I pulled off her pants—"

"In the middle of the movie theater?!" I asked.

"Yes! And I started fingering her. Two, three, four inside her . . . she soaked the entire chair!"

We were in the center of the hallway between classes. Students were running back and forth to different rooms while tears of laughter streamed down Barry Frommen's face as he told Tamar and me his story.

"Wha??" I asked, looking straight ahead, scared of my girlfriend's reaction.

"Then she grabbed my dick," Barry flipped his shaggy blond hair from his eyes, "and jerked me off." He made a vigorous masturbation motion with his hands. "I came everywhere! Completely ruined my pants!"

Frommen was overtaken with laughter and stopped trying to catch his breath. He was drunk on his story. His eyes were tiny slits, and he put his hands on his side like he had a cramp. It made me nervous. A person capable of laughing so hard without concern for vision or oxygen, I thought, was a person with little concern for anything.

"That's insane," I declared, still avoiding eye contact with Tamar at all costs.

I couldn't tell if his story was true or not. How could all those sex acts occur in a public place? Weren't there people around to tell him to put his pants back on? Wouldn't he be worried that someone would come in and see them? I would be a mess. I would be embarrassed for the characters in the movie looking down on me. Maybe if I could set up a tent or plywood stall that locked from the inside, I would feel remotely comfortable unzipping my fly. But even then, I would tuck myself away and sprint for the exit at the slightest movement outside the private hut. Could Barry be so daring as his story made him out to be?

And was it possible to completely ruin one's pants by coming on them? Did more somehow come out when a girl performed the act?

"Give it up, Bayme!" Barry managed to blurt out between cackles as he raised a palm in the air for me to slap. Whether I celebrated with him or not seemed trivial to him, like a little sugary flower bud on top of a cake already made entirely out of frosting.

"You're crazy," I murmured while giving him an understated five.

"You too, Tamar!" Barry cried, raising his hand for her to smack. "Give it up!"

Until this moment, I had avoided Tamar's death stare boring into me—searching for a semblance of empathy with his tale, something in my face that told her that I was in cahoots with him. That maybe I had fed Barry's hand job partner a hand job pill to make her perform against her will.

I couldn't let Tamar see my excitement, jealousy, utter disbelief of the whole situation. Barry didn't even have a girl-friend. This all took place with a classmate that he wasn't offi-cially together with. Tamar and I had been "going out" for months, yet we had barely touched. It took me hours to work up enough nerve to put my arm around her waist at the public bus stop, or take her hand in mine on the way to the mall. I wanted nothing more than to rub my face in her chest, yet I was too nervous even to joke about such a thing with her.

Sometimes, on Sunday afternoons Tamar and I would hang out on her bedroom floor watching television or studying the liner notes of the CDs in her collection. If I was feeling inti-mate and wanted to show her how I felt about the two of us, I would take a deep breath and grab hold of her foot. Firm and mighty, I gripped her from the sole and squeezed evenly, as though checking the ripeness of a cantaloupe.

You, Tamar, I was trying to tell her, *mean a lot to me.* It was the most physical intimacy I could bring myself to offer. A kiss was out of the question, as her lips were a sacred, beautiful part of her body that I was way too worried about offending. But her leg, the bottom part of it specifically, was an area that I felt comfortable getting close to. It was far from any erogenous zones, so Tamar could never mistake me for a sex fiend when I caressed it. And in contrast to her soft thighs, smooth belly, and round bottom, which I avoided meddling with like a sexual martyr, her feet were fortified and sturdily built; a hearty, load-bearing reason to like her.

Even seeing other people kiss made me uncomfortable around my girlfriend. When Tamar and I watched a VHS tape of the movie *Trainspotting* in her downstairs living room, we snickered and cringed as Ewan McGregor flushed himself down a filthy toilet to get his fix. When his friend Spud accidentally splattered his own shit all over the family of his new girlfriend in the middle of breakfast, we howled in laughter. But when McGregor and his young girlfriend sloppily made out in a taxi ride home, and then had quick sex in her bedroom, I sat quietly and affixed my gaze on the wide coffee table between us and the television.

"That was so dumb," I said lamely, after the scene was through.

Yet if Tamar weren't sitting next to me, I would have rewound the tape and paused it at its most explicit frame, so I could pull a chair right up to the screen and study exactly what was happening in the scene. Were the actors sweating? Were they completely nude? Was the sex simulated?

Next to Tamar, though, I thought I was supposed to show restraint and dismiss anything sex related. Meaningful relationships weren't about boobs and kissing; they were about respecting each other's boundaries and listening to one another—which I usually did while clasping my hands behind my back as we walked around school or the mall, like an attentive ice skater. My very mature notion of how to treat my girlfriend was really something Hollywood should take note of, I wanted to explain to Tamar. But it was also a convenient stance, since I was scared to death at the prospect of making a move.

Now, standing in the hallway and waiting for Tamar's reaction to Barry's story, I could steal a look and gauge her reaction. Who knows, I thought, maybe she was actually turned on by his tale. Maybe this was exactly the type of icebreaker we needed to put our relationship into the sexual high gear I desired.

That's so hot, perhaps she would say while looking at me and biting her bottom lip before lifting the hem of her skirt and bringing it down over my head. Then she'd shove me into a locker, and set up a series of gym mats around us for privacy.

"Jesus Christ, Frommen," she fumed instead. "You're an animal! I'm not high-fiving you!" Her lips were tightly pursed and her face was flushed red. She was breathing unusually heavy.

Barry shrugged and put his hand down. "That's right," he said, undeterred, "I'm an animal!" before walking off to class.

When the two of us were left alone, I again avoided looking in her eyes. It was too awkward.

I'd never discuss anything like that with anyone, I wanted to say to her. *It would be our secret.*

Yet even that was assuming too much. Tamar and I never spoke about touching each other's private parts. We had never even kissed. She might have hated hand jobs and blow jobs and sex jobs and thought they were all a gross violation of a woman's rights.

"Eytan," she said.

"What?" I replied distractedly, looking up and down the hallway, every which way except in her direction.

"Eytan!" she said louder, jolting me into focus.

"What?!" I screamed, locking eyes with her. Her face was red, her breath short and heavy. She looked like she had something important to tell me, something that she didn't want to say but was forced to, like news of a dying relative.

"Don't think that I'm going to do that to you."

"Of course not," I said, using my sleeve to wipe the sweat from my forehead.

It felt like a knife pierced my chest—like someone did actually die, someone who everyone thought was so great, yet I never got to meet.

CHAPTER 20

THE BIRDCAGE

"YOU NEED TO START making out with me," Tamar said sternly one evening. Only a month earlier, she had scolded me over our friends' mutual masturbation story and now she was demanding this.

Why don't you make out with me? I wanted to say to her. *Why don't you clean me with the silky, body lotion puff thing my mother keeps in the shower? Why don't you spread Vaseline evenly over my legs and chest, and then stack folded bath towels on top of my naked body?* I had needs too.

"Okay," I said sheepishly. "I'll do it."

The next day we cut class to see *The Birdcage* in a theater near school that had a lenient policy on underage kids and R-rated films. On weekends, thousands of moviegoers flooded the strip mall multiplex, but today, with only Tamar and me in the three-hundred-seat theater, it felt as though we were trespassing in an empty warehouse.

"Is this cool?" I asked her, wondering if she was uncomfortable being alone in such a large space with me.

"I guess." She shrugged and giggled.

Although we had been together for three months already, we never spent much time alone. During school we wandered the halls and sat near each other in class, always surrounded by others.

"I ate an entire bag of barbecued potato chips last night," I might whisper to Tamar in the hallways. "The big bag." In school, I spoke to Tamar in hushed, clipped tones. It was no secret that we were together, but if people overheard our conversations about food, music, or TV shows, I was worried they would think our relationship was fake.

That's not what real couples are supposed to talk about, I imagined they would say.

The few times I had visited Tamar's home in New Jersey, her parents insisted that her bedroom door remain open. As we sat on the carpeted floor and examined the sleeves of her father's Eric Clapton records, the wide-open space between the edge of her door and its frame seemed to be watching me, breathing on me, reminding me that, should I have the slightest inclination to try anything funny, it had its threshold on me.

Not that I would have attempted anything funny. With her parents liable to walk in at any moment, I wasn't expected to put my arm around Tamar, which I found difficult and nerve-racking. After all, what if I touched her somewhere that she didn't want to be touched and triggered deep personal issues that she had worked so many years to bury and overcome? What if my embrace made her start to cry, the way David's did to Donna in *Beverly Hills, 90210*?

With her parents about to walk in at any moment, there was no pressure for Tamar and me to cuddle. Who knew what they would do if they caught me with my arm around their daughter?

Get your filthy paws off my Tamar! I imagined her mother exploding as she burst into the room with her husband in tow. If

I somehow couldn't pull away fast enough, her father might rip his white T-shirt from his sweaty chest and roar at me like a werewolf under a full moon. After I visited her home for the first time, I mentally noted the route I would run, out of her house and down to the bus stop, should such an encounter ever take place.

Now as we stood alone in the empty theater, I wondered if she could sense the sexual tension. The next two hours would be dark, with no chance of her parents walking in. There were no more excuses for us not to cuddle.

"Let's sit over there," Tamar said, while skipping toward the back row of the theater. I followed behind and took the seat to her right. Between us, her arm lay on the armrest and her fingers splayed out over the edge into my seating area. I wondered if she had placed her hand there on purpose. Were her fingers encroaching into my zone because she wanted them to be close to me, or was this just a comfortable position for her hand?

I shook my head. This was my girlfriend, we were supposed to be intimate. I couldn't live my life being worried about whether or not her fingers were positioned purposefully or not. A move had to be made, and if she was uncomfortable with it, she'd have to let me know—I hoped not too harshly. I laid my arm on top of hers and intertwined her fingers in mine. There it was, an official cuddle.

From the corner of my eye, I watched my girlfriend not cry or become visibly ill; she was comfortable. I could relax. But in the next moment, she unlocked her fingers from mine and slipped her arm out.

No! I thought. I'm sorry, it won't happen again. I looked at her imploringly, wondering if this was the end of our relationship, but all she did was smile before taking a Snapple bottle from her jacket and twisting the metal cap loose with her free hand.

"Ahhhh!" she said satisfyingly, before replacing the bottle top and grabbing my hand this time. I could relax again.

As the lights dimmed and the previews began, we sank a little deeper into our seats. It was slightly uncomfortable keeping my hand clutched to hers above the armrest, but I couldn't let her go. Her hand was a trophy I wasn't ready to return.

"Eytan," she whispered close to me.

"Yeah?"

"Are you gonna kiss me during the movie?"

I looked at her seriously to see if she was joking or not. Aren't we already holding hands? Couldn't we take this one step at a time?

"You should," she said, a little louder.

My mind was soaked with thoughts. I felt like I couldn't do it but had to do it—like I wanted to do it, but didn't know if I should do it. What if I did it wrong and offended her? As my nerves rattled on, I realized I had to say something or she would feel hurt, her intimate request ignored.

"Sure," I said hastily and gave her a reassuring thumbs-up.

Tamar winked back at me. It was a most intimate gesture. Couldn't we just leave it at that for right now?

Suddenly an elderly lady with a walker pushed through the entrance and made her way into the theater. She abandoned her device in the aisle near the center row and supported herself on the seatbacks on the way toward a middle seat.

The lady hadn't even seen us, yet I felt intruded upon. Did she have any clue what this girl next to me wanted me to do? Obviously this wasn't the ideal location to make out with Tamar. I would have preferred a command center, located in a cave somewhere in rural Canada that had to be hiked to, with closed-circuit video cameras that allowed me to see anyone getting within a three-hundred-foot radius of the place. Couldn't this old fart find some other movie to go see while I did my best in here?

The movie started, and Robin Williams and Nathan Lane seemed to be doing something involving acting and costumes, but all I could see was a series of disconnected colorful images moving around and making noise. I couldn't focus. How was I supposed to put my face on Tamar's and rub my lips all over hers? It didn't matter that she wanted to make out; it felt disrespectful. What if my kiss changed her outlook on life and she started walking the streets at night wearing nothing but masking tape over her private parts?

"Hi, Tamar," I said, waving as though there may have been some confusion over who was trying to get her attention.

"Hi," she said, smiling.

"Listen, I'm kinda nervous about this."

"Really? Why?"

"Because I like you."

"Shouldn't that make it easier, then?"

"Yes, but what if you become like a slut afterward?"

Theoretically speaking, if Tamar became a slut it would be a cause for celebration. We could start renting cheap motel rooms on Sunday afternoons and play out all the fantasies I had mentally cataloged over the years.

"Don't worry about that," she said, rolling her eyes. "Relax."

I slunk back into my seat. What was the big deal? I'd kissed my parents countless times. But what if they skipped out on work and drove the forty-five minutes out to New Jersey in search of a matinee? The movie had already started, but we weren't so deep into it that a latecomer would wait for the next showing. There was a chance that my parents might some-how show up. I couldn't risk getting caught hooking up with my girlfriend. But while my dad would have fumed over catching me cutting classes from the "very expensive school" that he paid for, he probably wouldn't have minded that Tamar and I were cuddling.

"Did you brush your teeth?" he once asked while making his nightly, electricity-saving rounds, turning lights off in the apartment before we went to sleep.

"Maybe," I lied.

"You really should make it a habit," he explained. "No girls are going to want to kiss you if you have bad breath."

I looked up at him, confused.

"Good night, Eytan." He waved before shutting the light off in the bathroom opposite my doorway.

Had he just given me the green light to make out? I wondered, while flipping the light back on and giving my teeth a thorough scrub.

Yet his implied seal of approval made it no easier to perform what Tamar was asking.

You should kiss me, she had said. It was what she wanted. But what if I kissed in a way that she wasn't prepared for and our teeth knocked into each other or I drooled on her shirt and she screamed, *Rape!* The old lady up front would summon the police, Tamar would break up with me, and I'd be carted away to spend the rest of high school in prison.

"Ahem," Tamar cleared her throat and looked over at me with impatience. With a crooked index finger, she pointed to her lips.

It made no sense. All the porn I looked at and all the fantasies I devised were supposed to have led up to this very moment. This was the doorway toward making my sexual dreams come true and I couldn't take the first step. After I touched Tamar's lips to mine and felt an actual breast in my hand, would I be unable to walk down the school hallways without rubbing my body against every female in my path, like an addict looking for a fix?

I leaned over into her seat and inspected the bottom, kissing part, of her face. Her cheeks were smooth and slightly puffed out.

"I'm gonna do it, okay?" I phrased it as a question, wanting to hear one more time that she was comfortable with me defiling her.

"Uh-huh." She giggled.

I came closer to her face and looked in her eyes. Just like in the movies, they closed. As I inched even closer, her lips parted a few millimeters, and then my heart started beating fast and my body started shaking.

Tamar felt me shivering and opened her eyes.

"Are you cold?" she asked.

"I'm not sure."

"You're shaking like crazy."

"I know."

"You're really nervous."

"Uh-huh."

I leaned back in my seat, leaving her unkissed.

"Why?"

"I'm not sure."

"Maybe I should kiss you?"

Yes! I thought. *Just do it, rape me!*

"Okay," I said.

Tamar leaned over into my seat. Thank God, I thought, finally. I closed my eyes and puckered my lips, waiting for her worst. But after a few moments, nothing happened, and when I opened my eyes, Tamar was still staring at me.

"I can't do it, either," she admitted. "Now I'm nervous."

"See, it's not easy," I said. "Maybe we should wait?"

She leaned back into her seat. "No, you have to do it."

The movie seemed to be wrapping up. People were shaking hands, hugging. Based on the looks on their faces, whatever problems the characters were trying to figure out appeared to be resolved. It was now or never.

Shaking hysterically once again, I leaned in and squeezed the sides of her cheeks a little, puffing her lips out slightly. In I went, fast and hard, pushing my face against hers and laying down a loud smacking kiss. No tongue. After a second or two, I pulled back, still shaking, but triumphantly this time.

Back in my seat, I smiled wide and looked beyond the movie screen. John Tesh's *NBA on NBC* theme song played on a loop in my mind. I wanted to ride on the shoulders of my friends and parade out of the theater like Rudy Ruettiger after sacking the Georgia Tech quarterback.

When the lights came on, I stood up and stretched this way and that, brimming with confidence, unafraid to reach my hands in every direction available to me.

"Let's get outta here," I said, offering Tamar a gentlemanly hand to assist her from the seat.

"I hope you enjoyed the film," I told the elderly lady while holding the door for her.

Tamar and I walked out of the theater hand in hand. Even though the sky was cloudy and a light rain had fallen since we entered the theater, it felt like a new day. The asphalt on the parking lot smelled like progress. The clouds sped across the sky optimistically. I looked over at my girlfriend and felt a warm pressure on my heart. We hugged easily and unself-consciously.

"How'd you like that?" I asked, with my face close to hers.

"Yeah, it was great," she said, looking away. "Maybe just slow it down a little next time, Eytan."

"Okay," I mumbled meekly.

CHAPTER 21

THE RULES OF NEGIAH

I LEANED OVER THE CENTER armrest and into the passenger side where Tamar sat. Our lips met and I slipped my tongue inside her mouth. She grabbed at my chest and pulled me closer. As Derek and the Dominoes played on the Toyota Corolla's CD player, I maneuvered my butt over the parking brake and almost into her lap.

It was a Saturday evening and we were parked in an empty lot on the Upper West Side. Tamar had recently gotten her license, but she let me sit in the driver's seat as we fooled around.

While we continued mashing our tongues together, I slowly began to slide my hand underneath her shirt. I felt her warm skin against my fingers as I crept up the side of her body. Finally, I was gonna feel some boob. I touched the nylon underside of her bra and was reminded of the ones I came across in my mother's laundry that I had to fold every now and then.

"Do you want me touching these?" I would shout across the apartment while holding up one of her beige-colored undergarments.

"Yes! Everything!" my mother said, referring to the pyramid of clothes she had dumped on the couch for me to organize.

"I don't even know how these are supposed to fold up," I explained, holding the bra up to the light and inspecting it like a bunch of grapes on the vine.

"I'm sure you can come up with something suitable," she said.

I shook the image from my mind and patted Tamar's bra. Her breast was round and soft and firm and heavy. So many years of my life had led up to this moment. I opened my hand to grab it properly, to feel how glorious and life-affirming a boob could be, when all of a sudden, before I could clamp my seventeen-year-old paw down, a police car came careening at us at full speed. Lights flashed, sirens blazed. It barreled toward the Corolla, before stopping short a few feet from the car's grill.

"Holy shit!" I screamed, scrambling back into the driver's seat.

The cruiser's high beams glared in our faces like floodlights over a nighttime road repair, and two crisply uniformed officers emerged from the Crown Victoria and moseyed their way to our vehicle.

"Are you okay, ma'am?" the one on Tamar's side asked her, while his partner shone a light on me from behind.

"Hands on the wheel, sir," he demanded of me. "Keep your eyes on your fingers." In my periphery, I could see the dark, toned skin of the policeman's arms shooting out of his short sleeves, like a couple of taut electrical cables. To my right, Tamar was slumped deep into the bucket seat, hugging her chest and staring hard at the glove compartment before her. I thought she might be crying.

I had almost touched her boob.

A few weeks earlier, my dad asked me if Tamar and I followed the rules of *Negiah*, referring to the Jewish law that prohibits men and women from touching in any way that could lead to sex acts.

"You . . . um . . . adhere to the laws of . . . *negiah*?" he asked hesitantly, perhaps more embarrassed by asking the question than I would be answering it. Talmudic rabbis disagreed on what the law actually forbid. Some said it only meant abstaining from hugging and kissing, while other, more salaciously imaginative clergy outlawed handshakes, winks, and even "wanton glances" at the opposite sex.

I wasn't sure how my father defined the rule, but whatever it was, I blurted, "Yes, yes, yes, of course," and waved the matter off.

"Okay, okay," he said, without missing a beat. There was no way that he believed me. Between all the porn and masturbation I had indulged in under his roof, he must have known that I would have humped anything that didn't protest. Yet he seemed satisfied by my answer and eager to end the conversation as quickly as it began.

A few days later, Tamar and I sat cross-legged on my bed, our mouths attached to each other's. As I pushed my tongue as far as it could reach into her, it felt okay, but I wondered if there was something more to it that we were missing. Our teeth knocked into each other, and not breathing directly into her mouth, like I was giving CPR, was difficult. Hopefully, if we kissed for a long enough time, something would eventually click and I would see why everyone enjoyed it so much.

After a few minutes, I placed my hands on her waist and slowly crept up her body.

"Is this okay?" I asked, in between kisses.

"Uh-huh," she said.

"How 'bout this?" I asked again with my hands lingering under her breast.

"Eh . . . ," she said unsure.

A moment later the doorknob to my room turned, and I quickly pushed Tamar away.

"Everything okay in here?" my dad asked, looking around the room at the walls above our heads.

"Yes," I said in a chipper voice, "everything's great."

Tamar sat up with her back toward my father. She hung her head low, her hair covering her face, and said nothing.

"I thought I heard something."

"Not sure," I said, smiling.

"Okay," he said as he began to close to door and leave, before stopping short and poking his head back in.

"You okay, Tamar?" he asked.

Of course she was okay, I thought, a sharp anger beginning to grow.

"Yeah," Tamar said without turning around, her voice cracking, sounding unconvincing.

My dad, in his worn jeans and button-down shirt, a hefty hardcover book clutched in his arms, stared at me, confused, before accepting her confirmation. As he backed out of the room again, pulling the door behind him, he paused and left a liberal gap open.

"That was close," I said, pulling Tamar back toward me.

"Yeah, close," Tamar said sarcastically, squirming out of my embrace.

"What's your problem?"

"You pushed me away," she said, her hair falling over her face.

"But I had to," I said, sitting up. "My dad could have seen us kissing."

"So what? Don't push me."

"He thinks we're *shomer negiah*," I said, referring to the touching rule.

"Why would he think that?"

"Because I told him."

"Why would you tell him that?"

I didn't know what to say. Were Tamar and I not on the same page? "Aren't we supposed to be?"

"Says who?"

"I thought you'd want me to tell my parents that."

"Why would I want that?"

"So they don't think that we're hooking up."

"Eytan," she said sternly, "your parents can think whatever they want. I don't care."

I had never looked at it her way. I just assumed that, like parents and porn, parents and sex didn't go together. But Tamar didn't care and my father probably didn't either. He had asked me if I *followed* the rules of *negiah,* but he never told me I was supposed to. Sometimes my siblings and I would find him and our mother holding each other in our narrow kitchen after dinner, making out themselves.

"Gross!" we'd scream and disperse in every direction.

Would parents who truly disapproved of such behavior do it so blatantly in front of their own children? Perhaps if Tamar and I were rolling around on the floor naked, my father would have done more than leave the door slightly open, but for some sloppily executed French-kissing he might have even given us a few practical tips.

Eytan, he might say, *there are three points I'd like to make in regard to kissing your girlfriend. First: Consent. Ensure that both parties are willing to kiss each other. Second: Set a date. Call her in advance and ask her to a romantic location. Touch base with her the night before to confirm. Lastly: Be patient and make sure you have acceptable oral hygiene.*

That afternoon I wouldn't be able to put any advice into action, though, because Tamar said she was done hooking up and wanted to dub some of my CD collection.

"Ma'am?" The officer in the parking lot asked Tamar, his dark eyebrows raised, his head imploringly lowered. *It will be okay,* he seemed to be trying to tell her. *You can tell us if he's mistreating you.*

I had been centimeters away from Tamar's breasts, and now my worst fears were coming true. The acts that I dreamed about, yet was too nervous to perform because I thought they would get me into deep, unknown trouble, were going to get me deep into unknown trouble.

No! I'm not all right! I imagined Tamar saying. *Everything he's ever done has been gross and against my will. He tried to touch my breasts! His friend got a hand job in a movie theater!*

I would then be asked to step out of the car and place my hands behind my back. Tamar would be given an itchy brown recovery blanket to keep her warm while she leaned against the side of her car and ignored me as I was driven off to jail.

I never thought that I was doing the right thing by wanting to kiss or feel up Tamar. I never thought I was doing the right thing by looking at porn, fantasizing about classmates, calling phone sex lines, or even talking to girls. And now, those doubts would be confirmed by the law of the land.

"I'm fine, sir," Tamar said to the police officer. "We're fine."

The cops aimed their flashlights at various points in the car. Tamar's face, her lap, the steering column, my crotch.

"You sure?" he asked again.

"I'm sure," she said.

"Okay. Be careful around here," the cop suggested before he and his partner returned to their car and drove off. "This isn't the safest place to be doing what you're doing."

After they left, their last line stayed with me. I thought there should be a legal term like "perjury" or "extortion" or "vehicular manslaughter" to better refer to fooling around in a car. Something other than "doing what you're doing." It all seemed so inconsequential.

"Whoa, that was scary," Tamar said.

"Yeah, but in some ways, I guess it's cool."

"What do you mean?"

"Well, we weren't doing anything wrong, right? They let us go."

"Yeah, I guess," Tamar skeptically agreed.

I wanted her to understand that fooling around was okay, sanctioned by officers of the law. "So"—I placed my hand on her leg and stroked it up her thigh—"it's cool."

Tamar smiled and removed my hand. "Yeah, Eytan, real cool."

"We're allowed to be doing this," I pressed forth, cupping my hands together and shaking them to demonstrate the profoundness of my revelation. "The world is a free place, don't you understand?"

"I get it," she said, staring above the lens of her eyeglasses. "But that was a bit intense for me. I think I should take you home now."

I lifted my chest and exhaled theatrically. "Fine," I mumbled, longingly watching my hands grasp and knead the tan leather steering wheel as if it were my girlfriend's chest. I had been so close.

"Hello?" She snapped a finger in front of my face. "Can I have my car back now? You're making this uncomfortable."

"Sorry," I offered, stepping out of the door and circling the front of the Corolla so Tamar could take the wheel.

CHAPTER 22

BEHIND THE ARK

THE SYNAGOGUE AT Beth Hebrew was a multipurpose room. At the front, there was a proscenium-arch stage where the Ark containing the Torahs was installed and where school plays were performed. On the floor, the walls separating the girls' and boys' praying sections could be removed and the chairs cleared out for an open, ballroom-style area. I sat at the edge of the stage and waited for Tamar to walk through the side entrance.

"Ey-tan!" she called, emphasizing the second syllable as she pressed past the heavy steel double doors and into the great room.

"What's up?" I asked with a quick head nod.

"Nada." She waltzed up to where I was seated and stopped.

We were alone in the massive auditorium. Outside, our fellow students rushed to their next class.

"Come up here," I said, offering her a hand up the stage. I led her behind a generous curtain to a dark area in the wings where actors waited for cues before their entrances. Jutting into the small space was the back of the *Aron Kodesh*, the armoire-like unit that housed all the school's Torahs.

Tamar leaned up against the Torah closet and pulled me toward her.

We kissed for a long time. A real kiss, with tongue and without teeth. Her heavy lips found their way between mine, and I pressed my hands against her back and neck with what I thought was a meaningful measure of passion.

Earlier that day, I had sat on one of the chairs in front of the stage and, like I did every weekday, wrapped leather prayer straps around my arms and head. Along with the rest of the student body, I recited the morning prayers and thanked God for the earth and sky. I thanked Him for letting me wake up this morning, and I thanked Him for making me a Jewish male.

Now I took Tamar's hand and sat down on the carpeted floor. We kissed some more and my hands grazed over her breasts on their way to her face. I rubbed the back of her neck and gently massaged her scalp.

"Do you want to lie back a little?" I whispered.

"'kay," she said without hesitation, and leaned all the way, flat on her back.

Toward the end of the service that morning, the rabbi leading prayers opened the Ark and removed one of the Torahs inside. He paraded it around the sanctuary for the male students to kiss before resting it down on a table and reading three passages from it.

Before one of the readings, I was called up to recite a blessing.

"Blessed God, who is to be blessed!" I declared for the entire student body to hear after kissing the calf-skin Torah parchment. Since there were so many male students in school and only a handful of opportunities to call one up to the Torah each week, it would be a few years before I was given the honor again. I wanted to make this one count. "Blessed is God, who is to be blessed *forever*!" I shouted louder and more articulately.

Now, as I grinded against Tamar, I thought about the blessing and how it related to my girlfriend beneath me. What Tamar and I were doing was wrong, disrespectful, and against everything we had been taught about how to act in a synagogue. This dry sex, as it was called, might be considered the ultimate failure of our religious day school. Thousands of hours of rabbinic man power had been spent educating us on how to thank God for everything in the world. There were ways to thank Him for the sun rising and ways to thank Him for a lasagna. He could be thanked via prayer, charity, study, respecting elders, honoring parents, not watching TV on Shabbat, and a hundred other ways. Like visiting Israel or circumcising a son, getting called to the Torah was an exceptionally strong way of showing your love for God. Dry-humping your girlfriend in a place of worship, on the other hand, was probably equally disrespectful.

While my good deed may have factored out my bad, I didn't care. I would have brought Tamar here even if I'd skipped prayer services that morning. This was everything I had dreamed: a girl who wanted to feel my body against hers. Not some random, one-afternoon synagogue romp, Tamar and I were in love and that love allowed me to live out a small fantasy. If God wanted to strike one of the beams holding up the synagogue roof and bring it crashing down on us, so be it. I would die happy.

He didn't, though. Instead, as I rocked back and forth on top of my girlfriend, she wrapped her arms around my back and held me closer. It felt as if I were back in the second grade, grinding against an inanimate table in ecstasy, except this time the table loved me and kissed me back. I pressed on Tamar faster and harder, and she breathed deep into my ear. I felt up and down her body, frisking her like an inappropriate concert security guard. I wasn't anxious about performing correctly or worrying that she would push me away. My mind was clear; it just felt right. As I was about to finish, I looked up toward the curtain to see Rosecrantz, the school janitor, quietly walk through.

Holy shit! I thought as I swiftly put my hands over Tamar's face to hide our simulated sex. Rosecrantz looked down at us and froze; the horror on his face matched mine. His eyes bugged out and his jaw dropped. We stared silently at each other, and I stopped grinding against Tamar.

"Eytan, I can't really breathe," Tamar whispered to me.

Rosecrantz slipped out as fast as he came in, and I pulled myself off Tamar to smooth out my clothes.

"Why'd you do that?"

"Shhhhhh," I whispered, realizing that she had not seen Rosecrantz. "I just, um, got really into it. Let's get out of here."

"Really?" She seemed surprised. "Are you, uh, finished?"

"Yeah. Pretty much," I said before peeking my head outside the curtain to ensure that the coast was clear. "That was totally great."

I kissed her on the cheek and blurted, "Whydon'tIgooutfirst-I'llseeyouinabit," before throwing back the curtain and exiting the wing with theatrical urgency.

Once again, my wildest dreams had led to my worst nightmare. For the rest of the afternoon I was a wreck, wondering if Rosecrantz would go to the principal and get us expelled for defiling the synagogue. Whenever the school sound system rang before an announcement was made, I braced myself for the worst. *Eytan Bayme, Eytan Bayme, come to the principal's office NOW. You've done the most horrible thing possible.*

Tamar was still unaware that we had been caught, and as she smiled and giggled between classes, blissfully clueless to our impending doom, I felt like a gangster husband hiding his secret from a loyal wife and family. With the authorities hot on my tail and my demise all but eminent, I resolved to take the full blame for our little stunt.

Who was beneath you behind the Holy Ark, Mr. Bayme? I imagined the head rabbi of our school interrogating me.

No one, sir, I'd tell him. *I was humping myself. It's a problem that I'm not particularly proud of.*

But the day was drawing to a close and I hadn't been called to the head office. The final bell had rung, and I was packing my bag and closing my locker for the day. As I walked down the hall toward the buses outside, the sunlight shone through the front doors of school. Not thirty feet ahead, freedom was within my grasp. But at the end of the hallway, immediately before the exit, Rosecrantz was making his final cleaning rounds.

Two custodians were responsible for cleaning up after the eight hundred students who tore through Beth Hebrew each day. Victor, the senior of the caretakers, had been working at the school for several years.

"Yo, Vic!" students would call to him when they passed by his office at the back of the cafeteria.

"Awright," he'd shout back from behind his steel desk, with a finger in the air pointing at the area just above your head. Victor wore heavy Coogi sweaters with vibrant color patterns and chunky textures that looked like contemporary pieces of art. Once, while waiting for my mother to finish shopping at Nordstrom, I had seen one selling for more than five hundred dollars. Victor was a cool member of the Beth Hebrew staff who dressed classy and never got angry with students, and we looked up to him.

Rosecrantz, on the other hand, was an unknown. He was

from Nigeria and spoke in a thick accent that sounded like a different language altogether. Each day, no matter the temperature outside, he wore a solid-color, synthetic-looking, short-sleeve T-shirt with the crest of some foreign soccer club affixed over his heart or the word "Invicta" running from the collar to the hem. Rosecrantz had been hired only a few months earlier and didn't have fans the way his coworker did. As we gleefully accepted Vic's index finger, Rosecrantz sat on the opposite side of his desk, feet square on the floor and hands clasped in his oversized lap, looking at us from the corner of his eye, not frowning, but not smiling either. It was as though he had paused in the midst of explaining to his colleague the plot of a TV show or a sporting event and was eager to pick up where our "Yo, Vic"s had interrupted him.

Only a few yards of hallway separated Rosecrantz and me. As I closed the distance between us, time slowed. I remembered each time I'd failed to throw out my tray after school breakfasts and lunches. There were mighty stacks of empty juice cans; steep hills of Styrofoam cereal bowls, each containing a small puddle of leftover milk with which to stain the leg of Rosecrantz's Marithé François Girbaud jeans; and crusts of pizza stretching from Paramus to Midtown Manhattan if lined up end to end. Rosecrantz was responsible for picking up this legacy of trash I had left behind. Would he now put an end to it once and for all?

A month earlier, Barry Frommen and I had been playing an impromptu game of cafeteria field goal kicking. Using only the untied shoes on our feet, the object was to hurl our footwear as far across the empty lunchroom as possible. Barry had booted impressive yardage past the sandwich machine and down in front of the pizza counter, but I had my sights a few lengths beyond that, by the water fountain near the boys' bathroom. I lined up, took an unnecessary running start, and waited an extra ham-footed moment to release my New Balance sneaker. It flew high, instead of long, and directly into the parallel fluorescent bulbs by the hot chocolate machine. A torrent of fine shards hailed down before Barry and I fled the scene and never spoke of the crime again. Rosecrantz was left to sweep the glass that lodged between gaps in lunchroom tiles, like transparent poppy seeds between teeth.

In the hallway, before passing Rosecrantz, I imagined three men in suits and dark sunglasses emerging from behind a corner and grabbing me like a fugitive.

He's the humper! Rosecrantz would say as I got slammed against a locker and handcuffed behind my back.

Open-and-shut case, one of the men would mutter as I was led to the head rabbi's office.

When I was steps away, Rosecrantz looked up from his massive ring of keys and down upon me. For what felt like an eternity, there was no expression on his face. Just a blank stare in his bloodshot corneas that reflected all my sins. I could see myself just as easily wearing all-white, prison-issue scrubs, and staring at the light pouring down from the only window in my cell. I stopped in the middle of the hallway.

"Hey!" said Rosecrantz. "You are the man!" And held a fist out for me to bump.

CHAPTER 23

HORIZONS BROAD

TAMAR AND I were in deep. Way deep. Each night, we would stay on the phone for hours, racking up hundreds of dollars in long-distance charges on our families' phone bills. We weren't talking about anything pressing. We just needed to be on the line with each other.

"What are you doing now?" Tamar asked one night.

"Staring at the side of my fifty-CD tower. How about you?"

"Playing with a 3D pin toy thing."

"Cool."

After that we were silent for several minutes. Time didn't move fast as I examined my music storage unit. Rather, each moment spent thinking about Tamar while she was close at hand was savored. Tamar there, me here. This was quality time spent together, existing as a couple. After a few more moments of silence I went on to describe, turn by turn, the exact directions from my house to hers.

BEEP BEEP. BEEEP, went the earpiece, as I mentioned the Fuddruckers along the eastbound lane of Route 4. From the firmly pushed, evenly timed tones, I could tell that it was my dad dialing the phone at the other end of the apartment. In the short intervals between each burst, he was confirming his digits in the phone book or from a scrap of paper nearby. BEEP BEEP BEEP. BEEEP.

I waited for him to finish and place his ear to the receiver before saying, "Daddy!"

"Eytan?"

"I'm on the phone!"

"But I'm confused. I just called Sid." My father was never quick with technologies.

"Yes, I'm aware," I said through my teeth, embarrassed that I had to explain how the device worked with Tamar listening in. "But I was already using the phone."

"Oh," he said without any tone of amusement, "I see. You realize you've been on it for two hours already?"

"I know," I snapped back. "I have a lot to talk about."

My dad paused for a moment. If he and Sid had pressing matters to discuss, he would have swiftly told me that he "needed it right now, Eytan." Instead he sighed and said, "Fine, I'll make my call tomorrow."

"Sorry about that," I told Tamar and continued describing Route 4.

A few hours later, I woke up sweating in my clothes, on top of my quilt. The digital clock on the windowsill read 3:43 a.m. and the phone lay off the hook next to me. On the other end, my girlfriend breathed gently.

"Tamar," I whispered, "Tamar."

"What's happening?" she asked, confused.

"We fell asleep. I'm still here."

"Oh."

"We should probably hang up."

"Okay."

"I love you."

"I love you too," she said, half asleep.

The end of junior year was coming to a close. For twelve months, we had been together, not just as a couple, but physically together, in each other's presence, either at school or on the phone or at each other's house. We were inseparable.

"I love you so much," I would often say to her.

"I love you too."

"No, you don't get it. I really, really love you."

"I do too."

"Like, I love you so much that I'm a crazy person filled with love for you." I held her face in my hand, not breaking eye contact. "Do you understand?"

Tamar held my gaze and slowly nodded, as if I had just told her what to do with my body after I died. "Yes," she whispered.

I needed Tamar bad. The love that I felt for her was different from what I felt for my family. It was heavier and constricting, like a Little League baseball helmet clamping down on the sides of my head and squashing my ears in the process. I couldn't pop it off, like the easily adjustable, baseball-cap love of my family. I would need to wedge my fingers underneath the hard edges, then bend over and shimmy my way out of it.

"Love you!" my mother would call out before I left for school in the mornings.

"Yeah, I know," I'd scream back, slamming the front door between the "I" and "know."

With Tamar, I needed to schedule a good half an hour to bid her farewell before leaving her side.

"And I can't wait to call you on the phone," I'd tell her,

mid-embrace on Sunday afternoons before parting company. "In barely forty-five minutes."

So at the end of that summer, right before our senior year began, I made what seemed like a completely logical decision. I broke up with her.

"I just think that we're a bit young for something this intense," I tried explaining one Sunday afternoon by the bus stop near her house. "We need to be able to experience the world while we can."

Tears were streaming down her face. I felt horrible. I still loved her as much as I had a few months before, but I thought that a girlfriend was keeping me from something. I wanted to hang out with my friends more, take full advantage of senior year, and pick up where I left off being cool.

"Does this make any sense?" I asked.

"Not really."

"I love you, but we need to broaden our horizons." Her tears were coming faster now. She put her hands over her face and sniffled. I hated myself for hurting her, but this was how adults acted. We should be shaking hands, smiling, patting each other on the back, and saying things like *I really enjoyed the time we spent together*, or, *What a delightful year this has been*, or, *Job well done*. I hadn't anticipated crying.

"If we can't stay friends," I continued, "I am going to hate myself."

"Well, sorry, Eytan," she replied, with a look of anger. "I wouldn't want you to do that."

"That came out wrong. I just want us to remain as close as possible without being together." My bus was coming down the block. "Can I give you a hug, please?"

She stood up and let me hug her before walking off without looking back. As I got on the bus, I quickly regretted everything

I had said. What the hell was I thinking? Girls didn't like me. I could barely speak to them. Tamar had given me a chance. She was nice to me. She let me kiss her. She understood how annoying it was when my parents asked me routine questions and when teachers assigned work that needed to be completed on time. Why was I throwing this all away and betraying my feelings for a theoretical idea about the way my senior year of high school should be experienced?

When I got home I called her.

"What is it, Eytan?" She sounded annoyed.

"Maybe I made a mistake?"

"A what?"

"A mistake. We have something really special going on," I said. "We shouldn't give up on it."

Tamar said nothing.

"Tamar?" I asked, wondering if she had hung up on me.

She took a deep, laborious breath, as though about to address a child who continually turns the TV on after being told not to. "Eytan," she began, "you just broke up with me. You can't go around asking me out again."

"But we're in love."

"You said yourself that it was too intense. That we needed to 'broaden our horizons,' whatever that meant. Now you don't feel that way?"

"No! It was an error in judgment!"

"I don't think so, Eytan."

I couldn't believe it. An hour ago, I was the one orchestrating the breakup. I was in control of my life and making forward-thinking decisions. Now the tables had turned and I was getting dumped. A pit formed in my stomach and tears began welling inside me.

"I really enjoyed the time we spent together," Tamar inex-

plicably continued. "But I think that trying to be apart would
a good idea for us. Like you said, we're really young for something this intense."

Fuck!

"Let's try to be friends, okay?"

"Noo," I whined.

"Yes."

Single life sucked. At night alone in my bed, with no one to lull
me to sleep on the phone, I would try to force myself to cry. It
had been almost five years since the last time I shed a tear, when
my father forgot to buy fried chicken for me before my bar
mitzvah, and I thought a few drops might magically free me
from the urge to hold Tamar in my arms. But nothing ever
came out and it was like standing in front of the toilet waiting
and waiting and waiting, but never peeing.

After school each day I started going home with my old
friend Shimon, who had also transferred to Beth Hebrew. We'd
watch TV and play guitar before I passed out on a pull-out
mattress next to his bed and go to classes in the same clothes
the following morning. We were seniors now and it was supposed to be a breezy year, with little responsibility before
graduating, yet I was still falling behind. In a course titled
"Philosophy," I scored 50 percent on a quiz about the movie
The Ice Storm that we watched during class. And while my classmates conjugated words from their thick, advanced-level volumes of *510 Hebrew Verbs*, I, after twelve years of study, was still
trying to grasp the basics of the language from a coloring book.

All around me, things were changing. Classes were rowdier
and the jokers in them were bolder than ever before.

"You are the oldest living man in the entire world!" shouted a boy named Dani Cantor after our elderly Talmud instructor, Rabbi Yosef, asked him to read the text aloud in class. It was believed that Yosef was hard of hearing, but no one had ever tested the theory to such a definitive extent.

"You have bushels of hay growing out of your ears, Rabbi," Dani pressed on. "It's gross!"

"Very good, Dani," Rabbi Yosef said in a slight Eastern European accent, "now translate."

Midway through the year, word got out that Barry Frommen had gotten laid.

"What?" I said to Shimon after he broke the news to me in philosophy class.

"Full-on sex," he explained. "At least that's what I heard."

I sat at my desk, stupefied. Barry wasn't even going out with the girl he supposedly had slept with; they were just "friends with benefits," as he described it. How could this not have happened to me? I looked at my palms as though the answer lay in them. Would Tamar and I be having sex if I had not broken it off? Would we be above the white foamy tiles of the drop ceiling quietly going at it right this very moment? I was livid with myself. The world seemed to be spinning, developing new modes of communication and transportation. Babies were being born and rapidly growing into functional human beings who could walk and talk and create. People everywhere were having sex for the first time, loving it and then doing it a second, third, and fourth time before I'd even done it once. Life wasn't fair.

"Tell me everything," I demanded of Barry later that day in the woods behind the school.

"Easy there, Eytan." He was so cool and relaxed about everything; it was killing me. "What are you talking about?" he asked before taking a drag of a cigarette.

"You got sex," I said.

"Yeah, I guess," he admitted.

"So . . ." I was searching for the right words. Something that would solve my problems and perhaps lay a clear and defined road map for my own path toward getting it on. "What was it like?"

"You know, it was pretty cool," said Barry. It was a cold day and our heavy ski jackets clung rigid off our bodies.

"'Pretty cool'?" I asked. *Did she scream? Who was on top? Did it smell? How long did it take? Is she pregnant?* Dammit, I had so many questions.

"Yeah," he continued. "It was pretty cool."

"And then what?"

"And then I took a cold shower."

"What?" I exclaimed. "Why?"

"'Cause that's what you do after a blow job."

"Uh, a blow job isn't sex," I corrected him.

"Yeah, but you gotta take a cold shower after one."

I shook my head. He was missing my point. "You didn't have actual sex."

"Well, some people consider it sex," he offered.

I calmed down a little. Things weren't as dim as they appeared. "Not me," I said.

"Good for you then, Eytan," he added. "But she said that if I took her to the prom, we would have actual sex."

I nodded my head and wondered if I could do the same.

That night I woke up in Shimon's room after dreaming about Tamar. In my sleep we had gotten married, purchased a houseboat, and were raising three sun-drenched boys in a landless waterworld. The only people we came in contact with were other nomadic sea gypsies who would ask us for berries. While Tamar taught our blond-haired children how to hustle at backgammon, I showed them the importance of everything on our vessel, from sail masts to simple buckets. The only time I had actually ever been on a boat was to whale-watch in Cape Cod, where I spent most of the two hours vomiting over the railing, but that didn't matter. The dream was clear: I was meant to be with Tamar.

It was three-thirty in the morning when I woke up in Shimon's dark, creaky old house. I tiptoed downstairs to his dad's home office, where a box on top of his TV could descramble premium cable and pay-per-view channels for free. Seven minutes were spent in the glow of the Spice channel with the sound off, trying to stop thinking about Tamar.

"I was actually pretty surprised that you guys broke up," Shimon told me at school the next day. "I thought you were, like, meant for each other."

It was a common sentiment around the hallways. Tamar and I had been inseparable for so long, and people were used to us always being together. We were like a favorite pair of jeans that hung perfectly, the way they did on the mannequin. Now, with one leg missing, the trousers were awkward and useless.

"I know," I said glumly. "I was too."

"Anyway," he said, moving along swiftly, "maybe you shouldn't come over every single night."

"Why?"

"Because people might think it's a little gay."

"Who would think that?" I asked.

"My parents, for starters."

"Why would they think we're gay?"

"Because they asked me so."

My face took on the hue of a pink grapefruit.

"They asked if you were my 'special' friend," he continued.

"Oh God! What did you tell them?"

"I told them we weren't gay," he said. "'Cause we're not. Right?"

"Right!"

Now that I had to go home most nights, my parents soon realized that something wasn't the same.

"Everything all right, Eytany?" my mother asked one evening.

"Yes, I'm fine," I said curtly, trying to resist the temptation to spill my emotional guts all over the dining room floor.

"What's going on with you and Tamar?" Her motherly senses easily struck the weakest part of my delicate armor. "She hasn't been calling so much lately."

I stared blankly at the cardboard and fabric sections that protected the smooth surface of her oak dining room table. We had owned the dining set for at least ten years, yet rarely had the protective pads ever come off the top. Even on Shabbat, when guests came over and sat on the expensive sectional sofa in the living room, my mom simply put a tablecloth over the pads for us to dine on.

"Why don't we ever take these things off?" I snapped, ignoring her question. "I can't remember the last time I've seen the actual dining room table."

"Eytan, what is going on?"

"I just think it's crazy," I raised my voice louder, "that we bought this really nice table, yet we've never actually eaten on it."

"Eytan, please."

"What?" I was screaming now. "What are you hiding from us?"

I lifted up one of the flaps and threw it off to the side, uncovering the shiny wood beneath. It was a dark red, closer to brown, with not a scratch in sight.

"What's going on out here?" my dad said as he came rushing out of his bedroom in his green bathrobe.

"I'm really not sure," replied my mother.

"Well, I don't like yelling in my house," he said. "People are trying to read."

"We broke up," I mumbled.

"You broke what?" asked my dad.

"Oh, Eytany," my mother said, "I'm so sorry." She pulled me in for a hug as I stood there with my arms motionless at my sides. Letting her embrace me felt good. Soothing relief to an open wound.

"What is going on?" my dad said, still confused. "Hon?"

"Him and Tamar, Steve," she whispered. "They broke up."

"Oooh," he said uncomfortably. "I'm sorry about that, Eytan."

As they made silent gestures to each other, trying to figure out how to handle the situation, I buried my face in my mom's shoulder and hugged her back.

The year went on and Tamar and I tried to stay friends. Occasionally we'd leave school to eat lunch at a nearby diner or meet up some Sundays in Manhattan, a neutral zone between our homes. Having her undivided attention was great, but I hated that I couldn't hold her hand or kiss her or tell her how much I loved her.

"Why don't we just get married?" I said one afternoon as we were browsing CDs at the Tower Records on the Upper West Side, six months after we had broken up.

"Very funny, Eytan," she said, while leafing through Blackstreet albums, "but I'll pass."

"Well then, let's make out instead."

"Not happening."

"Why not?"

"Eytan," she said sharply, "you broke up with me, remember?"

"So?"

"So I don't make out with boys who have broken up with me."

"But I love you."

"I love you too, but it doesn't matter."

It was so frustrating. After months of separation, I still wanted to be with her. I knew there was a reason that we broke up, and sometimes when we weren't together and I was drunk or high with my friends, I could remember what that reason was. But most of the time, I only knew how much it hurt to be without her.

"Can I just hold your hand?" I asked pathetically.

"Fine," she said and didn't pull away as I took hers in mine while she continued through the record collection, one-handed this time.

"Also, will you go to the prom with me?"

Tamar stopped flipping CDs and turned to look at me.

"Really?" She was smiling.

The prom was a few months away. It would be a black-tie affair, organized by fellow students, at a formal reception hall somewhere in New Jersey. No teachers or adult supervision of any kind would be in attendance. In fact, it was specifically unsanctioned by our yeshiva day school.

After the summer, I would be shipping off to Israel to study biblical law for a year at an all boys' yeshiva in a trailer park on the West Bank. Who knows, I thought, I might find the Talmud so engrossing and never want to look at the opposite sex again. The prom might be my last chance to be close to any girl. Tamar would also be going to Israel, but to a non-remote school in the middle of Tel Aviv, surrounded by boys, sweaty male soldiers, and falafel purveyors. Prom would be a fitting end to our high school love affair. All our friends would be there and we'd dance, drink, give flowers to each other, and ride in a stretch limousine. It would be like TV, and if my friend Barry, and Dylan from *Beverly Hills, 90210*, could get laid that night, maybe I could too.

"I'd like that a lot, Eytan," Tamar said in earnest. "But we're going just as friends."

"Of course," I said through a plastic smile.

CHAPTER 24

PROM

A FEW WEEKS LATER, thirty-four classmates and I crammed into a small classroom to hear the wisecracking Dr. Aubergine speak lively about mitochondria.

"What is it, Drucker?" He stopped mid-lecture to call on Sam Drucker, my locker neighbor and a strange, talkative member of the drama club, who waved his hand in the air as if it were a flag flapping in the wind.

"I was wondering if any classmates," Sam's eyes scanned the ceiling of the room as he spoke, "would be interested in attending the prom with me?"

Most found this hilarious and doubled up with laughter. But this was no joke; he needed a prom date and didn't know who or how to ask. I thought it took incredible balls for weirdo Sam, who dressed mainly in Hawaiian shirts and was prone to spontaneous break-dancing in the hallways, to ask the entire room out.

Aubergine stood about five and a half feet tall and wore a wild, fluffy brown beard. "Who in their right mind would go with you, Drucker?" he teased, not so lightheartedly, goading the class into further giggle fits.

I kept my head down and stared at the textbook in front of me. Personal abuse in front of this many peers was dangerous territory, and I didn't want to get caught up in the cross fire.

"Would anyone like to go to the prom with Sam?" dared Dr. Aubergine. We all looked around, dumbfounded, wondering if anyone would take him up on the offer, but not a hand was raised.

"No one?" the Ph.D-holder pressed forth. "That can't be. How 'bout you, Bayme? Would you like to go with Sam?"

Out of the entire, overcrowded class, I couldn't believe that Aubergine chose me to drag out into the spotlight that Sam squinted so boldly beneath. I never acted out or interrupted his soapbox biology lectures. I just kept my mouth closed and did poorly on his tests. Was that really worth whatever embarrassment was about to ensue?

"No, sorry," I said.

"Why not?" he teased further. "He's a good-looking fellow."

"I'm not into guys, thanks." Was this abuse even legal? I wondered.

"Who are you going with instead, Bayme?" He dug in deeper, hitting upon the very reason I didn't want to get embroiled in his antics. Eventually people would find out who my prom date was, obviously, but it didn't need to be proclaimed on this public a scale.

"Tamar," I mumbled, and the entire class joined in a collective "Aw."

"Not bad," my teacher continued. "Tamar, are you aware of this?"

"Yes," she said from a few rows behind me, "I am."

I should have been happy. Unlike Sam, I had a prom date locked down and had secured her consent in the privacy of a large retail outlet. But I wasn't happy. In fact, I regretted asking Tamar shortly after she said yes. My ex-girlfriend would not even let me kiss her.

"Whoa! Classy guy," she said sarcastically, pulling back after I dove in to lay a dry one on her cheek, the way I had seen an older boy greet my sister one time on a walk around her college campus.

"Watch the face, though," Tamar continued, drawing an invisible circle around her nose and chin. Prom or no prom, there was no way that she would let me perform the most holy of holy sex acts on her. Who was I kidding?

It stung to know that there were other girls in my grade who still needed dates to the prom, and I mentally abused myself at the thought of taking Shoshie, Sarah, or Miriam. One time, Natalie Sussdorf had even spoken to me when she graciously allowed me to photocopy her notes before an American history exam. She had wavy blond hair and seldom smiled and, as one of the smartest people in the grade, was out of my league. Yet knowing how poor of a student I was, she had even offered to explain her materials to me.

"If anything is unclear, feel free to call me," she had said before handing me her hardcover notebook and thick, pristine red folder. Inside, all the handouts the instructor had distributed since the beginning of the term were neatly laid out, each one with a translucent, fluorescent Post-it tab and a brief description, like "S. Johnson" or "D. of I.," flapping off the page. It was a study guide not meant for anyone but herself, yet it was the most organized and beautiful piece of schoolwork I had ever seen—a package worthy of filing in the library's reference section.

"Wow, thanks!" I said, assuming Natalie's invitation to follow up by phone was simply a polite pleasantry and not an actual offer to help. But maybe Natalie had wanted me to call and ask her what type of flower it was that she had so intricately drawn in the margins of her notebook. Maybe she would then broach the subject of prom herself and ask me if I would consider taking her. In retrospect, it seemed totally plausible, but now that could never happen because I belonged to Tamar, was attached to her, committed to her for the night—her boyfriend, but with none of the benefits that a real boyfriend was entitled to.

As the prom approached, I tried to be mean to my ex-girlfriend in some adolescent, George Costanza effort to get her to call off the date. One Sunday afternoon she had come over and we were hanging out in my bedroom, playing guitar. As she sat cross-legged on the floor, strumming the chords to "Tears in Heaven" on my Yamaha acoustic, I came up behind her and massaged her shoulders.

"Please stop, Eytan," she said, muting the strings with her palm.

"Fine," I replied, sour-faced, shifting back to my bed. All I wanted was to kiss her and shake our boundaries up a bit before prom, yet she knew me well and sensed my intentions before I could put them into action.

I leaned back on my bed as she continued the Clapton song. On the windowsill to my left lay a crumpled tissue. Inside it, stiff and crusted-over contents from the previous evening's activities cracked under the touch of my fingers. But before I could toss it behind my bed and forget about it for another few years,

Tamar abruptly stopped her tune and spattered out a loud and dramatic sneeze.

"Bless you," I said and passed her the tissue.

"Thanks," she replied, lightly rubbing her nostrils with it.

Time slowed down as I waited for her to process what was wrong. And in those extra moments I was able to reflect more fully on my actions. The word "pathological" came to mind, as did Hannibal Lecter's neighboring cell occupant in *Silence of the Lambs.*

"Huh?" said Tamar, crunching the tissue in her hand and cocking her head in confusion. "What the hell is this?"

"My babies," I mumbled, realizing that this honest yet asinine response would not improve the situation.

"Your what?" she asked.

"Nothing."

"Your babies?"

"What?"

"Your babies?!" she screamed louder this time. She threw the tissue at my face and it bounced off my lip. "That's disgusting, Eytan! Why would you do that?"

I frowned guiltily, wishing I could take it back. "I'm so sorry. That was wrong."

"You think?" She stood up and placed her hands on her hips. "Are we gonna have a problem here?"

"No way," I assured her. "I won't do that again."

She shook her head like I was a child misinterpreting her. "Do you even want to go to the prom with me?"

"Um," I said.

"What?" She couldn't believe her ears.

"Yes!" I shouted. "Of course I do."

I couldn't back out. Tamar was my friend, a very good

friend who, while we were together, I had felt closer to than anyone else. It didn't matter that I wanted to go with other girls; I had asked her to be my date, and I owed it to both of us to stand by my words.

"Are you sure?"

"Absolutely," I said. "But maybe we could have sex there?"

Tamar narrowed her gaze and raised an eyebrow, the pieces all falling together. "Sorry. You know me better than that."

On the night of the prom, I was nervous. Never had I been to a party with everyone from my school and without any type of supervision. This was the final blowout before we all went our separate ways. People could act however they felt with no real consequences.

You're a pathetic wannabe, a bow-tied classmate, martini glass in hand, might bellow at me before hopping back into his limo and riding off into the world to make his mark.

"You look sharp, Eytan," my dad said as I was ready to leave the apartment and meet Tamar at the party. I was wearing a rented tux with a flower fixed to the lapel.

"Thanks."

"Have a great time," echoed my mom, her head poking out of the apartment door as I waited down the hallway for the elevator to carry me off.

In front of the catering hall, the parking lot was packed. Dozens of our classmates, dressed in bow ties and bridesmaid dresses, were smoking cigarettes. Even those of us who didn't like tobacco puffed away, proving a point, by lighting one smoke with the flaming butt of one that had just been finished, that we were the designers of our destinies and no one could tell us what to do any longer.

"Ach! Ach!" I hacked up loudly after inhaling too deeply.

Tamar was dressed in a tight-fitting purple gown that covered her chest and stopped right above her knees.

"Isn't it cool?" she asked, pirouetting in place.

"Yeah, you look awesome!" I said enthusiastically, happy to have her by my side.

Shimon, dressed in a tuxedo and bow tie tied authentically imperfect, piled out of our limo with his date, Hannah, in a sharkskin green minidress. She took a swig from a flask before passing it to Tamar.

"Bleg," she said, sipping. "What is that?"

"Frangelico," Shimon replied. "The finest."

"Classy guy," Hannah said to Tamar.

The only adults I could spot were standing around the perimeter of the parking lot, wearing Oakley sunglasses and smoking their own cigarettes. They wore thinning dress pants and baggy vests and stood like sentries by the limousines they chauffeured. Would they break up a fight if punches started flying? If someone came down with an asthma attack or spilled wine all over their fancy clothes, would these grown-ups know how to respond? Did they even have any experience with people our age?

We stood around smoking our smokes and drinking our hazelnut liqueur. My old friend Gilad joined us with our classmate Devorah, whom I had sent to the nurse's office a few years before. Gilad was six feet tall now and towered over our little group while adjusting his grand blond Afro with a hair pick. He took a drag of a Parliament 100 and left his mouth ajar, mid-yawn-style, until exhaling loud and purpose-fully.

"My Hungarian grandmother loves this stuff," he pro-claimed before throwing back a healthy portion of the flask and paying it forward to Devorah, hanging dutifully on his arm.

There were larger groups of friends scattered around the lot, drinking more exciting alcoholic beverages, smoking longer cigarettes, and laughing harder than we were, but having Tamar and my friends in a circle felt like the proper ending to high school. I may not have graduated as the coolest guy in school or with the highest marks or without my virginity, but the moment felt honest as Tamar let me take her hand in mine.

Inside, the hall was elegant with high ceilings, a chandelier, and grand windows framed by silk curtains. There was a nonalcoholic bar off to one side with rows of carafes in three shades of yellow lined up before a man who might also have been a limo driver. Waiters scurried around offering kosher hors d'oeuvres on silver trays and little napkin triangles that I crumpled and stashed in my pocket to harden, later on, into a tight ball. On a small temporary stage a deejay played nineties rock music that no one danced to. Instead, those classmates who weren't smoking outside were hanging around in circles eyeing each other and picking at mini potato *bourekas* and pieces of sushi.

"It's like we're all getting married," said Gilad. "Or at least you guys are. I didn't go to this school."

"I'll go get us some drinks," I said to Tamar and excused myself to the bar to request four Shirley Temples, figuring they would mix well with the Frangelico. As I tried to gather the highballs off the black countertop, Natalie Sussdorf placed an order for some seltzer.

"Hey, Eytan," she said.

"Oh, hi," I said. Natalie was wearing a tight red dress that hugged her skinny body seamlessly, like an individually wrapped cucumber that offered no obvious point of extraction from its plastic sheath. She clutched a tiny black purse in front of her with both hands. My struggle to grasp the four drinks at once suddenly became something I needed to perform with bravado and grace.

"You having a good time?" she asked, almost unbearably casually.

"Uh, yeah. Sure," I said. "My friends are over there." I motioned to them with three of the drinks resting in my palms, as if their coordinates offered proof for my response. "How 'bout you?"

Natalie shrugged her shoulders and said, "Eh."

"Shit," I offered. "Sorry."

"Whatever." She smiled thinly. "You going to the party later?"

I had to place all three drinks back on the bar and try, again, to round them up with the fourth. Tamar and I hadn't decided about the after-party yet. It was at the house of a classmate who we weren't very friendly with. Supposedly there would be beer and a swimming pool and weed and everyone else in our class. I squeezed all the drinks together and hoisted them off the table. The glasses scratched against each other and I prayed they wouldn't shatter.

"For sure," I said to Natalie, before urgently running toward my group and demanding that they each take a glass.

More and more students found their way inside and ordered spike-able ginger ales and orange juices before taking seats at circular banquets surrounding the dance floor. Our clique staked a claim on a table in the back, away from the deejay, and we laid low behind charger plates and cloth napkins standing at attention.

A white-gloved waiter came around and offered us a choice of bread from a wicker basket he presided over with silver tongs.

"A roll, sir?" he asked, standing over my shoulder. I turned back and realized that he was only two or three years older than I was. Why was he dressed like a butler and talking to me as though I had a job? It felt like we were actors playing adults in a school theater production. I wanted to go back outside, walk a couple of blocks down the street, and as per standard teenage protocol, hide between two parked cars as I smoked a cigarette. This game of grown-up was making me sweat through my tuxedo.

"Can I get two?" I asked.

"Yeah, man," the waiter said, breaking character. "You guys can have the whole basket, actually." And he placed the pile of bread in the center of the table and walked back to wherever he came from.

"Beth Hebrew Class of 1998, let's see you get dowwwwwn," cried the deejay, after a thick cut of prime rib was served for dinner.

Tamar and I watched our classmates shyly climb from their chairs and bop and duck modestly to West Coast hip-hop music and the Goo Goo Dolls. From our perch on the sidelines, even the most popular kids in our class didn't look particularly cool.

"Are we gonna dance?" she asked as "Smells Like Teen Spirit" cranked out of the speakers.

I looked over at Gilad and Shimon, who were safely trying to pretend they had not noticed everyone else getting down on the dance floor.

"You wanna grab a smoke?" Shimon caught my eye and asked.

"Maybe a little later," I told him and offered my arm to Tamar.

On the floor, in the midst of people whom I had become

friends with or tried to ignore over the past three years, Tamar and I moved our bodies the way we had seen on *Club MTV*. I rolled my arms and grinded my butt at the ground, while Tamar raised her hands toward the chandelier and wriggled her hips like a blade of sea kelp. A few feet away, Sam Drucker danced wildly with a group of kids who had all come dateless. Through the crowd, I saw Barry dancing with his date the way an adult might have, by holding her hand in front of them and placing his arm around the small of her back.

"What up, Bayme? What up, Tamar?" he shouted over his shoulder, directing his way across the floor through heavy dance traffic, still holding his date at an elegant distance.

"Looking good!" called Tamar. I grinned and scanned the room for places that they might have already had sex in. The bathroom stalls were a good option as well as a tall fake tree in the back corner of the room that might provide decent cover.

"You guys coming to the party afterwards?" he asked, maneuvering his dance partner between him and Tamar and myself so we could all talk over her shoulder.

"Not sure yet," said Tamar.

"Totally!" I exclaimed at the same time.

"Tamar, we need you there!" Barry hollered.

"Yeah, you should come." His date strained her head around to address us, before Barry shuttled her off like a carnival teacup ride.

"Should we go?" Tamar asked me over the music.

"Yeah, maybe," I said and placed my arms around her shoulders to look beyond her.

"Okay," she matched my noncommitment, gently peeling from my embrace.

Between songs, Tamar and I caught our breaths and giddily squeezed out stomach cramps until the beat kicked back in. The deejay spun a House of Pain record and it seemed like the floor might buckle from everyone jumping in place. Soon, even Gilad and Shimon had left their refuge with Devorah and Hannah, and we were all in a circle singing along. Everything seemed so simple. Move to the music. Smile. Laugh. Whatever was supposed to happen, would. And if it didn't, something else was waiting around the corner.

"Good one, Bayme," Tamar shouted as I spun her around.

I shot a finger in the air and held it, like John Travolta on the cover of the *Saturday Night Fever* VHS. All I wanted was the moment.

CHAPTER 25

A VIRGIN SO LONG

PROM ENDED AT ELEVEN O'CLOCK and the limo dropped Tamar and me off at my house to change cars.

"You look so pretty!" my mother announced when we entered.

"Thanks, Mrs. Bayme," said Tamar. My father shuffled out of his bedroom in blue jeans and a green polo shirt when he heard our entrance.

"Tamar," he said, surprised. "Nice to see you again."

"Nice to see you too, Dr. Bayme." She giggled.

"Listen," I interrupted their reunion, "we're gonna get changed and drive out to a party."

"Whose party?" my mom asked.

"Just a girl in our class."

"Where?"

"New Jersey."

"Will adults be there?" She continued her interrogation with a tactful smile, as if this line of questioning were her way of making pleasantries.

"I don't know," I told her impatiently.

"Will there be boozing?"

"God, Ma. Maybe."

"Hon," my dad interjected. "I'm sure it will be fine."

"Yes," I promised them, "it will."

"Okay." My mother grinned, giving Tamar and me warm kisses on our cheeks and rubs on our backs. "It's so nice to see you again, Tamar." She turned toward me. "And you smell like cigarettes, Eytan."

"Some kids at the prom were smoking," I said. "It was pretty gross, actually."

After changing out of our fancy clothes, I drove us out to the party in my mother's tan Nissan Maxima.

"Prom was fun," I told Tamar on the George Washington Bridge, wondering if she understood my underlying meaning. The prom, which I asked her to, *was* fun, but it was over now.

"Yeah, I'm having a great time," she said. "Thanks."

The after-party was in full swing when we arrived. Cars were scattered on the sides of the street. Some were parked parallel; others had been left at 70-degree angles. I found an opening and, not wanting to upset the ragtag organization, backed into it without bothering to straighten out.

Inside, pictures of hand-drawn arrows led Tamar and me from the front door through a well-carpeted living area and modest kitchen and down a reinforced staircase to an unfinished basement. A few bare lightbulbs cast hot spots on corners of the room and a blue glow spilled through two small windows looking out onto a pool outside. Dr. Dre's *The Chronic* bounced out of speakers somewhere while a group of boys I'd never seen outside of school sat on the floor inhaling whippits next to a foosball table.

"Yo, Bayme," mumbled one of them when our eyes met, a yellow balloon inflating magically from the side of his fist.

"Hey," I said, liking the way my name came out of his mouth.

Off to the side, by a couch in the corner, a member of the wrestling team had taken off his shirt and flexed the muscles on his bare chest for another classmate with a video camera. His smile shone in the glare of the camcorder's spotlight and his pecs swelled proudly at their audience.

"What the hell?" I winced at Tamar.

"Hubba hubba," she responded with raised eyebrows.

In the opposite corner, several prom-goers, still in their suits and gowns, congregated around Sam Drucker, handstanding impressively on top of a keg of Miller Lite.

"Crazy," Tamar said coolly. On the other side of the room, Barry, Shimon, Gilad, and their dates were huddling over a Ping-Pong table.

"Heyyo!" they proclaimed at our entrance. Tamar and I doled out hugs and hand slaps, avoiding the ember tips of glowing Marlboro Mediums.

"Easy there," said Barry as I jostled next to him. He held the top half of a two-liter bottle of soda in one hand and protected the bottom half of a three-liter bottle, filled with water, with his other.

"What's that?" asked Tamar.

"Gravity bong!" shouted Barry heroically. "You taking one?"

Tamar blushed. Once, when we were still together, we had smoked cheap pot out of a rolled piece of silver foil. We didn't get high, and the drug left us sleepy and suffering from stomach cramps. Since our breakup, I had fallen into a habit of smoking with friends several times almost every weekend. Tamar had asked me to try it again with her, but I had resisted and confided in her that I actually hated the way it made me feel and did it only out of social pressure. Now, with the inhalant crew to our left and the upside-down drinkers keg-standing their way to glory on our right, this might not have been the most ideal setting for my sweet ex-girlfriend to get blasted out of her mind from a two-liter gravity bong. But something inside me said she should.

"Go for it, babe," I said, dropping my arm around her.

"Who you 'babe'-ing?" she said, flipping my limb off her shoulder.

"Yeah," Gilad chimed in before drawing Tamar in close to him. "Who you 'babe'-ing?"

"Yeah, Eytan." Shimon pulled me in for another hug. "Who you 'babe'-ing?"

Tamar and I had not even had a beer, but drunk courage seemed to be seeping into the air like nitrous oxide fumes.

"All right," Tamar declared, "I'll have one."

"Heyyo!!" the boys all cried in unison.

Tamar moved over to counsel nervously with Hannah and Devorah, when I realized that Barry's date was nowhere to be seen.

"What happened?" I whispered as he held a flame to a few small crumbs of weed at the top of the two-liter bottle. He pulled up attentively, releasing a shower of milky smoke into the chamber above the three liters of water.

"Where?" he asked.

"With your girl?" I said impatiently.

"Oh, we broke up."

"Why? What happened?"

"Eh, she was nuts." He waved the matter off.

Something wasn't right. Only a few hours earlier, they looked like they were having a great time on the dance floor. He was about to get laid. Why would he break it off at such a pivotal point? A deep anger started boiling inside me. Barry took too much for granted. He was spoiled and irrational, and it didn't even bother him enough to acknowledge. I wanted to shove him over the Ping-Pong table and crash the bong onto the floor. *What the fuck is wrong with you?* I would scream as a hush fell over the booze and laughing-gas squads and the videographer panned across the room to document me demanding of him: *Don't you even want to have sex?*

But then it occurred to me. "She wouldn't do it!" I said out loud. "That's why you broke up!"

"Dude, lay off," Barry said, the bong hit ready. "Get over here, Tamar," he called playfully.

I watched wide-eyed as my little ex-girlfriend put her mouth over the top of the two-liter bottle and sucked down a sizable lungful of White Rhino pot. After she had inhaled, she looked up at me, glassy-eyed, and blew out softly. As if the cubic foot of smoke she held in her lungs were nothing more than sweet Palisade's air over the Hudson River.

"Holy shit!" cried Gilad. "You're a beast!"

"That was a ton of smoke," Shimon agreed.

"Give it up!" Barry called, raising a palm in the air, which Tamar spanked with humble pride. It was an impressive display of stoner lung capacity that even I probably would not have been able to match. I watched as Barry made preparations for further bong hits that Devorah and Hannah were lining up for, after feeling empowered by Tamar.

I felt like I was receding into the center of the room as four different parties raged forth around me. I could have stayed put, not really part of a group, not really alone either, and pretended or tried to have a good time until the sun came up, but that's not why I had come all this way.

Up the wooden staircase and in back of the house, several groups of classmates congregated around the pool. In contrast to the mixed piñata of drug and alcohol use downstairs, these festivities felt tame and grown-up. Most of the kids around the pool had taken Advanced Placement classes over the past year. They held bottles of Corona near the parts of their Princeton and Cornell T-shirts that tucked into their jeans. These were the people whom I watched and wondered about as they were called up to receive their diplomas at graduation the previous week. Is he proud? I remember asking myself at the event while scanning the face of Yair Techinsky, our valedictorian, as he shook hands and smiled for a photograph with our head rabbi. My friend Jack, who had not attended the prom because he followed the rules of *shomer negiah*, which forbade mixed dancing, stood across the pool holding forth in a hushed tone over the barely audible sound track seeping from the basement. A yarmulke rested high on his head, standing more stately and solitary in this dress-code-less environment than it ever did back at school. He caught my eye and raised his beer at me in recognition. One of the girls in the group he was talking to was Natalie.

My chest heaved and fell, and I tried to breathe some courage out of a wet bottle of Yuengling from a cooler nearby. There was no opener, though, so I retreated to the kitchen to find one and procrastinate.

"Hey, Eytan," Natalie said, catching me inside the house opening and closing drawers in search of the appropriate utensil.

"Oh hi, Natalie," I said, swinging around to face her. She had changed from her dress into a pair of jeans and fitted V-neck T-shirt.

"I was hoping you'd make it," she said so matter-of-factly, swiftly kick-starting my heart.

"Do you have a bottle opener?" I shot back, ignoring her confession and applauding myself for the fine, unself-conscious conversation opener.

"I think I can do it with a lighter," she offered, pulling one out of her jeans pocket and popping the top off my beer.

"Nice," I replied, genuinely impressed. "Do you wanna have a smoke out front?"

"Sure," she said.

On a short concrete staircase leading up to the front of the house, we took seats beside each other. Two bottles of beer rested by our feet and the shadow of a wide green lawn intersected by a stone pathway spread out before us under the moonlight.

In school, rabbis often spoke about the *yetzer hara*, or evil inclination, as a spirit that compels man to sin. It was sometimes illustrated as a wicked vapor moving from room to room, urging anyone who sniffs at it to gossip or mistreat his parents or flee the scene of a car accident. I had been manipulated by a powerful form of *yetzer hara* that specialized in awkwardness and fear of the opposite sex, but I refused to ruin my chances with Natalie and succumb to it. So I committed myself, on those stairs, to do whatever necessary to engage Natalie in conversation that did not lull or veer bizarrely off course. And I ran with a tight line of questioning.

"Did you end up having fun at prom?" I asked.

"Not really."

"I'm sorry about that. Why?"

"I didn't really like my date."

"That's too bad. Why?"

"He's boring," she said.

Don't be boring, don't be boring, don't be boring, I chanted to myself while tilting the bottle back into my mouth.

"Why is he so . . . boring?" I asked, emphasizing the word as though it were a concept I had never really understood.

Natalie let out a clipped laugh. "Have you ever spoken to him?"

"Actually, no," I admitted.

"Well," she looked for the right way to explain, "he's just not my type."

"Fair enough," I said, swallowing a flake of jealousy. I wasn't a type that could be easily classified in the strong and silent or tall, dark and handsome phylums. I was something different, part nervous and part shy, part goony and skinny-limbed, five foot nine inches and a user of hair gel and Polo Sport. I wasn't so much a type as a bunch of slapdash characteristics that weren't always consistent (I sometimes wore a knockoff Calvin Klein cologne called CJ Won). People who could be summed up easily, as Natalie indicated about her date, made me envious. Their lives seemed simpler and laid out clearer, and left me unsure of myself.

The short silence was conveniently broken when Gilad stumbled out from around the back of the house with his arm around Hannah, Shimon's date. He had a forty-ounce bottle of Country Club malt liquor in his free hand and had stripped down to a gray tank top undershirt.

"Eyyyy-tan!" he pronounced, before stopping at the foot of the staircase and leaning up against the iron railing to our left. Soggy, bong-induced grins were spread across both their faces. Hannah's cheeks were flushed red and her breathing was deep and sparse, as though she were surfacing after an extended dive before each gasp. Gilad silently cocked his head toward Natalie and raised his eyebrows up and down at me. "There's a girl sitting beside you," he whispered.

"Thanks." I rolled my eyes, shooing him away.

"Just letting you know," he added before he and Hannah continued into the house.

"Sorry about that," I said to Natalie.

"It's fine," she said.

I thought about school ending and college and our graduation ceremony and the rapidly approaching summer, and I realized that there was an utterly endless supply of conversation topics to cover with Natalie. Talking was easy; it could go on for days. I took this newfound confidence and boldly slid closer to her.

"You know, Gil is kind of buff," she said, "in, like, a skinny type of way."

"Right," I said softly. It wasn't the ideal response to my bare arm grazing her bare arm. I was hoping for some further encouragement. Something like, *I was hoping you'd do that*, or, *You have a nice amount of arm hair.*

At that moment, Tamar and Shimon slowly emerged from the side of the house. With heads down and hands in their pockets, they moved in step with each other, like monks strolling around a cloister—except they looked like they were on the verge of an intense fit of giggles. As they circled the lawn from the side of the house all the way out to the curb by the street, I felt Natalie's eyes watching me watch them. By the edge of the street, Tamar looked up and stopped smiling, her weed seemingly wearing off within moments. She looked confused and shocked, as if witnessing me participate at a white supremacist rally.

"What's the deal with you and Tamar?" Natalie asked, after they disappeared behind a tree at the property line.

"What do you mean?" I responded, downing the last couple of inches of beer in two generous gulps.

"Aren't you guys, like, in love?"

"We used to be." I shrugged. "I guess."

"But you went to the prom together?"

"Yeah," I said curtly. "As friends."

"I saw you guys dancing," Natalie confessed after a pause. "It looked like you were having fun."

"We were," I explained, before swinging my arm around her and moving in to meet her lips. We kissed for a few moments before she pulled away.

What? I asked without saying anything. Natalie squinted at me. "We're not together anymore," I told her, exasperated.

"Okay," she said finally. "We should go inside and find a room."

Basement impulses were making inroads aboveground. In the kitchen, a classmate with a top-tier university touted across his shirt ducked under a funnel full of beer. Through an attached hose, he breathed down a liter and a half of fluid like an unclogging toilet.

"Pretty gross," I whispered to Natalie, hoping to appear more mature than my ambitious peer.

"You think so?" she asked, a villainous smile flashing across her face.

"I mean . . . I guess."

"You should try it, Eytan," she urged.

"I don't think that's the best idea," I said, moving down a hallway lined with doors. What was the point of beer at this point? I thought. We've already kissed and committed to fooling around. Wasn't alcohol just a tool to reach this level of intimacy? Besides, I didn't know how to funnel anyway.

Behind one door was a bathroom, and behind another was a bed with two people on it.

"Get the fuck out!" yelled one, as the light from the hallway glared off their outlines under a blanket.

"Whoops," I said to Natalie with a wink she ignored.

Behind the third door lay a simple guest room with two perpendicular beds, one of which was occupied by a moaning figure under a brown felt blanket.

"What?" groaned an ill and familiar voice.

"Devorah?" I asked. "Are you okay?"

"No," she mumbled.

"Okay, well, we're just gonna take this other bed," I replied, shutting off the light and taking Natalie's hand.

Shimon's prom date turned toward the door to see who was invading her drunk and stoned slumber. "Noooo," she responded.

Natalie held back, seemingly weighing her feelings. If I had been with Tamar, the answer would have been a clear, *We're finding another room*, but Natalie seemed bolder.

"Shh," she said to Devorah and closed the door behind the three of us.

Standing up in the blackness, I explored the coastlines of her lips with my own, and confirmed the softness of our cheeks against each other. I placed my hand on her back and bravely led it up to her slim neck and down across her sloping waist and butt.

"Listen," I whispered, throaty and deep, "do you wanna lie down with me?" Any smooth or subtle easiness was absent from my voice. This was the most serious question I'd asked anyone in months. If Natalie wished, we could review the pros and cons of her decision on a dry erase board beforehand.

"Sure," she responded, upbeat and chipper before turning

around in the dark to feel her way toward the bed. With our clothes on, we climbed under a bedsheet on the narrow, single mattress. To our left somewhere, Devorah emitted a sound like my stomach would after skipping breakfast and lunch, and I drew my arm up and over Natalie's shoulder to bring her in close.

Without speaking, we kissed some more. Time seemed to pass in blocks, each mile marked by bolder acts of passion. Like TV shows that start every half hour on the hour, the first episode was strictly about making out; the second, punctuated by heavy petting over the shirt; the third, featuring a labored unhooking of a bra and a respectful stroke of a bare boob.

Between Devorah's wet blanket moans and disapproving, "You guys . . . ," I asked Natalie what she wanted to do.

"I'll do anything," she said evenly.

I pulled my face back and cocked my eyebrows.

"Anything?" I asked incredulously, my body starting to shake.

"Anything," she confirmed.

"No . . . ," peeped Devorah.

Never did I believe that it would come to this. I had wanted sex for as long as I could remember, but the reality of this wish coming true was something I had never truly fathomed. It was like collecting karate belt after karate belt with the safety of knowing that I would never get into a fight. In my imagination, I was King Fuck, who charmed legions of women in the fields and town squares before bedding many of them at once in my silk-festooned chambers. But actual flesh-and-blood passion ceased for me after dry-humping or the scarce hand job. Sex was something that I assumed would occur after marriage. Once my life was busy with a full-time job, wedding thank-you cards, and a tasteful silverware set for my wife and me to use on Shabbat, then we'd wriggle in some intimacy under a heavy duvet. An offer for real and present sexual intercourse, as this appeared to be, forced me to confront a scenario that existed only in my fantasies. It was so foreign to me that I couldn't even bring myself to ask Natalie for it.

"Maybe we should . . . ," I said after several minutes of silence, holding Natalie close against my body, trying to will away nervous body quaking. "You know?"

"No." She laughed. "What?"

"Sleep together," I said seriously.

"You're tired?"

"Not like that," I stammered, my teeth chattering like a frozen dog's.

"Sure," she replied, cheerful and perky.

I pulled her in for a hard, deep kiss. It wasn't so much that I longed for her, but rather I hoped her warm and stable body would relax my vibrating, nerve-racked frame. Still, my mind reeled. Did I actually want to lose my virginity to Natalie? Or did I simply like the idea of having sex? This would be a significant life decision, as my dad might have put it. Had I taken proper account of my feelings and any consequences that might arise from such an arrangement?

"Are you okay?" she asked, coming up for air. "I can feel your heart beating like crazy."

"Yeah, I'm fine," I said, trying to drive back the onslaught of introspection and stay in the moment. "I've just been waiting for this for so long."

"What?" Natalie asked, pushing me back and looking crooked.

"What?" I asked.

"What do you mean, you've 'been waiting for this for so long'?"

"Um . . ."

"Why have you been waiting for this for so long?" she cut me off. "And what exactly do you mean by 'this'?"

I tried to think about her questions and offer an honest response, but I didn't know what I meant. The words had just come out. If I had to break it down, "this" could mean both sex and, specifically, sex with Natalie. I had been waiting for it for so long because I was a mildly repressed kid with an overactive imagination. And I had been waiting to do it with her because she was a girl and had flirted with me a few hours, or "so long," ago. But I was in no state to present such a concise explanation behind my thought process, so instead, I offered a noncommittal "I'm not sure."

"You're not sure why you just said that you've been waiting for this for so long?"

"No," I doubled down.

"Maybe this is a bad idea," Natalie said as she started to feel around the bed for her bra.

"What?" I asked, sitting up. "Why?"

"I don't know," she huffed, moving around in the dark. "You just got out of a relationship and we've never really talked. It just doesn't feel right."

"Tamar and I broke up over a year ago," I argued. "That doesn't make any sense."

"Well, I'm just not feeling it all of a sudden," she admitted, climbing over me and fixing her clothes. In the dark, she stood up straight and paused before saying, "Sorry," and marched out the door.

"Shit," I said, flopping back on the bed, burying my face in the pillow.

"Thank God," uttered Devorah.

A few moments later, I pulled myself back up and straightened out my own clothes before peeking outside the door. Music and hollering had been replaced by a few sparse murmurs in the distance. On the carpeted hallway floor before me, the beer-draining, future Ivy Leaguer slept like a fetus. I toed out and over him, slipping through the kitchen and into the living room, where more slumbering partygoers were strewn about. Gilad and Hannah sat next to each other on a large sectional sofa in a deep state of snooze. Their hands rested in plain view on their own laps, four hands on four thighs, as if an officer had asked them to keep them where he could see them. Lengthwise, on the opposite side of Gilad, Barry had furnished himself with a frilly red throw blanket and was snuggled beneath it, neck to toe. For a moment, I thought about waking him up and staking a space of my own along the friendly couch, where I could sleep or pretend to sleep and lend the appearance that I had ended my night in a healthy stupor of substances surrounded by people that cared about me. But instead, I continued out the front door and into the early morning.

I strode across the lawn, the grass coating my New Balance sneakers in morning dew, and breathed in what smelled like a new batch of air, freshly stocked and still cool from a truck that rode through the night to deliver it. The only sound was a breeze hustling through the tall trees across the street from the party house, now to my right and behind me as I made my way toward the car down the block.

There were fewer vehicles scattered over the street at this hour, and from the distance, it was easy to see the rear, driver's-side door of my mother's car ajar. I jogged the extra yardage, whispering, "No, no, no, no," at the thought of a robbery following the evening's soul-stealing dramatics. But when I reached the Maxima, a pair of feet extended out the open door, and upon closer inspection, they were attached to Shimon's body, asleep in the backseat.

"What are you doing?" I asked, resting an arm over the door.

"Sleeping," grumbled Shimon, lifting his head up for a moment before letting it plop back down against the gray leather interior.

It was going to be a beautiful June morning—perfect for eating an oversized bagel stuffed with an inch-thick layer of cream cheese and wrapped in wax paper. Maybe a plastic bottle of chocolate milk to wash it down. I was about to suggest to sleeping Shimon that we go find one—maybe even shove his legs inside, shut the door, and take him for a ride like loose cargo. But I noticed another body, sleeping upright in the driver's seat with her forehead against the window. Tamar's cheeks were rosy and soft-looking, her red hair stuck in an intricate bun designed special for the prom. She had removed her glasses and was gripping them lightly in her hands by her leg. It was a simple, responsible act that probably took no deep consciousness to remember before falling asleep, yet it struck me as incredibly wise and grown-up of her. As though, no matter how messed up and stoned and out of her mind she might get, there were basic instincts and ways to respond to the curveballs life threw her: *Sleeping with my head against a window would break my eyeglasses, so I'll remove them first.*

"Shimon," I whispered. "Shimon."

He didn't answer.

"Shimon."

"What?"

"Get up." I offered him a hand.

"No."

"Yes."

"Why?"

"Because I need to shut this door."

"Please just let me sleep."

"No, the battery is going to die if the door is left open."

He made a great show of pulling himself upright and nod-ded at me. "You're right," he said before taking my hand and standing up on the pavement.

"We can lay out on the front," I told him and closed the door.

I crept up onto the silver hood, careful not to dent it or shake Tamar too much, and lay my back upon the windshield. Shimon stretched out beside me and shut his eyes as though auditioning for an Excedrin commercial. From our perch, I watched the sky turn a dark and moody crack-of-dawn blue, to a vibrant and optimistic full-swing turquoise. The vast sec-tion of tree hanging near the car swept leaves against the sky like a giant mop on a shimmering floor.

Beyond the embarrassment of saying the wrong thing to Natalie, I felt relief. Maybe I needed to master schoolwork first or find a new girlfriend or establish habits like Tamar did with her glasses before going to sleep, but something told me that I wasn't ready to lose my virginity. I needed to live a little further outside my mind and in the real world before seeing the fantasies I had obsessed over come to life. Maybe I needed the experience that the following year in Israel would offer or the upcoming summer as a camp counselor? Or maybe I would be ready tomorrow or the following week or an hour from now with a ten-pack of ribbed condoms and a jug full of lubricant in my knapsack. Or perhaps I was fooling myself, and the only reason I didn't lose my virginity was because I screwed up and said something stupid and scared Natalie away. Whatever the reason, it didn't make much difference; I would still be lying next to my friend with my ex sleeping in the car underneath me.

But what if I hadn't screwed up and we had sex, and I emerged from that room as a man with more hair under his armpits and more gait in his step and a wider smile and fingernails that weren't bitten down to quarter-inch lengths? And what if I had stomped on the word "Dartmouth" in the hallway and downed every last bit of beer pooling in the bottom of plastic cups in the kitchen? And what if I had screamed, "Guess who just got laid?!" to all my sleeping classmates in the living room while pointing two thumbs at myself, parading on the front lawn like a band leader, slapping each leaf right off the branches they sprouted from, and then baking fresh bagels from scratch on the hood of my mom's car?

"I didn't get laid," I admitted to Shimon.

He opened his eyes and searched my face for the appropriate response.

"Sorry?"

"Yeah, it's fine," I told him, waving off the fantasy. "Thanks."

ACKNOWLEDGMENTS

So much gratitude to Daniela Rapp and the team at St. Martin's Press for believing in this book. I still get a big smile on my face whenever an e-mail from you lands in my inbox.

A huge thank-you to Laurie Abkemeir for her patience, vision, and herculean editorial efforts. You are the best agent.

To Jacqueline Mckeon, Lee Roberts, Phillippa Garson, and Lynn Schapiro for their honest feedback and close readings. And to Carol Bergman, Adam Sexton, and NYU for their early support and guidance.

Love and thanks to Ilana, Ari, Ian, William, and Samantha Milstein for their ongoing support and tireless championing. And to Yehuda for not putting up too much of a fuss about the contents of this book.

And to Cymbeline Kellett for being my favourite person. Thanks for believing in me like no one else does.